Long D₁
Walkers' Handbook

Long Distance Walkers' Handbook

The LDWA Directory of Long Distance Paths

Fifth edition

A&C Black · London

Published by A & C Black (Publishers) Ltd
35 Bedford Row, London WC1R 4JH

Fifth edition 1994

First edition 1980 and second edition 1982
published by Greenaway, Surrey
Third edition 1986 (reprinted 1988)
and fourth edition 1990 published by
A & C Black (Publishers) Ltd

ISBN 0 7136 4039 1

A CIP catalogue record for this book is available from the British Library

Acknowledgements

Maps by ML Design. Front cover photograph by Ian Johnson. Back cover photograph by Alan Pearson, courtesy of Ian Johnson.

Printed and bound in the United Kingdom by Bell & Bain

CONTENTS

INTRODUCTION

This is a fully revised and updated version of the *Long Distance Walker's Handbook*, first published in 1980 and going through four editions, the last in 1990.

Walking as a recreational activity is now one of the most popular leisure-time pursuits, and one that continues to grow in popularity. Part of this post-war growth industry has been the development of named routes that link up individual footpaths and rights of way to create longer-distance walks; national governments hope thereby to encourage a largely urban society to enjoy the recreational benefits of the countryside, rambling groups and footpath societies to increase the use of their local paths, local governments and tourist authorities to attract visitors to their area, and walkers to find routes that have been chosen to be as interesting and easy to follow as possible; many authors simply want to share their enjoyment of a particular route with others.

The first edition of this book contained a modest 130 routes; by the last (fourth) edition, the number had grown to 350. To simplify keeping track of so many routes and their associated publications, a computer database was set up in the mid-1980s; at first this was known as the National Register of Long Distance Paths, but it is now maintained by the Long Distance Paths Advisory Service under the Long Distance Walkers Association. This database now contains in excess of 700 routes, and the number continues to grow. This is the first edition of this book to be produced from the database, and contains details of nearly 500 routes, of which roughly 40% are waymarked.

SCOPE

For the purposes of this book, we include any named walking route known to LDPAS at April 1994 that has some form of waymarking or published description, and that is at least 20 miles long or provides links to and from such routes. Routes for which an essential publication is out of print, or which are known to no longer be maintained, and those for which LDPAS has been unable to obtain current information, are not included. Some routes under development at the time of publication have been included, but we do not include routes that are primarily road walks, or that are used mainly by runners or in competitions.

Though routes vary considerably, there are several broad categories. The English Countryside Commission has distinguished between National Trails (which they maintain) and Regional Routes (local authority routes for which they grant aid), but there is no rigorous definition of these, and it does not take into account the large number of other routes for which they do not grant aid. For our purposes, we distinguish on the maps at the back of this book between National Trails, Regional Routes and other waymarked trails, and described routes (i.e. routes which are not way-marked, but only described in a publication). These are listed in alphabetical order in the main section of the text, and the number to the right of the path name is that on the map.

The so-called anytime challenge walks have been separated out into their own section in the book. The great majority of these are 20–30 mile circular routes mainly on the moors and fells of North-ern England, and it is difficult to represent these on the overview maps in this book. For this reason, they are not mapped, but sorted by region. Each region is identified by a letter, and these letters are shown on the overview map on the first page of the anytime challenge walk section.

The inclusion of only formal named routes in this book does have the unfortunate side effect of making it seem that there are few long distance walking routes in Scotland. This is of course not true; it is simply that the more open access in the Highlands and other upland areas means that there is less need for formal named routes. There are however a large number of other publications that deal with Scottish hill walks, and the Scottish Rights of Way Society (see address list at the end of this book) publishes information on glen passes and other long dis-tance rights of way.

Another type of walking route that fits uneasily into our classi-fication of long distance path is the canal towpath. These provide excellent ways of walking off-road for long distances, and also provide good links from and through towns and cities, but few of them are marketed as long distance paths, and few have any sort of publication concerned with walking the towpath. For this rea-son, most of them are not listed in this book, though you can get a map of the inland waterway network, almost all of which has a walkable towpath, from any good bookshop. For further informa-tion contact British Waterways at the address given at the back of this book.

Cycling and riding routes are not included in this book unless they are also intended for walking and are mainly off-road; con-verted railway lines often form part of these and are generally multi-use, including walking, but are rarely long enough in them-selves to qualify for inclusion in this book unless they form part of a longer route, in which case they are listed under that route (see for example Trans Pennine Trail).

DISTANCES

These can vary depending on how they are measured; we generally use the official length, even where this is known to be wrong. For general interest, a list of routes sorted by length is given at the end of the book.

MAPS

The numbers shown in the map section of the book correspond to those listed to the right of the path name in the individual entries in the main section, so it should be easy to match the maps with the text entry.

The map numbers given in the individual entries refer to the Landranger 1:50,000 series of the Ordnance Survey, though on many routes the 1:25,000 Pathfinder or Outdoor Leisure series may be preferable. If the route is shown by the OS on these maps, the text reads "On OS maps"; if not, it reads "OS maps"; this is based on information provided by the OS, though note that a new route can only be added to the next edition of the map concerned — for Landrangers, this is roughly once every 3–4 years. Note too that, though the exact course of routes is shown on the Outdoor Leisure and 1-inch-to-1-mile Touring maps, there is only a rough indication of them on Landrangers and Pathfinders. Map numbers in the route entries are given in numerical sequence, which may not necessarily be that for the walk itself.

WAYMARKING

Waymarking refers to the marking specific to that route, which may be a symbol (for example, an acorn on English National Trails), or named discs and signposts; it does not refer to the standard marking of rights of way (for example, in England, yellow arrows for footpaths and blue for bridleways), as this does not tell the walker if he/she is on the correct right of way.

Although a fundamental distinction can be drawn between routes that have a specific waymark and those that don't, standards of waymarking vary widely, according to the needs of the terrain and the diligence of those responsible. A converted railway line will need only a sign at either end, whereas a route through a complicated pattern of fields or through an extensive woodland area may need a large number of waymarks. Generally, routes maintained by the Countryside Commission in England and the equivalent bodies in the other countries are well waymarked and maintained; other waymarked routes are usually, but by no means always, also well looked after, though some routes are only waymarked along certain sections, for example in one county and not in another. On unwaymarked routes, there will generally be nothing on the ground at all to tell a walker that he/she is on the correct route; here, use of a guidebook, and probably also of map and possibly compass, will be essential.

USER GROUPS

Many of the major routes have their own association, who are generally a good source of information on the route, and may publish regular guides to accommodation, transport, etc. These groups are generally membership-based.

Many of these groups grew out of the local groups of the Ramblers Association, who have been instrumental in establishing many of our LDPs. Anyone interested in maintaining our heritage of public footpaths should consider membership — details can be obtained from the address given at the back of this book.

PUBLICATIONS

Publications vary even more widely than the routes they describe, from glossy coffee-table books to slim hand-written booklets or copies of typewritten A4 sheets. We distinguish hardbacks, paper- and softbacks, leaflets, looseleaf, and "folders"; the latter is a catch-all for any set or pack of leaflets, laminated cards or typesheets — these may be obtainable separately, but space precludes listing them all. Details can be obtained from the publisher. Publications are listed alphabetically by title. Sizes are in standard international measures or in millimetres; A4/3 means A4 folded into 3.

Books published by the larger publishers should be available through any bookshop, even internationally; for this reason, the ISBN is given where known. Other publications will normally only be obtainable locally or by post from the address given or from a local tourist office. When requesting information from a private address, remember to enclose return postage. Though most local authorities have some sort of postal sales, it is often better to try the local tourist office first. Postage charges are given in brackets where known.

Both Stanfords (12-14 Long Acre, London WC2E 9LP (071 836 1321)) and Cordee (3a De Montfort St, Leicester LE1 7HD (0533 543579)) stock a wide range of maps and books which can be ordered through the post.

It is in the nature of publishing that books and especially leaflets go quickly in and out of print. So, although the details in this section are believed correct at the time of going to press, the information presented will be soon out of date, and, for this reason, should be regarded as guidelines only; current information on availability and price should be checked with the publisher concerned.

Note also that the countryside does change, mainly as a result of human activity (changes in land use, housing and road development), but also through natural erosion, particularly on coastal paths; consequently sections of a route shown in a publication that has not been recently updated may no longer be walkable as described. Any problems encountered with a right of way should be reported to the appropriate highways authority; guidebooks should normally give details of these.

BADGES

Badges and certificates for a particular route have been listed where known; in addition, P&R Publicity Ltd, 13d Queensway,

Stem Lane Industrial Estate, New Milton, Hampshire BH25 5NN (0425 611911) sell badges for over 120 routes.

ADDRESSES

To save on space, these have been separated out and listed in a section at the back of the book.

ACCOMMODATION

Several routes have a user group (see above), which will usually publish a regular, normally yearly, accommodation list. Where this is not the case, most towns have a tourist office which is generally the best source of accommodation lists and can book ahead if required. Any tourist office can provide a list of tourist offices in other areas, together with a map showing their location.

Other sources of accommodation information are the Ramblers Association's Yearbook, distributed free to members but also available in bookshops (ISBN 0900613750, £4.99), which includes a list of camping barns and a large section of bed and breakfast addresses that have been recommended by members; and the Youth Hostels Association, which maintains both youth hostels and camping barns.

CHANGES TO THE NETWORK

The list of routes in this book is a snapshot of the status of the route network at a particular time, and of course changes will occur, as new routes are created and old ones revised or extended. Anyone wanting to keep up-to-date with these developments is recommended to join the Long Distance Walkers Association, membership of which includes a copy of *Strider*, published every four months, which carries a regular "News of LDPs" column, besides articles on all aspects of long distance walking. The current membership secretary is Mr Geoff Saunders, 117 Higher Lane, Rainford, St Helens, Merseyside WA11 8BQ.

DISCLAIMER

As with previous versions, this book is not intended to be a guide to any particular route, but a guide to which routes are available, and where further information can be obtained. Inclusion of a route in this book cannot be taken as an indication of the quality of a route, either scenically or in terms of usability.

Although this book represents the result of a large amount of investigation and correspondence, with such a large and ever increasing volume of data it is probably inevitable that errors and omissions have crept in, in spite of the best efforts of the compilers. Neither LDPAS nor the LDWA nor the publishers can be held responsible for any inconvenience caused thereby. Please send information on any errors or omissions to LDPAS at the address below, so problems can be rectified in future editions.

ACKNOWLEDGEMENTS

The work of many people has gone into the contents of this book over the years. Barbara Blatchford, who was involved in the compilation of the first three editions, and John Margetts and Sue Ramsay, who compiled the fourth, will no doubt recognise much of the material in this edition. Various people were involved in setting up the LDP database now maintained by LDPAS, and this book is a result of their labours.

For the current edition, Keith Warman compiled the information on anytime challenge walks, and Ann Sayer the maps. Information was provided by the multitude of local authorities, rambling groups, footpath societies, publishers, writers, LDWA members and other walkers now involved in the creation and maintenance of LDPs. I stitched the whole together into what is, at least for the moment, the definitive list of such routes.

Peter Robins
Manager
Long Distance Paths Advisory Service Ltd
11 Cotswold Court
Sandy Lane
Chester   CH3 5UZ

ABBREVIATIONS USED IN THE BOOK

AONB	Area of Outstanding Natural Beauty
CC	County Council
DC	District Council
GR	Grid reference *or* Grande Randonnée
LDWA	Long Distance Walkers Association
NT	National Trust
OS	Ordnance Survey
OSNI	Ordnance Survey of Northern Ireland
RA	Ramblers' Association
SSSI	Site of Special Scientific Interest
YHA	Youth Hostels Association

LONG DISTANCE ROUTES

Abbott's Hike   1

Cumbria, N Yorks, W Yorks	171 km / 107 miles

The Hike, named after its originator, links 25 miles of the Dales Way, 14 miles of the Three Peaks Walk and three miles of the Pennine Way to provide a scenic route from Yorkshire to the eastern side of the Lake District. It is essential to carry OS maps.

Start	Ilkley, W Yorks	SE117476
Finish	Pooley Bridge, Cumbria	NY470247
OS maps	90, 91, 97, 98, 104	

Publication(s)
Paperback: *Abbott's Hike* by Peter Abbott (Peter Abbott). 1980 \ 210 x 149 \ 64pp \ £2.00.

Ainsty Bounds Walk   2

N Yorks	70 km / 44 miles

The Ainsty is a low-lying area to the west of the city of York, and at one time was annexed by it. It is bounded by the rivers Wharfe, Nidd and Ouse. A description of the route across pleasant agricultural land and past many buildings of historic interest was first published in 1975 by RA members to publicise rights of way in the area. As far as possible it follows footpaths along the banks of the rivers bounding the area, passing through Boston Spa, Wetherby, Moor Monkton, the outskirts of York and Bolton Percy.

Start and Finish	Tadcaster, N Yorks	SE488434
OS maps	105	

Publication(s)
Paperback: *Ainsty Bounds Walk* by Simon Townson (Dalesman Publishing Ltd). ISBN: 0852067909. 205 x 135 \ 48pp \ £1.10.

Allerdale Ramble   3

Cumbria	87 km / 54 miles

From central Lakeland the route heads northwards along the western side of Borrowdale and Derwent Water to Keswick. Here there is a choice of route, either across the foothills of Skiddaw or over its summit, before heading west along the Derwent valley to

Cockermouth. The Ramble then crosses the agricultural land of mid-Allerdale to reach the coast at Maryport, where it turns north along the flat coastline past Allonby and Silloth, giving easy walking and extensive views across the Solway Firth.

Start	Seathwaite, Cumbria	NY235119
Finish	Grune Point, Cumbria	NY145571
On OS maps	85, 89, 90	

Publication(s)
Booklet: *The Allerdale Ramble* by Fred Harper and Harry Appleyard (Allerdale District Council). 1986\A5\32pp\£0.99.

Alternative Pennine Way 4

Borders, Cumbria, Derby, N Yorks, Northumb, S Yorks, W Yorks	429 km / 268 miles

As its name suggests, this route was devised as an alternative to the somewhat overused "official" Pennine Way, and is a more varied route divided into 20 daily stages ranging from 7.5 to 31km with accommodation at the end of each stage. Although keeping to the Pennines, it does not keep to the tops, and therefore entails more climbing than the Pennine Way.

From Ashbourne, the Way heads through the eastern part of the Peak District via Dove Dale, Youlgreave, Chatsworth, the Derwent Edges, Dunford Bridge and Marsden, to reach Hebden Bridge and Haworth.

The Aire is crossed at Bingley, and the Yorkshire Dales via Ilkley, Pateley Bridge and Hawes to Kirkby Stephen. After crossing Dufton Fell, the route descends to the Tyne valley via Allendale, crosses the Kielder Forest to Byrness, and finishes in Jedburgh, where there is a connecting route to the S Upland Way.

Start	Ashbourne, Derby	SK178469
Finish	Jedburgh, Borders	NT651204
OS maps	74, 80, 87, 91, 98, 99, 104, 110, 119	

Publication(s)
Paperback: *The Alternative Pennine Way* by Denis Brook and Phil Hinchliffe (Cicerone Press). 1992\116 x 176\£8.99.

Altrincham Circular 5

Cheshire, Gtr Man	27 km / 17 miles

A clockwise route around the town of Altrincham, passing along the district boundary to Davenport Green, through Halebarns to the Bollin and Ashley Heath, Bow Green and Little Bollington, returning via Dunham and Oldfield Brow.

Start and Finish	W Timperley, Gtr Man	SJ771901
OS maps	109	

Publication(s)
Paperback: *The Altrincham Circular* by Altrincham WEA (Willow Publishing). ISBN: 0946361282. 1989\A5\56pp\£3.75 (+ 80p).

Angles Way   6

Norfolk, Suffolk	124 km / 78 miles

The Angles Way was devised by the Ramblers' Association and was waymarked by the County Councils. It was opened in 1989, and, together with the Peddars Way, Norfolk Coast Path and Weavers Way, forms the 220-mile Around Norfolk Walk. From Great Yarmouth the route goes by Bredon Water, along the River Waveney to its source, and by the Little Ouse through heathland and marsh to Knettishall Heath.

Start	Great Yarmouth, Norfolk	TG522081
Finish	Knettishall Heath, Suffolk	TL944807
On OS maps	134, 144, 156	
Waymark	Disc with "Angles Way" round perimeter	

Publication(s)
Paperback: *Angles Way* (RA Norfolk Area). 1989\210 x 143\18pp\£1.20 (+ 25p).
Booklet: *The Angles Way* (Suffolk County Council). £1.00 (+ SAE).
Leaflet: *The Angles Way* (Suffolk County Council). A5\Free (+ SAE).
Paperback: *The Angles Way — Walking in an Historic Landscape* by Kate Skipper and Tom Williamson (Suffolk County Council). 132pp\£5.00.

Anglesey Coast Path   7

Gwynedd	194 km / 121 miles

First created by the Ynys Mon (Anglesey) Group of the RA, this circuit around the island uses existing rights of way, linked by roads which form about a quarter of the route, to follow the coastline as closely as possible. It passes attractive bays, fine cliff scenery, marshes and sands, the port of Holyhead and several nature reserves.

Start and Finish	Menai Bridge, Gwynedd	SH556716
OS maps	114	

Publication(s)
Paperback: *A Walker's Guide to the Anglesey Coastal Path* by Harry Ashcroft (Walker's Guides). 1991\147 x 210\76pp\£3.25.

Paperback: *Walking the Anglesey Coast* by Jan Harris (Walking Routes). ISBN: 095181480X. 1994 \ 118pp \ £4.95.

Paperback: *Walking the Anglesey Coast / Cerdded Arfordir Mon* by Jan Harris (Walking Routes). ISBN: 0951814818. 1994 \ 122pp \ £5.95.

Paperback: *Walking the Isle of Anglesey Coastline* by John Merrill (Trail Crest Publications Ltd). ISBN: 1874754136. 1993 \ 60pp \ £4.50.

Badge and certificate (£2.75 / post free) available from Trail Crest Publications Ltd.

Around the Carneddau   8

Gwynedd   64 km / 40 miles

A circuit around the edge of the Carneddau. From Capel Curig, the route visits the lakes of Llyn Crafnant, Lllyn Cowlyd, Melynnllyn and Llyn Dulyn. It then descends to the Aber Falls via the Roman Road over Bwlch y Ddeufaen, and traverses Moel Wnion to Gerlon and Ogwen. It then skirts Llyn Ogwen, and follows the bridleway back to Capel Curig.

Start and Finish	Capel Curig, Gwynedd	SH721583
OS maps	115	

Publication(s)
Looseleaf: *Around the Carneddau* (Dave Irons). Free (+ 9"x4" SAE).

Around the Lakes   9

Cumbria   232 km / 145 miles

Based on the Bob Graham Round, a circular route, primarily for fell-runners, of 72 miles, 42 peaks and 27,000ft of ascent, this route also includes Kentmere and the Far Eastern and Coniston Fells, and provides a circular taking in all the peaks of the Lake District and involving 50,000ft of ascent.

Start and Finish	Grasmere, Cumbria	NY339072
OS maps	89, 90, 96, 97	

Publication(s)
Paperback: *Walking Round the Lakes* by John and Anne Nuttall (Cicerone Press). ISBN: 1852840994. 116 x 176 \ 240pp \ £6.99.

Avon Community Forest Path   10

Avon   75 km / 47 miles

A route around the Bristol/Avon Community Forest, currently under development by Avon County Council, this path will encircle

Bristol, using the northern part of Two Rivers Walk, and most of the 7-mile Dramway Footpath to the east of the city. It is due to open in mid 1994.

Start and Finish	Keynsham, Avon	ST659690
OS maps	172	

Publication(s)
None at time of writing.

Avon Valley Path 11

Dorset, Hants, Wilts	55 km / 34 miles

The Path follows the lower reaches of one of S England's best-known chalk rivers, through a valley much of which is designated as an SSSI, and of great botanical interest, besides being known to anglers for its salmon.

Though much of the Path does not follow the riverbank, it aims to keep as close to it as possible, passing from the Cathedral at Salisbury through Downton, Fordingbridge and Ringwood before ending at Christchurch with its 11th-century priory and Harbour.

Start	Salisbury, Wilts	SU143297
Finish	Christchurch, Dorset	SZ160925
On OS maps	184, 195	
Waymark	Green and beige with bridge	

Publication(s)
Leaflet: *Avon Valley Path* (Hampshire County Council). A4/3 \ Free.

Avon Walkway 12

Avon	50 km / 31 miles

A path which provides a mixture of rural and urban walking through the heart of two historic cities, the Walkway follows the river Avon from Pill, near its mouth, through the wooded Avon Gorge and under the Clifton Suspension Bridge to the floating harbour in the centre of Bristol. It continues along the Avon valley to Bath and then follows the Kennet and Avon Canal towpath to the Dundas aqueduct.

Start	Pill, Avon	ST525759
Finish	Dundas Aqueduct, Avon	ST785626
On OS maps	172	
Waymark	"AW" logo	

Publication(s)
Paperback: *Face the Dawn: the Bristol to London Long Distance Path* by Eddie Critchley (Ramblers' Association). ISBN: 0900613556. 1984\A5\50pp\£2.00 (+ 70p).
Paperback: *The Kennet & Avon Walk* by Ray Quinlan (Cicerone Press). ISBN: 1852840900. 1991\116 x 176\200pp\£6.99.

Aylesbury Ring 13

Bucks, Herts	50 km / 31 miles

Originally created by the Aylesbury and District group of the Ramblers Association, the route has since been adopted by the local county and district councils.

Though never more than 5 miles from the centre of Aylesbury, the route aims to encompass some of the remoter areas of the Vale, passing through Gt Kimble, Upton, Waddesdon, Whitchurch, Hulcott and Aston Clinton.

Much of the western section is coincident with the North Bucks Way.

Start and Finish	Wendover, Bucks	SP869078
On OS maps	165	
Waymark	Aylesbury duck	

Publication(s)
Leaflet: *The Aylesbury Ring* (Buckinghamshire County Council). 1993\A4/3\Free (+ SAE).
Paperback: *Vale of Aylesbury Walker* by Peter Gulland and Diana Gulland (RA Buckinghamshire). ISBN: 090061367X. A5\140pp\£3.00.

Baker Way 14

Cheshire	13 km / 8 miles

One of four interlinked, waymarked walks conceived by the late Jack Baker and developed by him and other members of the Mid-Cheshire Footpath Society. From the edge of the Delamere Forest the Way runs south-west along farmland paths to the outskirts of Chester.

Start	Brines Brow, Cheshire	SJ524706
Finish	Christleton, Cheshire	SJ443654
On OS maps	117	
Waymark	Black spot on standard waymarks	

Publication(s)
Booklet: *Waymarked Walks in Central Cheshire* (Mid-Cheshire Footpath Society). 100 x 223\16pp\£0.75.

Barnsley Boundary Walk 15

S Yorks, W Yorks	118 km / 74 miles

Created by Barnsley Borough Council in association with the publishing arm of the "Barnsley Chronicle", the Walk aims to provide the walker with a view of the varied countryside, industrial heritage and other points of interest in the Borough.

From Langsett Reservoir, it uses the former salt road to Dunford Bridge, and then heads west past several reservoirs to Upper Denby and the Country Parks at Cannon and Bretton Halls. From here it crosses farmland to the north of Royston before crossing the coalfield to the east of Barnsley where there is currently much reclamation in progress. It then heads west via Elsecar Heritage Centre through country parks and woodland to reach Langsett again.

Start and Finish	Flouch Inn, S Yorks	SE197016
OS maps	110, 111	

Publication(s)
Booklet: *Barnsley Boundary Walk* (Wharncliffe Publishing Ltd). ISBN: 1871647177. 1993\A5\48pp\£3.95.

Beacon Way 16

W Midlands	27 km / 17 miles

This "green" route from Handsworth via the outskirts of W Bromwich and Walsall through the heart of the W Midlands conurbation to the Staffordshire border runs through Beacon Country Park past lakes, through nature reserves and woods, and along the banks of canals.

Plans are under way to link the northern end with the Heart of England Way.

Start	Sandwell Park, W Midlands	SP018913
Finish	Chasewater, W Midlands	SK040070
On OS maps	139	
Waymark	Named posts and standard arrows	

Publication(s)
Leaflet: *Beacon Regional Park* (Walsall Metropolitan Borough Council). 1989\A4/3\Free.
Leaflet: *The Beacon Way* (Beacon Regional Park). A4/3\Free.

Beeches Way 17

Bucks, Gtr London	25 km / 16 miles

This route connecting the river Thames at Cookham with the Grand Union Canal at W Drayton passes through several ancient woodlands now designated as SSSIs, including part of Burnham Beeches. It also passes several remnants of lowland heath, and the village of Stoke Poges, the setting for Thomas Gray's "Elegy in a Country Churchyard".

Start	Cookham, Bucks	SU898858
Finish	West Drayton, Gtr London	TQ061801
OS maps	175, 176	
Waymark	Named standard discs and posts with beechnut logo	

Publication(s)
Leaflet: *The Beeches Way* (Buckinghamshire County Council). A4/3 \ Free (+ SAE).

Best of Lakeland 18

Cumbria	96 km / 60 miles

By following well-used paths, this walk makes route finding fairly easy. With care, the reasonably fit walker should be able to complete the walk well within the eight days allowed for in the guide. The start at Ravenglass offers a choice of walking up Eskdale, or of taking the narrow-gauge steam train to Boot-in-Eskdale; both are enjoyable, but the train is mainly a summer service. The route takes in most of the well-known Lakeland landmarks: Wast Water, Wasdale Head, Great Gable, Sty Head Tarn, Patterdale, Ullswater, Angle Tarn, High Street, Troutbeck and Orrest Head. It finishes at Windermere.

Start	Ravenglass, Cumbria	SD084963
Finish	Windermere, Cumbria	SD413987
OS maps	89, 90, 96	

Publication(s)
Paperback: *Footpath Touring: Best of Lakeland* by Ken Ward (Footpath Touring). ISBN: 0711701458. 1985 \ 221 x 114 \ 64pp \ £3.50.

Black and White Village Trail 19

Heref & Worc	99 km / 62 miles

Originally conceived by David Gorvett as a route for car-drivers, the Trail provides a similar route for walkers through the villages between Leominster and Kington, an area characterised by the large number of timbered and half-timbered buildings. The land-scape is generally undulating farmland, and provides good views of the surrounding hill ranges. The villages concerned are Dilwyn, Weobley, Almeley, Eardisley, Kington, Lyonshall, Pembridge and Eardisland.

Start and Finish	Leominster Station, Heref & Worc	SO502589
OS maps	148, 149	

Publication(s)
Paperback: *The Black and White Village Trail* by David Gorvett and Les Lumsdon (Scarthin Books). ISBN: 0907758479. 1991\A5\64pp\£4.50.

Blackwater Valley Footpath 20

Berks, Hants, Surrey	30 km / 19 miles

This route along the Surrey/Berks/Hampshire border via Sand-hurst, Farnborough and Aldershot is planned to link eventually to the North Downs Way at Farnham, and via the Loddon Valley to the Thames between Reading and Henley. The main route to Swallowfield is due to be completed by 1995.

Start	Farnham, Surrey	SU844468
Finish	Swallowfield, Berks	
OS maps	175	
Waymark	Named posts and arrows with waterfowl and reed logo	

Publication(s)
Looseleaf: *Explore the Blackwater Valley* (Blackwater Valley Team). A4\4pp\Free.

Blue Man Walk 21

N Yorks	26 km / 16 miles

A short walk developed and fully waymarked by the Forestry Commission through its upland coniferous forests on the east side of the North York Moors.

Start	Reasty Bank Top, N Yorks	SE965944
Finish	Allerston, N Yorks	SE876830
OS maps	101	
Waymark	Blue man	

Publication(s)
Looseleaf: *Blue Man Walk Route* (Dalby Forest Visitor Centre). A4\1pp\Free.
Badge (£0.70) available from Dalby Forest Visitor Centre.

Bollin Valley Way 22

Cheshire, Gtr Man	40 km / 25 miles

The River Bollin rises in the Pennine Foothills and flows through Macclesfield, Prestbury, Wilmslow, Hale and Bowdon, eventually running into the Manchester Ship Canal (i.e. the Mersey) at Bollin Point.

The Bollin Valley Project was established in 1972 by a consortium of public bodies as an experiment into land management. This Project produced a series of leaflets on footpaths in the valley, which developed into a Way from source to mouth.

Start	Macclesfield, Cheshire	SD920739
Finish	Partington, Gtr Man	SJ706912
OS maps	109, 118	
Waymark	Named discs with river logo	

Publication(s)
Leaflet: *Bollin Valley* (Bollin Valley Project). A4/3 \ Free.

Bowland-Dales Traverse 23

Lancs, N Yorks	152 km / 95 miles

An upland route across the Forest of Bowland and the Yorkshire Dales, contrasting Bowland's heather-clad gritstone hills with the limestone terraces of the Dales. Besides visiting the villages of Slaidburn, Settle, Malham, Kettlewell, Aysgarth and Reeth, the route passes Attermire Scar, Malham Cove, Kilnsey Crag and Buckden Pike, the latter being the route's highest point at 2302ft.

Start	Garstang, Lancs	SD492450
Finish	Richmond, N Yorks	NZ171009
OS maps	92, 98, 99, 102, 103	

Publication(s)
Paperback: *The Bowland-Dales Traverse* by John Gillham (Grey Stone Books). ISBN: 0951599623. 1991 \ 105 x 150 \ 64pp \ £3.75.

Bradford Ring 24

W Yorks	51 km / 32 miles

Fourteen easy-going walks (each with a return route), forming a chain encircling Bradford, make up the main ring walk and its alternatives, and provide very flexible walking routes. From Cottingley the walk heads east along the Aire valley to Shipley and Apperley, where it loops south across parks, golf courses, reclaimed mine working areas and along field and beckside paths to Pudsey,

Birkenshaw and Scholes. It then loops north, passing to the west of Bradford via Shelf and Thornton.

Start and Finish	Cottingley Bridge, W Yorks	SE112380
OS maps	104	

Publication(s)
Booklet: *Bradford Ringwalks* by Arthur Gemmell and Paul Sheldon (Stile Publications). ISBN: 0906886449. 1989\200 x 120\128pp\£1.50.

Brandon/Bishop Auckland Walk 25

Durham	16 km / 10 miles

One of a series of railway-lines bought by local authorities, and developed for use by walkers and cyclists; horseriders may use them with a permit. The Brandon/Bishop Auckland Walk connects the Deerness and Lanchester Valley Walks on the western edge of Durham City with Willington and Bishop Auckland. The 4-mile Auckland Walk does not connect to this route.

Start	Broompark, Durham	NZ254415
Finish	Bishop Auckland, Durham	NZ207301
On OS maps	88, 92, 93	

Publication(s)
Folder: *Railway Walks in County Durham* (Durham County Council). 1990\A5\10pp\£0.99 (+ 75p).

Bronte Way 26

Lancs, W Yorks	64 km / 40 miles

Originally a short route linking Haworth with Wycoller Hall, the Way was extended in 1992 to provide a cross-Pennine route linking various places associated with the lives and works of the Bronte sisters.

From Gawthorpe Hall west of Burnley, the Way runs through Burnley and the Thursden Valley to Wycoller Hall (Ferndean Manor in "Jane Eyre"), over the moors to Top Withins (Wuthering Heights) and down to Haworth Parsonage, where the Brontes lived and where there is now a Bronte Museum.

From here the route runs east to the Brontes' birthplace at Thornton, south along the hills west of Bradford to the Spen Valley (Shirley country) before finishing at Oakwell Hall (Fieldhead in "Shirley", and now a country park).

Start	Gawthorpe Hall, Lancs	SD805340
Finish	Oakwell Hall, W Yorks	SE217271
On OS maps	103, 104	

Waymark	Named posts

Publication(s)
Leaflet: *Bronte Way* (Lancashire County Council). 1992\A5\Free.
Folder: *The Bronte Way* (Lancashire County Council).
1992\A5\£1.60 (+ 74p).

Burnley Way 27

Lancs	64 km / 40 miles

A circuitous route around the town of Burnley. Conceived by
Burnley and District Civic Trust and adopted by the Borough
Council, the Way crosses a wide variety of terrain from moorland
tops to canal towpath. Passing via Widdop and Hurstwood reservoirs, Thieveley Pike, Clowbridge Reservoir, Hapton and Padiham,
it links with the Bronte, Rossendale, Hyndburn and Pendle Ways.

Start and Finish	Weavers Triangle, Lancs	SD838329
On OS maps	103	
Waymark	Stylised B and bird logo	

Publication(s)
Folder: *The Burnley Way* (Burnley Borough Council). 1993\A4/3\
5pp\Free.

Calderdale Way 28

W Yorks	80 km / 50 miles

The Way is a clockwise circuit around Calderdale, which was
officially opened in 1978. It was pioneered by local civic trusts and
developed by West Yorkshire County Council. The main and link
routes to the valley bottom are designed so that they can be
completed in short stages. The walk encircles Halifax, Hebden
Bridge and Todmorden, following old packhorse ways across the
open gritstone hillsides, which are mainly used for sheep farming,
and passing through hillside villages (the majority of which were
developed to house the weaving communities) and old mill towns
on the banks of the river Calder.

Start and Finish	Greetland, W Yorks	SE097214
On OS maps	103, 104, 110	
Waymark	CW trefoil	

Publication(s)
Paperback: *The Calderdale Way* by Calderdale Way Association
(Metropolitan Borough of Calderdale). ISBN: 0906651042.
1983\A5\56pp\£2.00.

Cambrian Way 29

Dyfed, Gwent, Gwynedd, Mid Glam, Powys, S Glam	438 km / 274 miles

Described as the "Mountain Connoisseur's Walk", this north-south route through upland Wales involves 61,540ft of ascent and requires much stamina to complete. It is a tough, high-level route which is not only longer than the Pennine Way but has twice as much climbing and should not be underestimated or attempted without map, compass and the ability to use them.

First proposed in 1968, the then Countryside Commission showed great interest in designating the route as a National Trail, but bowed to opposition in 1982. The Ramblers' Association however remains keen on it being given official status in the future.

From Cardiff on the south coast, it follows a meandering northerly route over the Black Mountains, Brecon Beacons, Carmarthen Fan, Plynlimon, Cadair Idris, the Rhinogs, the Snowdon massif and the Carneddau to reach Conwy on the north coast.

Tony Drake pioneered the route, and his guide includes a comprehensive accommodation and services list (with periodic update insert). Richard Sale's book describes a somewhat different route.

Tony Drake is willing to give advice and information on the route, and update the accommodation list as necessary (2 Beech Lodge, 67 The Park, Cheltenham, Glos GL50 2RX (0242 232131)).

Start	Cardiff, S Glam	ST180765
Finish	Conwy, Gwynedd	SH783775
OS maps	115, 124, 135, 147, 160, 161, 171	

Publication(s)

Paperback: *Cambrian Way: the Mountain Connoisseur's Walk* by A J Drake (Ramblers' Association). ISBN: 0950958034. 1994\210 x 128\96pp\£4.50 (+ 40p).

Hardback: *A Cambrian Way* by Richard Sale (Constable and Co Ltd). ISBN: 0094691800. 171 x 114\270pp\£14.95.

Camel Trail 30

Cornwall	30 km / 19 miles

Two sections of disused railway line along the river Camel: firstly from Padstow via Wadebridge and Boscarne Junction to Bodmin (12 miles owned by Cornwall CC), and secondly, from Boscarne Junction to Poley's Bridge on the edge of Bodmin Moor (7 miles owned by N Cornwall DC). The Padstow to Wadebridge section is along the Camel estuary, the rest through densely wooded landscapes.

Start	Padstow, Cornwall	SW920754
Finish	Poley's Bridge, Cornwall	SX082742
On OS maps	200	

Publication(s)
Leaflet: *The Camel Trail* (Cornwall County Council). 1993\
A4/3\Free.

Centenary Circle   31

Essex	36 km / 23 miles

A circular route around Chelmsford. Passing via Sandon, Galley-wood, Writtle, Broomfield and the river Chelmer, the Circle is one of a series of walks devised by the Borough Council and published under the name "Country Ways".

Start and Finish	Sandford Mill, Essex	TL740060
On OS maps	167	
Waymark	Profiles of Queens Victoria and Elizabeth II in garland	

Publication(s)
Folder: *Country Ways* (Chelmsford Borough Council). A5\11pp\£3.00.

Centenary Way (North Yorkshire)   32

N Yorks	133 km / 83 miles

A route devised by North Yorkshire County Council to celebrate the 100th anniversary of Yorkshire County Council. It runs across the Howardian Hills and Yorkshire Wolds via Castle Howard and Wharram Percy, linking York and the Foss Walk with the Wolds and Cleveland Ways. It combines riverside walks in deep valleys with forest tracks.

Start	York, N Yorks	SE603522
Finish	Filey Brigg, N Yorks	TA126817
OS maps	100, 105, 106	
Waymark	"CW" on standard waymarks	

Publication(s)
Booklet: *The Centenary Way from Filey Brigg to York Minster* (North Yorkshire County Council). 1989\A5\36pp\£1.00.

Centenary Way (Warwickshire)   33

Warks	156 km / 98 miles

An easy figure-three-shaped route through the finest scenery in Warwickshire, the Way was devised to celebrate one hundred years of Warwickshire County Council. From Kingsbury, south of Tamworth, it passes via the Tame Valley, Atherstone Ridge and George Eliot country around Nuneaton before passing to the east of Coventry to Kenilworth, Warwick and Leamington Spa.

From here it heads east to the Burton Dassett Hills, south to Edge Hill and Shipston-on-Stour, and then west to Ilmington Downs and Meon Hill north of Chipping Campden.

Start	Kingsbury, Warks	SP204959
Finish	Meon Hill, Warks	SP176454
OS maps	139, 140, 151	
Waymark	Bear and ragged staff	

Publication(s)
Folder: *Centenary Way* (Warwickshire County Council). 1989\A4/3\11pp\£4.00.

Cestrian Link Walk 34

Cheshire, Clwyd, Derby	180 km / 113 miles

Designed to link the Pennine Way with Offa's Dyke Path, from Edale, the Link leaves the Peak District via Castleton and the Goyt valley and takes a meandering route across the Cheshire lowlands. It loops south to avoid the northern industrial areas, crosses pasture and woodland, and follows river and canalside paths, lanes and tracks to pass through many Cheshire villages, including Gawsworth, Church Minshull, Beeston and Aldford. From Mold in Clwyd it follows a route north-west along the lower Clwydian hills to reach Prestatyn.

Start	Edale, Derby	SK125858
Finish	Prestatyn, Clwyd	SJ081838
OS maps	116, 117, 118, 119	

Publication(s)
Hardback: *A Cestrian Link Walk* by John N Davenport (Westmorland Gazette). ISBN: 0902272454. 1983\116 x 177\108pp\£2.50 (+ 40p).

Chalkland Way 35

Humberside, N Yorks	64 km / 40 miles

A tour around the most northerly chalk outcrop in Britain – the Yorkshire Wolds, noted for green, dry valleys. A circular route, it runs clockwise via the villages of Great Givendale, Bugthorpe, Thixendale, Fimber, Wetwang, Huggate and Millington.

Start and Finish	Pocklington, Humberside	SE802488
OS maps	100, 101, 106	

Publication(s)
Looseleaf: *The Chalkland Way* (Ray Wallis). 1994\Free (+ SAE). Badge (£1.00 / SAE) available from Ray Wallis.

Cheshire Ring Canal Walk 36

Cheshire, Gtr Man, Staffs	156 km / 98 miles

A circular route following the towpaths along six historic canals of various ages and character, this Walk offers the solitude of quiet countryside, the hustle and bustle of city streets and "high tech" factories, plus views of the Cheshire Plain and Peak District hills. It is an easy route to follow, as the only place where the path leaves the canal side is where the canal continues through long tunnels, when the route follows the old horse paths over the top. There is also a short section along a road connecting the Rochdale and Ashton canals in central Manchester.

Start and Finish	Marple, Gtr Man	SJ962884
On OS maps	108, 109, 117, 118	
Waymark	Metal plaque with bridge and barge	

Publication(s)
Folder: *Cheshire Ring Canal Walk* (Cheshire County Council). 100 x 210\11pp\£8.00 (+ £1.15).
Paperback: *The Cheshire Ring* by John N. Merrill (Trail Crest Publications Ltd). ISBN: 0907496636. 80pp\£4.95.
Badge and certificate (£1.00 / £0.50 / SAE) available from Frank Hodson.

Chesterfield Round 37

Derby	80 km / 50 miles

This walk was created by the Chesterfield Town Group of the Ramblers' Association as a celebration for the national Association's Golden Jubilee. Starting just north of the town, it is a circular walk which starts by going around and to the east of the town. Just south of the village of Heath, it then goes west for some two miles before turning north to follow an undulating route around the west side before swinging around to the east and back to Troway.

Start and Finish	Troway, Derby	SK412792
OS maps	119	

Publication(s)
Folder: *Chesterfield Round Walk* (RA Chesterfield & NE Derbyshire). A5\3pp\£1.00 (+ SAE).

Chilterns Hundred 38

Berks, Bucks, Herts, Oxon	160 km / 100 miles

Designed as a circuitous tour of the Chilterns, the route aims to pass some of the most picturesque villages and scenery of the AONB, besides visiting numerous historic churches and inns.

From Amersham, it passes south and west to the Chiltern Society's Open Air Museum at Chorley Wood and the Quakers' Meeting House at Jordans to reach the river Thames at Cookham and Marlow. It then continues to Stonor, north to Watlington, Princes Risborough and Wendover to Tring, before heading south to Great Missenden and back to Amersham.

Start and Finish	Amersham, Bucks	SU964982
OS maps	165, 166, 175, 176	

Publication(s)
Paperback: *Chilterns Hundred* by Jimmy Parsons (Chiltern Society). 1988 \ 210 x 149 \ 32pp \ £1.80.

Cistercian Way 39

Cumbria	53 km / 33 miles

The Cistercian Way is a walk along the paths, tracks and byways of the low Carboniferous Limestone hills that fringe the northern shores of Morecambe Bay.

From Grange-over-Sands, the route goes via woodlands to Hampsfell (220m) and Cartmel Priory to Cark and Holker Hall. The route then continues over the sands of the Leven Estuary, but this is dangerous and should only be attempted with the recognised Sand Pilot. Otherwise, until the estuary path is completed, the train should be caught to Ulverston.

From the pleasant market town of Ulverston, the Way continues by Dalton to Furness Abbey and the coast at Roa Island.

Start	Grange-over-Sands, Cumbria	SD412781
Finish	Roa Island, Cumbria	SD232648
On OS maps	96	
Waymark	Monk	

Publication(s)
Leaflet: *Cistercian Way* (South Lakeland District Council). 1990 \ A4/3 \ Free.
Paperback: *The Cistercian Way* by Ian O. Brodie (Carnegie Press). ISBN: 094878931X. 1989 \ A5 \ 64pp \ £3.50.

Clarendon Way 40

Hants, Wilts	39 km / 24 miles

Named after Clarendon Park on the eastern edge of Salisbury, the Way links that city on the river Avon with Winchester on the river Itchen. Crossing the river Test at Kings Somborne, its scenery ranges from the water meadows of the valleys with their charming villages through woodland to chalk downs with their fine views.

Start	Salisbury, Wilts	SU143297
Finish	Winchester, Hants	SU483293
On OS maps	184, 185	
Waymark	Bishop's mitre	

Publication(s)
Leaflet: *Test & Clarendon Way* (Hampshire County Council). 1986\A4/3\Free.
Paperback: *The Test Way and The Clarendon Way* by Barry Shurlock (Hampshire County Council). ISBN: 0948176032. 210 x 125\128pp\£3.95.

Cleveland Way 41

Cleveland, N Yorks	176 km / 110 miles

Officially opened in 1969, this is Britain's second-oldest National Trail. From Helmsley the Way climbs to the North York Moors at Sutton Bank, from where there is a short extension to the Kilburn White Horse, and heads north along the western edge of the high heather moors to Osmotherley. From here it follows tracks along the northern escarpment of the moors over Carlton Bank, Cringle Moor and Hasty Bank to Greenhow Moor. There the Way turns north over Kildale Moor, Roseberry Topping and Gisborough Moor to leave the North York Moors National Park and cross farmland to reach the coast at Saltburn-by-the-Sea. From here it follows a varied and undulating coastal path southwards along clifftops, over the sands and past harbours and resorts including Runswick, Whitby, Robin Hood's Bay and Scarborough to reach Filey Brigg.

Start	Helmsley, N Yorks	SE611839
Finish	Filey Brigg, N Yorks	TA126817
On OS maps	93, 94, 99, 100, 101	
Waymark	National Trail Acorn	

Publication(s)
Softback: *Cleveland Way* by Ian Sampson (Aurum Press). ISBN: 1854100211. 1989\210 x 130\144pp\£8.99.

Leaflet: *Cleveland Way* (Countryside Commission Postal Sales). 1991\A4/3\Free.
Paperback: *Cleveland Way* by Bill Cowley (Dalesman Publishing Ltd). ISBN: 0852069065. 1987\205 x 135\72pp\£3.95.
Booklet: *Cleveland Way Accommodation and Information Guide* (North York Moors National Park). 1993\A4/3\24pp\Free (+ large SAE).
Softback: *Cleveland Way Companion* by Paul Hannon (Hillside Publications). ISBN: 1870141172. 1987\175 x 117\88pp\£4.95.
Paperback: *Great Northern Walks: Where to Stay* by John Morrison (Leading Edge Press and Publishing). ISBN: 0948135247. 1991\188 x 105\160pp\£3.25.
Hardback: *Guide to the Cleveland Way* by Richard Sale (Constable and Co Ltd). ISBN: 0094672202. 1987\171 x 114\224pp\£7.95.
Stripmap: *The Cleveland Way* (Footprint). £2.95.
Paperback: *The Cleveland Way* by John Merrill (Trail Crest Publications Ltd). ISBN: 0907496709. 80pp\£4.95.
Paperback: *Walking the Cleveland Way and the Missing Link* by Malcolm Boyes (Cicerone Press). ISBN: 1852840145. 1989\116 x 176\144pp\£5.99.
Badge and certificate (£2.75 / post free) available from Trail Crest Publications Ltd.

Cleveland Way (Missing Link) 42

N Yorks	80 km / 50 miles

The route utilises public rights of way and Forestry Commission tracks to provide a scenic link between the two ends of the National Trail. It predates the North York Moors Park's Tabular Hills Link.
From the coast it climbs the eastern flank of the North York Moors to Reasty Bank Top and the start of the Forestry Commission's Blue Man walk, which is followed through the Langdale Forest to Crosscliffe. The Link then leaves the trail and crosses open moorland, passing the Hole of Horcum to Levisham, from where it goes through Cropton Forest to Hutton-le-Hole and Shiplam Moor to reach and follow the river Riccal to Helmsley.

Start	Crook Ness, N Yorks	TA026936
Finish	Helmsley, N Yorks	SE611839
OS maps	100, 101	

Publication(s)
Paperback: *Walking the Cleveland Way and the Missing Link* by Malcolm Boyes (Cicerone Press). ISBN: 1852840145. 1989\116 x 176\144pp\£5.99.
Badge and certificate (£1.25 / £0.30 post free) available from Missing Link Recorder.

Clopton Way   43

Cambs	17 km / 11 miles

The walk offers commanding views over much of south-west Cambridgeshire, as it follows the top of an escarpment through the deserted medieval village of Clopton. It connects the Wimpole Way with the Greensand Ridge Walk.

Start	Wimpole Hall, Cambs	TL343511
Finish	Gamlingay, Cambs	TL226533
OS maps	154	
Waymark	Clopton Way posts and discs	

Publication(s)
Leaflet: *Clopton Way* (Cambridgeshire County Council). 1990\A4/3\£0.40 (+ 50p).

Clyde Walkway   44

Strathclyde	80 km / 50 miles

The Clyde Walkway, a riverside path through the centre of Glasgow, is currently under development. At the time of writing, it is planned to extend from Bonnington Linn, south of Lanark, via Strathclyde Park to Bell's Bridge by the Exhibition Centre, where it continues as part of the Glasgow to Loch Lomond Cycle Path to Dumbarton, linking with the Leven towpath to Balloch on Loch Lomond. At present, the sections from Dumbarton to Cambuslang and from Uddingston to Strathclyde Park are open, as are various short sections further upstream.

At Bell's Bridge, it links with the 14-mile Kelvin/Allander Walkway to the start of the West Highland Way at Milngavie, and with the 33-mile Glasgow to Irvine Pedestrian Cycle Route, which in turn links at Johnstone with the 14-mile Johnstone and Greenock Railway Path. Note that the Glasgow-Irvine route contains a long road section.

Start	Lanark, Strathclyde
Finish	Dumbarton, Strathclyde
OS maps	63, 64, 72

Publication(s)
Leaflet: *Glasgow-Loch Lomond-Killin Cycle Way* (Sustrans Scotland). A4/3\Free (+ SAE).
Leaflet: *Long Distance Pedestrian and Cycle Routes* (Strathclyde Regional Council). 1993\A4/3\Free.

Coast to Coast Trek   45

Cleveland, Cumbria, N Yorks	192 km / 120 miles

This is a shorter (by some 70 miles) alternative to the now classic Wainwright route. Devised by Richard French, it starts further south and finishes further north. Following well-defined tracks and footpaths, it is generally an easy-going route, although some upland sections can be difficult in poor weather. From the west coast at Arnside the route heads east, over the limestone pavement around Hutton Roof to Kirkby Lonsdale; it reaches and crosses the Yorkshire Dales National Park via Ribblehead and Wensleydale, going on to Leyburn. At Osmotherley the route joins the Cleveland Way through the North York Moors National Park to the finish at Saltburn on the east coast.

Start	Arnside, Cumbria	SD461788
Finish	Saltburn-by-the-Sea, Cleveland	NZ668216
OS maps	93, 97, 98, 99	

Publication(s)
Booklet: *A One Week Coast to Coast Trek Irish to North Sea* by Dick French (Richard French). 1994 \ 105 x 150 \ 24pp \ £3.00 (+ A5 SAE).

Coast to Coast Walk   46

Cumbria, N Yorks	304 km / 190 miles

This route, written by Wainwright in 1972 partly to encourage others to devise their own routes, is now followed by many walkers, but it has caused some problems where the route does not follow rights of way. It links the two coasts and three National Parks, and favours a high-level traverse (often with alternative routes) wherever possible.

From the west coast, the walk crosses the coastal plain to Ennerdale Water and the Lake District National Park, which is traversed via the Honister Pass, Grasmere, Grisedale Pass or Striding Edge and Haweswater to reach Shap. From Shap Fell the Westmorland limestone plateau is crossed to Kirkby Stephen. The route then climbs to the Pennine watershed on Nine Standards Rigg and passes through Keld, Reeth and Richmond before crossing the flat agricultural Vale of Mowbray to reach and follow the Lyke Wake Walk route over the North York Moors for 16 miles. It then crosses Glaisdale Rigg to Grosmont and Robin Hood's Bay.

To take into account the problems with non-rights of way, the route was slightly amended in 1994; this amended route is that shown in the 1994 Michael Joseph guide, and on the OS strip map.

Start	St Bees, Cumbria	NX959119
Finish	Robin Hood's Bay, N Yorks	NZ953048
OS maps	89, 90, 91, 92, 93, 94, 98, 99, 100	

Publication(s)

Softback: *A Northern Coast to Coast* by Terry Marsh (Cicerone Press). ISBN: 1852841265. 1993\116 x 176\280pp\£7.99.

Booklet: *Coast to Coast Accommodation Guide* (Mrs Doreen Whitehead). 1994\100 x 150\56pp\£2.00 (+ SAE).

Paperback: *Coast to Coast Walk* by Paul Hannon (Hillside Publications). ISBN: 1870141180. 1992\152pp\£6.95.

Hardback: *Coast to Coast Walk* by A Wainwright (Michael Joseph). ISBN: 0718140729. 1994\£9.99.

Booklet: *Coast to Coast Walk* (YHA Northern Region). 1993\A5\20pp\£2.00.

Booklet: *Coast to Coast Walk Accommodation Guide* by Ewen Bennett (North York Moors Adventure Centre). 1994\A6\36pp\£3.00.

Stripmap: *Coast to Coast Walk: Keld to Robin Hood's Bay* (Ordnance Survey). ISBN: 031926047X. 1994\£4.99.

Stripmap: *Coast to Coast Walk: St Bees Head to Keld* (Ordnance Survey). ISBN: 0319260461. 1994\£4.99.

Paperback: *Great Northern Walks: Where to Stay* by John Morrison (Leading Edge Press and Publishing). ISBN: 0948135247. 1991\188 x 105\160pp\£3.25.

Leaflet: *The Coast to Coast Walk* (Richmondshire District Council). 1988\A4/3\£0.20.

Hardback: *Wainwright's Coast to Coast Walk* by A Wainwright (Michael Joseph). ISBN: 071812622X. 1987\250 x 215\208pp\£16.99.

Paperback: *Wainwright's Coast to Coast Walk* by A Wainwright (Michael Joseph). ISBN: 071813107X. 1989\250 x 215\208pp\£12.99.

Coed Morgannwg Way   47

Mid Glam, W Glam	58 km / 36 miles

The Way, most of which is on Forestry Commission land, was opened in 1977 to celebrate the Queen's Silver Jubilee, and extended to meet the Taff Trail in 1993. It crosses part of the Coed Morgannwg, a complex of four upland forests covering over 41,000 acres of the rolling hills of the south Wales coalfields.

From Gethin it heads west to the Dare Valley and Craig y Llyn, then south-west, climbing to several more viewpoints, to reach Afan Argoed Country Park. From here the route follows less elevated paths past a number of archaeological remains from prehistoric to industrial times, to Margam where an easterly extension goes to Gilfach.

Start	Gethin Woodland Park, Mid Glam	SO057032
Finish	Margam, W Glam	SS814852
On OS maps	170	
Waymark	White footprint on brown background	

Publication(s)
Leaflet: *Coed Morgannwg Way* (West Glamorgan County Council).
1994\A4/3\Free.

Consett and Sunderland Railway Path 48

Durham, Tyne & Wear	32 km / 20 miles

The Railway Path is one of many disused railway lines throughout the country that have been converted by Sustrans Ltd to cyclepaths for use by non-motorised transport. It connects Sunderland via Chester-le-Street and Stanley to the Derwent and Waskerley Ways south of Consett.

Start	Hownes Gill, Durham	NZ099495
Finish	Sunderland, Tyne & Wear	NZ385570
OS maps	88	

Publication(s)
Leaflet: *Consett & Sunderland Railway Path* (Sustrans Ltd).
A4/3\Free (+ SAE).
Folder: *Railway Walks in Derwentside* (Derwentside District Council). A4/3\4pp\£0.80.

Cook Country Walk 49

Cleveland, N Yorks	64 km / 40 miles

The route aims to show some of the countryside in which Captain James Cook was born. It starts at his birthplace in Marton, and passes through Great Ayton, Staithes and Whitby, in all of which Cook lived. Partly coincident with the Cleveland Way, it passes a mixture of moorland, forest and sea-cliffs.

Start	Marton-in-Cleveland, Cleveland	NZ516162
Finish	Whitby, N Yorks	NZ900117
OS maps	93, 94	

Publication(s)
Booklet: *The Cook Country Walk* (North York Moors National Park). ISBN: 0907480152. A5\32pp\£1.70.

Cotswold Way 50

Avon, Glos, Heref & Worc	165 km / 103 miles

A route along the Cotswold edge was first suggested by the Gloucestershire District Committee of the RA in 1953 and the creation of new rights of way proposed, but it was not until 1970 that the county councils opened the present route using existing rights of way. The route is currently the subject of a proposal for upgrading to National Trail status, which would include some improvements to the current line.

The Way meanders along the western edge of the Cotswold Hills, mainly following the top of this limestone escarpment, from where there are extensive views over the Severn Vale to the Malverns and the distant hills of the Mendips and the Welsh border, but descending from time to time to visit attractive villages nestling under the shelter of the edge. It crosses stone-walled farming countryside, passing villages and country houses built from the local limestone, and many sites of archaeological interest.

From Chipping Campden the route goes via Broadway, Stanway, Beckbury Camp, the ruins of Hailes Abbey (NT) and Winchcombe, from where it climbs to Cleeve Cloud (the highest point on the route at 1,083ft), Crickley Camp, Birdlip, Painswick and Haresfield Beacon. It crosses the Frome valley and continues on an undulating route past Hetty Pegler's Tump (long barrow), Dursley, Wotton-under-Edge and Tormarton to reach the city of Bath.

Start	Chipping Campden, Glos	SP152392
Finish	Bath, Avon	ST751647
On OS maps	150, 151, 162, 163, 172	
Waymark	White spot	

Publication(s)
Paperback: *Aerofilms Guide: The Cotswold Way* by Ted Fryer (Ian Allan Publishing). ISBN: 0711020434. 286 x 140\128pp\£8.99.
Paperback: *Complete Guide to the Cotswold Way* by Mark Richards (Penguin Books Ltd). ISBN: 0140469168. £5.99.
Booklet: *Cotswold Way Handbook* (RA Gloucestershire Area). 1993\£1.00 (+ 30p).
Softback: *Guide to the Cotswold Way* by Richard Sale (Constable and Co Ltd). ISBN: 0094691304. 1988\171 x 114\£8.99.
Paperback: *The Cotswold Way* by Kev Reynolds (Cicerone Press). ISBN: 1852830498. 116 x 176\£6.50.
Paperback: *The Cotswold Way* by Mark Richards (Thornhill Press). ISBN: 0904110931. 1982\120 x 175\72pp\£1.50.
Badge (£1.25 / 25p) available from RA Gloucestershire Area.

Cotswolds   51

Glos, Heref & Worc, Warks	133 km / 83 miles

Linking many of the north Cotswold villages and other places of interest, this walk, beginning at Shakespeare's birthplace, goes south to Mickleton, then on to Chipping Campden, the finest of the Cotswold wool towns with many attractive and historic buildings. The walk continues south and then west to Broadway, and on to Stanton; then it turns east to Blockley. After a visit to Batsford Arboretum, the walk turns south to pass through Stow-on-the-Wold and Upper and then Lower Slaughter. At Bourton-on-the-

Water it turns north-west to Wood Stanway, then south-west to Sudeley Castle, Winchcombe and on to the finish in Cheltenham.

Start	Stratford-upon-Avon, Warks	SP204549
Finish	Cheltenham, Glos	SO947222
OS maps	150, 151, 163	

Publication(s)
Paperback: *Footpath Touring: Cotswolds* by Ken Ward (Footpath Touring). 221 x 114 \ 64pp \ £3.50.

Cown Edge Way 52

Derby, Gtr Man	30 km / 19 miles

This generally U-shaped route on the eastern edge of Gtr Manchester, rising to Cown Edge Rocks via Strines and Mellor, and returning via Charlesworth and Werneth Low, was originally created in 1970 as part of National Footpath Year. There is a mixture of terrains from urban to moorland, and most of the route is easily accessible by public transport.

Start	Hazel Grove, Gtr Man	SJ925875
Finish	Gee Cross, Gtr Man	SJ945930
On OS maps	109, 110	
Waymark	Named posts and amber discs and arrows	

Publication(s)
Booklet: *The Cown Edge Way* (RA Manchester Area). 1985 \ A5 \ 29pp \ £1.00.

Cross Bucks Way 53

Beds, Bucks	38 km / 24 miles

This route across northern Buckinghamshire was designed to link the Greensand Ridge Walk and Two Ridges Link at Leighton Buzzard with an extension of the Oxfordshire Way at Stratton Audley; however, this extension has yet to be completed.

Passing mainly through agricultural land, the route visits the villages of Marsh Gibbon, Twyford, Addington (where it crosses the N Bucks Way), Winslow, Swanbourne (where it appropriately crosses Swan's Way), Stewkley with its Norman church, and Soulbury.

Start	Stratton Audley, Bucks	SP609260
Finish	Linslade, Beds	SP912262
On OS maps	165	
Waymark	Named standard waymarks	

Publication(s)
Leaflet: *Cross Bucks Way* (Buckinghamshire County Council).
A4/3 \ Free (+ SAE).

Cumberland Way 54

Cumbria	128 km / 80 miles

The Way takes a meandering route from the Irish Sea across the
historic county of Cumberland and the Lake District National Park
to reach the former Westmorland boundary and the old market
town of Appleby. It avoids the mountain summits and follows old
tracks and footpaths, and provides a safe route across the open
fells, over passes and along lakesides. The Way visits Strands,
Wast Water, Black Sail Pass, Buttermere, Keswick, Castlerigg
stone circle, Aira Force, Brougham Castle and Cliburn.

Start	Ravenglass, Cumbria	SD084963
Finish	Appleby-in-Westmorland, Cumbria	NY683204
OS maps	89, 90, 91, 96	

Publication(s)
Softback: *Cumberland Way* by Paul Hannon (Hillside Publications). ISBN: 1870141113. 1985 \ 110 x 162 \ 96pp \ £4.95.

Cumbria Coastal Way 55

Cumbria	200 km / 125 miles

The Way follows the west coast of Cumbria from Roa Island, where
it links with the Cistercian Way, to Carlisle, passing from Victorian
industry at Barrow via the peaceful Duddon estuary, Sellafield
nuclear station, St Bees Head (start of Wainwright's Coast to
Coast), Georgian Whitehaven and the little-known Solway coast.

Start	Roa Island, Cumbria	SD232648
Finish	Carlisle, Cumbria	NY400554
OS maps	85, 89, 96	
Waymark	Named posts	

Publication(s)
Leaflet: *Cumbria Coastal Way* (Cumbria County Council).
1993 \ A5 \ Free.

Cumbria Way 56

Cumbria	112 km / 70 miles

The Way provides a relatively low-level south-to-north crossing of
the Lake District National Park, following tracks and paths along

valleys and over passes in the midst of splendid and varied scenery. From Ulverston it passes Coniston Water, Tarn Hows and Dungeon Ghyll and crosses the Stake Pass to Borrowdale, Derwent Water and Keswick. The Way continues to Caldbeck either via Dash Falls or over High Pike, and then follows the Caldew valley to Carlisle.

Start	Ulverston, Cumbria	SD284785
Finish	Carlisle, Cumbria	NY400554
On OS maps	85, 89, 90, 96, 97	

Publication(s)
Paperback: *The Cumbria Way* by John Trevelyan (Dalesman Publishing Ltd). ISBN: 1855680009. 1994\130 x 200\56pp\£3.95.

d'Arcy Dalton Way   57

Oxon, Warks, Wilts	104 km / 65 miles

The Way, published in 1985 to mark the RA Golden Jubilee, is named after the late Col WP d'Arcy Dalton who worked for over half a century to preserve rights of way in Oxfordshire. The Way takes a meandering southerly route, first crossing ironstone hills to Epwell and Hook Norton, and then following footpaths and tracks for 28 miles across the limestone uplands of the eastern Cotswolds via Great and Little Rollright, Churchill, Fifield, Great Barrington and Holwell. The river Thames is crossed at Radcot Bridge and the Way continues across the flatter farmland of the Vale of the White Horse, finally climbing to the crest of the chalk ridge of the Oxfordshire Downs, along which the Ridgeway Path runs.

Start	Wormleighton, Warks	SP448518
Finish	Wayland's Smithy, Wilts	SU281853
OS maps	151, 163, 164, 174	
Waymark	Named signs	

Publication(s)
Paperback: *d'Arcy Dalton Way* (Oxford Fieldpaths Society). 1987\210 x 148\60pp\£2.00 (+ 40p).

Dales Way   58

Cumbria, N Yorks, W Yorks	130 km / 81 miles

The Way, conceived by Colin Speakman and Tom Wilcock of the West Riding Group of the RA, mainly follows, as its name suggests, attractive dales through the Yorkshire and Howgill Fells and the south-eastern part of the Lake District. From Ilkley it heads along Wharfedale past Bolton Abbey, The Strid, Grassington and Buckden before crossing Cam Fell and the Pennine Way to descend to Dentdale. From here the river Dee is followed westwards to Sedbergh, then the Lune to the Crook of Lune. The Way crosses farmland to reach Burneside and the river Kent, which is traced for several miles before the path branches off to Bowness-on-Windermere.

There are three link routes to the main Ilkley to Bowness one: from Leeds (Leeds–Dales Way), Harrogate (Harrogate–Dales Way) and Shipley/Bradford (Shipley–Dales Way). See these path entries for further information.

Start	Ilkley, W Yorks	SE117476
Finish	Bowness-on-Windermere, Cumbria	SD402968
On OS maps	96, 97, 98, 104	
Waymark	Named signposts in Dales NP	
User group	Dales Way Association	

Publication(s)
Paperback: *Dales Way* by Colin Speakman (Dalesman Publishing Ltd). ISBN: 1855680726. 1994\200 x 130\128pp\£4.95.
Paperback: *Dales Way Companion* by Paul Hannon (Hillside Publications). ISBN: 1870141091. 96pp\£4.95.
Booklet: *Dales Way Handbook* (Dales Way Association). 1994\A5\£3.00.
Booklet: *Dales Way Route Guide* by Arthur Gemmell and Colin Speakman (Stile Publications). ISBN: 0906886538. 1991\197 x 120\44pp\£2.80.
Paperback: *Great Northern Walks: Where to Stay* by John Morrison (Leading Edge Press and Publishing). ISBN: 0948135247. 1991\188 x 105\160pp\£3.25.
Paperback: *The Dales Way* by Terry Marsh (Cicerone Press). ISBN: 1852841028. 1992\116 x 176\£5.99.
Stripmap: *The Dales Way* (Footprint). £2.95.
Badge (£1.50) available from Dales Way Association.

Darent Valley Path   59

Kent	24 km / 15 miles

From the river Thames at Dartford, this riverside route (devised by Kent Area RA in conjunction with local and county councils) runs along the Darent Valley via Farningham, Eynsford and Shoreham to Otford, where it meets the North Downs Way, and finally Sevenoaks.

Start	Dartford, Kent	TQ543744
Finish	Sevenoaks Wildfowl Res., Kent	TQ515564
On OS maps	177, 188	
Waymark	Yellow "D" on timber posts	

Publication(s)
Folder: *Countryside Walks in North-West Kent* (Kent County Council). ISBN: 1873010109. 1991\A4/3\£1.95.

Dark Peak Boundary Walk

60

Derby	125 km / 78 miles

A mainly high-level route circuit of the three great moorland masses of Kinder Scout, Bleaklow and Black Hill, the Walk passes via Glossop, Marsden, Hathersage and Bradwell, and traverses gritstone edges, moorland, wooded cloughs and stone villages, and passes numerous reservoirs.

Start and Finish	Hayfield, Derby	SK037869
OS maps	110	

Publication(s)
Looseleaf: *Dark Peak Boundary Walk* by Dave Irons (Dave Irons). 1992 \ A4 \ 1pp \ Free (+ SAE).

Dartmoor Perambulation

61

Devon	80 km / 50 miles

The Perambulation marks the boundary of the ancient forest of the moor and is one of the oldest and longest "set" walks on Dartmoor. In 1240, a writ was issued by Henry III asking the sheriff of Devon to "beat the bounds" of his brother's land. Twelve knights were summoned to ride the 50-mile boundary. In recent years, the route has become popular with walkers, who follow a similar course, visiting some of the same landmarks. From Cosdon Beacon the route heads south through Thirlstone, King's Oven, Dartmeet and Ryder's Hill. At Eastern White Barrow the Perambulation reaches its most southerly point. The return journey north passes Nun's Cross, Great Mis Tor and Yes Tor and goes back to the cairn on Cosdon Beacon.

Start and Finish	Cosdon Beacon, Devon	SX633939
OS maps	191, 202	

Publication(s)
Looseleaf: *Dartmoor's Ancient Boundary Walk* (Ian & Caroline Kirkpatrick). Free (+ SAE).
Paperback: *Dartmoor's Greatest Walk: the Perambulation of Dartmoor* by Bill Ranson (Devon Books). ISBN: 0861148002. 1987 \ A5 \ 80pp \ £3.95.
Badge and certificate (£2.00 / SAE / £0.30 / A4 SAE) available from Ian & Caroline Kirkpatrick.

Daugleddau Trail 62

Dyfed	80 km / 50 miles

This route around the Daugleddau estuary, devised by the Pembrokeshire Coast National Park and which will link with the Knights Way, is currently the subject of a dispute with a landowner, and has hence not been officially opened. A suggested route is however marked on OS maps.

Start and Finish	Haverfordwest, Dyfed
On OS maps	157, 158

Publication(s)
None at time of writing.

Dearne Way 63

S Yorks, W Yorks	48 km / 30 miles

A varied traverse from rural west to the industrialized east of Barnsley district following the River Dearne from its source near Birds Edge, Denby Dale, in Kirklees, to its meeting with the River Don at Mexborough in Doncaster.

The first third is in unspoilt Pennine countryside tracking fields, woods and villages. After Bretton Country Park the mining heritage area of Barnsley is met with canals, bridges and riverside walking providing interest for students of industrial archaeology. The route bypasses Barnsley town centre (but not some good real ale pubs), before heading east for Darfield and Mexborough, passing Monk Bretton Priory by way of fields, riverside paths and woods to end near Mexborough and the Denaby Ings Nature Reserve.

Start	Birds Edge, W Yorks	SE202079
Finish	Mexborough, S Yorks	SE490002
On OS maps	110, 111	
Waymark	Named discs with miners lamp logo	

Publication(s)
Folder: *Dearne Way* (Barnsley Metropolitan Borough Council). A4/3 \ £0.50.

Deerness Valley Walk 64

Durham	12 km / 8 miles

One of a series of railway-lines bought by local authorities, and developed for use by walkers and cyclists; horseriders may use them with a permit. The Deerness Valley Walk links the

Lanchester Valley and Brandon/Bishop Auckland Walks on the western edge of Durham City with Crook.

Start	Broompark, Durham	NZ254415
Finish	High Wooley, Durham	NZ172390
On OS maps	88, 92	

Publication(s)
Folder: *Railway Walks in County Durham* (Durham County Council). 1990\A5\10pp\£0.99 (+ 75p).

Delamere Way 65

Cheshire	35 km / 22 miles

One of a series of four interlinked, waymarked walks developed by the Mid-Cheshire Footpath Society. From Stockton Heath, south of Warrington, the Way runs south along farmland to the Delamere Forest, where it loops north to meet the northern end of the Sandstone Trail at Frodsham.

Start	Stockton Heath, Cheshire	SJ615858
Finish	Frodsham (Beacon Hill), Cheshire	SJ517767
On OS maps	109, 117, 118	
Waymark	Green spot on standard waymarks	

Publication(s)
Booklet: *Longer Trails in Vale Royal* by Carl Rogers (Vale Royal Borough Council). 1993\A5\76pp\£1.95.
Booklet: *Waymarked Walks in Central Cheshire* (Mid-Cheshire Footpath Society). 100 x 223\16pp\£0.75.

Derwent Walk 66

Durham, Tyne & Wear	19 km / 12 miles

One of a series of railway-lines bought by local authorities, and developed for use by walkers and cyclists; horseriders may use them with a permit. The Derwent Walk runs from the south bank of the Tyne through Rowlands Gill to Consett, where a recently opened extension links it with the Waskerley Way and Consett and Sunderland Railway Path.

Start	Swalwell Old Station, Tyne & Wear	NZ199621
Finish	Hownes Gill, Durham	NZ099495
On OS maps	88	

Publication(s)
Folder: *Railway Walks in County Durham* (Durham County Council). 1990\A5\10pp\£0.99 (+ 75p).

Folder: *Railway Walks in Derwentside* (Derwentside District Council). A4/3 \ 4pp \ £0.80.

Derwent Way 67

Humberside, N Yorks	144 km / 90 miles

The Way follows the river Derwent from its confluence with the Ouse to its source on the North York Moors. It crosses the Vale of York, passing Kexby and Stamford Bridge, and skirts the Howardian Hills to reach Malton. Then the Way, which has followed footpaths, tracks and roads along or close to the river valley, goes to the south of the river as it runs through the Vale of Pickering, and climbs to the northern foothills of the Yorkshire Wolds before crossing the Vale to rejoin the river at West Ayton. The last part of the route follows the river, gradually climbing the foothills of the North York Moors and passing through forestry plantations to reach open moorland at Lilla Howe Cross on the Lyke Wake Walk route.

Start	Barmby-on-the-Marsh, Humberside	SE690285
Finish	Lilla Howe, N Yorks	SE889987
OS maps	100, 101, 105, 106	

Publication(s)
Paperback: *Derwent Way* by Richard Kenchington (Dalesman Publishing Ltd). ISBN: 0852064438. 205 x 135 \ 80pp \ £1.25.
Badge available from Richard Kenchington.

Doncastrian Way 68

S Yorks	53 km / 33 miles

A circular walk around the old County Borough boundary of Doncaster. The walk follows a route from the urban fringes to open fields, river banks and green lanes towards the settlements of Barnby Dun and Dunsville, in a clockwise direction. The circle is completed by a similar route through villages, fields and riverside paths towards Sprotbrough and along the river Don and back to the start.

Start and Finish	Doncaster, S Yorks	SE566041
OS maps	111	
Waymark	Named signposts	

Publication(s)
Leaflet: *Doncastrian Way* (Doncaster Metropolitan Borough Council). A5 \ Free.

Douglas Way 69

Gtr Man, Lancs	58 km / 36 miles

The Way, devised by Lawrence Hubbard of the Bolton Group of the RA, follows the river Douglas from its source to its confluence with the river Ribble near Hesketh Bank, south of Preston. It descends from the open moorland of Winter Hill to salt marshes, via farmland and urban areas around Wigan where there are many sites of interest to industrial archaeologists.

Start	Winter Hill, Gtr Man	SD661145
Finish	Longton, Lancs	SD458255
OS maps	108, 109	

Publication(s)
Softback: *The Douglas Valley Way* by Gladys Sellers (Cicerone Press). ISBN: 1852840730. 1991\116 x 176\64pp\£4.99.
Paperback: *The Douglas Way* by Lawrence Hubbard (RA Bolton Group). 1987\150 x 208\36pp\£3.15.

Downs Link 70

Surrey, W Sussex	48 km / 30 miles

This is a north-south bridleway link between two national trails which was developed by Surrey and West Sussex County Councils. From St Martha's Hill on the North Downs Way the Link follows bridleways over wooded heath and farmland to meet and follow the trackbed of the former Horsham and Guildford direct railway through Cranleigh to Christ's Hospital near Itchingfield. Here the trackbed of the former Shoreham to Itchingfield Junction line is followed through Partridge Green and Bramber, crossing farmland to meet the South Downs Way.

Start	St Martha's Hill, Surrey	TQ032483
Finish	Botolphs, W Sussex	TQ193094
On OS maps	186, 187, 198	
Waymark	Green/white disc with bridge	

Publication(s)
Leaflet: *Downs Link Route Guide* (West Sussex County Council). A4/3\Free.
Paperback: *The South Downs Way and Downs Link* by Kev Reynolds (Cicerone Press). ISBN: 1852840234. 116 x 176\136pp\£5.99.

Ducal Nottinghamshire   71

Derby, Notts	51 km / 32 miles

Two circular 18-mile bridleways (Western and Eastern Circuits) can be linked together to form this figure-of-eight route through the rolling countryside to the south of Clumber Park, and reaching as far west as Cresswell Crags.

Start and Finish	Bothamsall, Notts	SK675734
OS maps	120	
Waymark	Signposts and standard (blue) waymarks	

Publication(s)
Leaflet: *Ducal Nottinghamshire Eastern Circuit* (Nottinghamshire County Council). 1993 \ A5 \ Free (+ 35p).
Leaflet: *Ducal Nottinghamshire Western Circuit* (Nottinghamshire County Council). 1993 \ A5 \ Free (+ 35p).

Dyfi Valley Way   72

Dyfed, Gwynedd, Powys	174 km / 109 miles

The Dyfi (English Dovey) valley is one of the most beautiful valleys in Wales. This route follows the north side of the Dyfi, from Aberdyfi going in a north-easterly direction, through Pennal and the Centre for Alternative Technology at Llwyngwern Quarry. Across the site of King Arthur's last battle at Camlan, the going is fairly easy before the strenuous climb up to the summit of Aran Fawddwy, which at 2,971ft is the highest peak south of Snowdon. At Llanuwchllyn the route retraces its steps, then returns in a south-westerly direction south of the Dyfi, then on through Llany-mawddwy and Machynlleth to the finish at Borth.

Start	Aberdyfi, Gwynedd	SN614959
Finish	Borth, Dyfed	SN609901
OS maps	124, 125, 135, 136	
Waymark	DVW in shape of salmon	

Publication(s)
Paperback: *Guide to the Dyfi Valley Way* by Laurence Main (Kittiwake Press). ISBN: 0702808873. 1988 \ 211 x 121 \ 96pp \ £3.95 (+ 57p).

East Devon Way   73

Devon	64 km / 40 miles

An easy route that follows the estuary of the river Exe to Lympstone and then turns east over the commons and rolling hills of the East Devon AONB via Harpford, Sidbury, Farway and

Colyton. It can be combined with the South West Coast Path to form a large circular walk.

Start	Exmouth, Devon	SX999814
Finish	Uplyme, Devon	SY333933
OS maps	192, 193	
Waymark	Foxglove (logo of AONB)	

Publication(s)
Booklet: *The East Devon Way* by Norman Barns (East Devon District Council). 1993\60pp\£4.95 (+ 40p).

East Mendip Way   74

Somerset	.	30 km / 19 miles

As the West Mendip Way does not cover the whole of the Mendip range, a continuation eastwards to Shepton Mallet was created to mark the fortieth anniversary of the Rotary Club of Shepton Mallet; this was called the Mendip Forty, and signposts and waymarks for this were erected. In 1993, this route was incorporated into the East Mendip Way, and extended through to Frome.

Though a continuation of the W Mendip Way, the scenery on the E Mendip Way is surprisingly different, being softer with fewer high summits, and having hedgerows instead of dry stone walls. Few villages are passed on the route, but it does pass Shepton Mallet, and after that Chelynch, Downhead and Chantry. At the end, in Frome, the Way passes through Trinity, the largest surviving area of pre-industrial-revolution workers' housing in Britain.

Start	Wells, Somerset	ST549461
Finish	Frome, Somerset	ST777481
OS maps	183	
Waymark	Named signposts and ash key logo waymarks	

Publication(s)
Leaflet: *The East Mendip Way* (David Wright). 1993\A2/4\£2.00 (+ SAE).

East Riding Heritage Way   75

Humberside, N Yorks	136 km / 85 miles

This is the overall name given to four linked walks devised by Glen Hood (then of Shakespeare Junior High School, Hull), and developed and waymarked in conjunction with Humberside County Council. The walks are:

1. **Beverley Twenty**
20 miles from the Humber Bridge at Hessle, west along the Humber Estuary and then following a meandering north-easterly

course, with several variations, on field paths and tracks across flat to gently undulating farmland to Beverley.

2. Hutton Hike
23 miles from Beverley Minster along farmland and riverside paths and dykes, passing through Arram, Cranswick and Hutton to Driffield.

3. Rudston Roam
21 miles from Driffield following river, beckside and field paths over level to gently undulating farmland via Nafferton, Burton Agnes and the Rudston monolith to Bridlington.

4. Headland Walk
21 miles from Bridlington along the chalk cliffs of the Heritage coast to Flamborough Head and Bempton and Buckton cliffs to the promenade at Filey, with an alternative finish at the Brigg.

Start	Hessle (Point), Humberside	TA026253
Finish	Filey Brigg, N Yorks	TA126817
OS maps	101, 106, 107	
Waymark	Standard waymarks with path initials	

Publication(s)
Folder: *Beverley Explorer* (Humberside County Council). A5 \ £2.00 (+ 30p).
Folder: *Bridlington / Driffield Explorer* (Humberside County Council). A5 \ £2.00 (+ 30p).
Looseleaf: *East Riding Heritage Way* by Glen Hood (Glen Hood). 1993 \ A4 \ 9pp \ Free (+ SAE).
Badge and certificate (£1.00 / SAE / £0.15 / 9"x6" SAE) available from Glen Hood.

Ebor Way   76

N Yorks, W Yorks	112 km / 70 miles

A relatively gentle walk, taking its name from Eboracum, Roman York. From Helmsley it heads southwards to Hovingham and crosses undulating farmland to Strensall, from where the river Foss is followed to York. The city is crossed on the path along its medieval walls and is left along the banks of the river Ouse. At Tadcaster the route turns west and continues along the Wharfe valley and the Ainsty bounds to Wetherby and Harewood. Here the Way climbs to the gritstone outcrops of the Chevin and Cow and Calf Rocks on the edge of Ilkley Moor before descending to Ilkley in Wharfedale.

Start	Helmsley, N Yorks	SE611839
Finish	Ilkley, W Yorks	SE117476
On OS maps	100, 104, 105	

Waymark	Ebor Way signposts

Publication(s)
None at time of writing.

Eddisbury Way   77

Cheshire	28 km / 18 miles

One of a series of four interlinked, waymarked walks developed by
the Mid-Cheshire Footpath Society. From Frodsham Bridge near
the northern end of the Sandstone Trail, the Way runs south along
farmland and riverside paths and the western side of the Delamere
Forest to Kelsall and Duddon. It then continues via Huxley to
rejoin the Sandstone Trail at Higher Burwardsley.

Start	Frodsham (Beacon Hill), Cheshire	SJ517767
Finish	Burwardsley, Cheshire	SJ525567
On OS maps	117	
Waymark	Blue spot on standard waymarks	

Publication(s)
Booklet: *Longer Trails in Vale Royal* by Carl Rogers (Vale Royal
Borough Council). 1993\A5\76pp\£1.95.
Booklet: *Waymarked Walks in Central Cheshire* (Mid-Cheshire
Footpath Society). 100 x 223\16pp\£0.75.

Eden Valley Walk   78

Kent, Surrey	24 km / 15 miles

This walk explores the valleys of the rivers Eden and Medway
between Edenbridge and Tonbridge, and passes through the High
Weald AONB. It follows the Eden valley past Hever Castle to the
confluence with the Medway near Penshurst Place; it then follows
the Medway past Haysden Water into Tonbridge.

Start	Cernes Farm, Surrey	TQ425445
Finish	Tonbridge, Kent	TQ590465
On OS maps	187, 188	
Waymark	Tree, castle and river	

Publication(s)
Booklet: *Eden Valley Walk* (Kent County Council). ISBN:
1873010060. 1991\210 x 210\28pp\£2.45.

Eden Way 79

Cumbria	124 km / 78 miles

Starting north-west of Carlisle, where the river Eden flows into the Solway Firth, the walk follows the river through quiet, unspoilt countryside to its source high up on Mallerstang Edge south of Kirkby Stephen.

Start	Rockcliffe Marsh, Cumbria	NY333619
Finish	Black Fell Moss, Cumbria	SD807998
OS maps	85, 86, 90, 91, 98	

Publication(s)
Paperback: *Eden Way* by C Emett (Cicerone Press). ISBN: 1852840404. 1990\176 x 116\184pp\£5.99.

Elham Valley Way 80

Kent	37 km / 23 miles

This valley walk through the Kent Downs, opened in 1994, gives striking panoramic views and passes through a diverse landscape of downland, woodlands, orchards, parkland and farmland.

From Canterbury, the Way follows the North Downs Way to Patrixbourne, but then heads south to Kingston (where there are spurs to Barham), Elham and Lyminge. The main route finishes in Hythe, but there is an alternative ending in Sandling. The route is well served by public transport.

Start	Canterbury, Kent	TR150579
Finish	Hythe, Kent	TR170345
OS maps	179, 189	
Waymark	Named posts	

Publication(s)
Booklet: *Along and Around the Elham Valley Way* (Kent County Council). ISBN: 1873101389. 1994\210 x 210\48pp\£2.45.

Epperstone Park to Southwell Minster 81

Notts	32 km / 20 miles

A circular bridleway created by Notts County Council in conjunction with the British Horse Society, this route passes through the rolling countryside to the southwest of Southwell; it passes through the villages of Halloughton and Morton, and skirts to the south of Southwell.

Start and Finish	Epperstone, Notts	SK648487
OS maps	120	

Waymark	Signposts and standard (blue) arrows

Publication(s)
Leaflet: *Epperstone Park to Southwell Minster* (Nottinghamshire County Council). 1993\A5\Free (+ 35p).

Epping Forest Centenary Walk   82

Essex, Gtr London	24 km / 15 miles

The route was published to mark the hundredth anniversary of the Epping Forest Act of 1878, which preserved this remnant of the Great Forest of Waltham from development. From Manor Park on the urban fringe the Walk heads north through a narrow strip of forest to Leytonstone, Highams Park, and the outskirts of Chingford. From here the route becomes more undulating and tree-covered as it passes Connaught Water and High Beach Conservation Centre to reach Epping.

Start	Manor Park Station, Gtr London	TQ419858
Finish	Epping, Essex	TL465012
On OS maps	166, 167, 177	

Publication(s)
Booklet: *Epping Forest Centenary Walk: Manor Park – Epping* by Fred Matthews and Harry Bitten (Epping Forest Superintendent). ISBN: 0852030215. 1992\A5\16pp\£1.00.

Esk Valley Walk   83

N Yorks	56 km / 35 miles

This route through the North York Moors National Park starts with a circular walk over Danby and Westerdale moors from Castleton to the source of the river at Esklets, and then follows the river valley through Glaisdale and Grosmont to the sea. There is a variety of countryside from open moorland to riverside pastures, and the route is easily accessible by the Esk Valley railway line.

Start	Blakey, N Yorks	SE683989
Finish	Whitby, N Yorks	NZ900117
OS maps	94, 100	
Waymark	Leaping salmon emblem	

Publication(s)
Booklet: *Esk Valley Walk* (North York Moors National Park). ISBN: 090748039X. 1992\120 x 170\32pp\£2.95.
Booklet: *Regional Routes Accommodation Guide* (North York Moors National Park). 1993\120 x 170\12pp\Free (+ SAE).
Badge (£1.00) available from North York Moors National Park.

Eskdale Way 84

Cleveland, N Yorks	132 km / 83 miles

A very varied circuit of the fields, woodlands, moors and country lanes of Eskdale, from the fishing port of Whitby along the northern side of the valley via Glaisdale and Commondale and looping over the Gisborough Moors before returning to the valley at Kildale. The return route meanders along or near the south side of the dale, looping south to visit Wheeldale and Goathland before returning to Whitby.

Start and Finish	Whitby, N Yorks	NZ900117
OS maps	94	

Publication(s)
Paperback: *Eskdale Way* by Louis S Dale (Dalesman Publishing Ltd). ISBN: 0852067445. 1983\205 x 135\48pp\£1.25.

Essex Way 85

Essex	130 km / 81 miles

This route was developed by the Council for the Protection of Rural Essex and RA members, and has recently been adopted by Essex County Council.
   From Epping it heads north-east across gently undulating agricultural land, passing through or near many attractive old villages including Willingale, Pleshey and Coggeshall. It continues north-eastwards, passing through Dedham, which has connections with the painter John Constable, and Manningtree, and then goes along the Stour Estuary to Harwich.

Start	Epping, Essex	TL465012
Finish	Harwich, Essex	TM259329
On OS maps	167, 168, 169	
Waymark	Named green discs and posts	

Publication(s)
Booklet: *The Essex Way* (Essex County Council). ISBN: 1852810874. 1994\A5\32pp\£3.00.

Etherow/Goyt Valley Way 86

Gtr Man	19 km / 12 miles

This route linking Stockport to the western edge of the Peak District follows the river Goyt upstream to where the Etherow runs into it north of Marple, and then follows the latter upstream through Compstall and Broadbottom to the county boundary at Woolley Bridge. Though an urban fringe walk, it is largely through attractive woodland. The northern section from Idle Hill forms part of the Trans Pennine Trail. See also Goyt Way.

Start	Stockport, Gtr Man	SJ893903
Finish	Woolley Bridge, Gtr Man	SE008958
OS maps	109, 110	
Waymark	Signposts with white footprint	

Publication(s)
Booklet: *Etherow–Goyt Valley Way* (Etherow/Goyt Valley Wardens). A5 \ 16pp \ £0.50.
Leaflet: *The Etherow and Goyt Valleys* (Etherow/Goyt Valley Wardens). A4/3 \ Free.

Exe Valley Way   87

Devon	34 km / 21 miles

For the most part the route follows quiet country lanes and footpaths along the Exe Valley via Bickleigh, Tiverton and Bampton, with a brief stretch of road through Tiverton. It is mostly flat, and is usable by horseriders and cyclists except between Bickleigh and Tiverton, and Bampton and Exebridge.

Start	Stoke Canon, Devon	SX937980
Finish	Exebridge, Devon	SS935249
On OS maps	181, 192	
Waymark	Named discs with stylised V symbol	

Publication(s)
Leaflet: *The Exe Valley Way* (Devon County Council). 1993 \ A4/3 \ Free.

Exmoor & Lorna Doone   88

Devon, Somerset	161 km / 101 miles

Designed as an eight-day walk taking in some of the most attractive scenery of the National Park and the countryside in which R.D. Blackmore's "Lorna Doone" is set, the route passes Dunkery Beacon (at 1,703ft, the highest point on Exmoor), then goes on to Dulverton and Withypool via the famous Tarr Steps. It continues through Simonsbath and down through the Doone valley to finish at Lynmouth.

Start	Dunster, Somerset	SS992437
Finish	Lynmouth, Devon	SS724494
OS maps	180, 181	

Publication(s)
Paperback: *Footpath Touring: Exmoor and Lorna Doone* by Ken Ward (Footpath Touring). ISBN: 0711701954. 1985\224 x 114\ 64pp\£3.50.

Fife Coast Path 89

Fife, Lothian	131 km / 82 miles

The Fife Coast Path keeps faithfully to the shore between the Forth Road Bridge and St Andrews Bay, though, for convenience, this route starts and finishes at railway stations. It includes numerous castles, fishing villages, remarkable rock formations, caves and long sandy beaches. The coast is a haven for bird life and flora. Apart from an exposed chain walk at Kincraig Point, the walking is easy, though times of high tide are best avoided in some places as the walk uses the foreshore.

Start	Dalmeny Station, Lothian	NT139779
Finish	Leuchars Station, Fife	NO449207
OS maps	59, 65, 66	

Publication(s)
Hardback: *The Fife Coast* by Hamish Brown (Mainstream Publishing Co Ltd). ISBN: 1851586083. 1994\155 x 232\226pp\£12.99.

Fife Interbus Walks 90

Fife	306 km / 191 miles

A series of ten interconnecting walks in Fifeshire, which all start and finish at bus stops. The ten walks are: Kincardine to Ballingry (23 miles), Colinswell to Wester Balgedie (23 miles), Dunfermline to Kirkcaldy (18 miles), Balfarg to Abernethy (14 miles), E Wemyss to Kettlebridge (9 miles), Crail to Gateside (38 miles), Boarhills to Leven (22 miles), Ceres to Luthrie (13 miles), Dairsie to Gauldry (11 miles) and Tayport to Newburgh (20 miles).

Start and Finish	Various
OS maps	58, 59, 65, 66

Publication(s)
Paperback: *Fife Between Bus Routes* by Owen Silver (Owen Silver). ISBN: 0951398318. 1991\A4/3\40pp\£1.00 (+ SAE).

Forest Way 91

Essex	40 km / 25 miles

The Way, designated and waymarked in 1972 by Essex County Council to mark European Conservation Year, links two forests and several open spaces in south-west Essex. From the edge of Epping Forest it runs north over farmland, from where there are views over the Lea valley, and crosses Latton and Harlow Commons to Hatfield Heath, Woodside Green (NT) and Hatfield Forest.

Start	Loughton Station, Essex	TQ423956
Finish	Takeley Street, Essex	TL534213
On OS maps	167, 177	
Waymark	Bright green Forest Way signposts & plaques	

Publication(s)
Paperback: *The Forest Way* (Essex County Council). ISBN: 1852810238. 1991\A5\14pp\£2.50.

Foss Walk 92

N Yorks	45 km / 28 miles

The Walk follows footpaths along or near the river Foss, from its confluence with the Ouse in the historic city of York to its source at Pond Head, four miles from the finish. The Walk passes through Strensall, Sheriff Hutton, Crayke and Oulston.

Start	York, N Yorks	SE603522
Finish	Easingwold, N Yorks	SE528698
On OS maps	100, 105	
Waymark	Named signposts and named arrows with frog logo	

Publication(s)
Paperback: *The Foss Walk* by Mark W Jones (River Foss Amenity Society). 1988\210 x 135\14pp\£1.50 (+ 30p).

Frome Valley Walkway 93

Avon	22 km / 14 miles

The Walkway links the northern outskirts of Bristol to the Cotswold Way by way of Frampton Cotterell, Yate and Chipping Sodbury. It passes through sandstone gorges, and by old mills, before rising to the Jurassic limestone of the Cotswolds.

Start	Frenchay, Avon	ST640772
Finish	Old Sodbury, Avon	ST752812
On OS maps	172	
Waymark	Kingfisher logo	

Publication(s)
Booklet: *Frome Valley Walkway* (Northavon District Council). 1993\100 x 180\Free.

Furness Boundary Walk 94

Cumbria 177 km / 111 miles

The Walk describes a clockwise circuit around the boundary of the Furness area of the historic county of Lancashire, which is enclosed by two river systems: to the west the river Duddon from its source at the top of Wrynose Pass to the sea; and to the east the river Brathay, Lake Windermere and the river Leven. It is bounded by the Irish Sea to the south. 60 miles of the route follow the coast around the Furness Peninsula, and the rest is on riverside and lowland paths following the river systems.

Start and Finish	Barrow-in-Furness, Cumbria	SD190688
OS maps	90, 96	

Publication(s)
Leaflet: *Walking Round High Furness* (Paddy Dillon). 1990 \
A3/9 \ £0.40.
Leaflet: *Walking Round Low Furness & Cartmel* (Paddy Dillon).
1990 \ A3/9 \ £0.40.
Paperback: *Walking the Furness Boundary* by John Llewellyn (St Mary's Hospice Appeal Centre). £4.95 (+ 50p).

Furness Trail 95

Cumbria 96 km / 60 miles

Described as an explorer's guide to Southern Lakeland, this route links seven South Cumbrian towns: Kendal, Levens, Cartmel, Newby Bridge, Ulverston, Coniston and Bowness. It is designed to include as many places for sightseeing and more active pursuits as possible.

Start and Finish	Kendal, Cumbria	SD520931
OS maps	96, 97	

Publication(s)
Softback: *The Furness Trail: Walking and Discovering South Lakeland* by Tim Cappelli (Sigma Leisure). ISBN: 1850583285. 1993 \ A5 \ 176pp \ £6.95.

Gipping Valley River Path 96

Suffolk 27 km / 17 miles

A riverside walk developed by Suffolk County Council, and passing through their Countryside Project Area. For most of the way it follows the towpath of the former Ipswich to Stowmarket Navigation (1793-1932), and the remains of eleven locks can be seen along the river Gipping. The Path leads through the industrial area of

Stowmarket to open countryside, passing farmland, old water-meadows, gravel pits and seven former water mills before meeting the Orwell Estuary at Ipswich.

Start	Stowmarket, Suffolk	TM050588
Finish	Ipswich, Suffolk	TM163439
OS maps	155, 169	
Waymark	Water-wheel logo	

Publication(s)
Leaflet: *The Gipping Valley River Path* (Suffolk County Council). A5 \ Free (+ SAE).

Glen Feshie 97

Grampian, Highland	51 km / 32 miles

One of the three main north-south passes across the granite massif of the Cairngorms, providing a challenge for fit walkers, but in bad or winter conditions it should only be attempted by well-equipped and experienced hill walkers.

From Braemar, it goes west to Inverey and the Linn of Dee, and then west to Glen Feshie, which it follows to Kincraig.

See also Lairig an Laoich, Lairig Ghru.

Start	Braemar, Grampian	NJ152915
Finish	Kincraig, Highland	NH830057
OS maps	34, 36	

Publication(s)
Leaflet: *The Cairngorm Passes* (Scottish Rights of Way Society). A2 \ £0.25 (+ 25p).

Glyndwr's Way/Ffordd Glyndwr 98

Powys	193 km / 121 miles

Named after Owain Glyndwr (the English form is Owen Glendower), an early-fifteenth-century warrior statesman who attempted to establish an independent Welsh nation, the route passes by, or close to, many sites connected with Glyndwr's rebellion, and the central point of the walk is Machynlleth, where Glyndwr held parliament as "Prince of Wales".

A varied and scenic route through mid Wales, it links with Offa's Dyke Path at each end, and although some sections provide easy walking, there are areas of open moorland and remote hillsides, where it is essential to carry an OS map and compass.

From Knighton the Way meanders north-west, passing through Abbeycwmhir and Llanidloes, and across the foothills of the Plynlimon range to the old market town of Machynlleth. From here it turns eastwards, recrossing Wales via Llangadfan, Dyfnant Forest, Lake Vyrnwy and Meiford to Hope village near Welshpool.

Start	Knighton, Powys	SO283724
Finish	Welshpool, Powys	SJ229071
On OS maps	124, 125, 126, 135, 136, 137	
Waymark	Yellow arrow on "Glyndwr's Way" plaque	

Publication(s)
Folder: *Glyndwr's Way / Ffordd Glyndwr* (Powys County Council). A4/3 \ 15pp \ £1.60.
Softback: *Owain Glyndwr's Way* by Richard Sale (Constable and Co Ltd). ISBN: 0094713103. 1992 \ 116x172 \ 206pp \ £9.95.
Paperback: *Owain Glyndwr's Way: A Pocket Companion Guide* by Gillian Walker (Management Update Ltd). ISBN: 0946679398. 1990 \ A5 \ 80pp \ £4.95 (+ 95p).

Goyt Way 99

Derby, Gtr Man	16 km / 10 miles

Linking with the Etherow/Goyt Way at Compstall, this easy route continues the river path along the Goyt via New Mills to Whaley Bridge.

Start	Whaley Bridge, Derby	SK012815
Finish	Compstall, Gtr Man	SJ965909
On OS maps	109, 110	
Waymark	GW logo with wavy line	

Publication(s)
Leaflet: *The Goyt Way* (Etherow/Goyt Valley Wardens). A4/3 \ Free.

Grafton Way 100

Bucks, Northants	21 km / 13 miles

The Way, named after the Dukes of Grafton who owned large areas of land in the southern part of Northamptonshire during the eighteenth and nineteenth centuries, links the North Buckinghamshire Way at Wolverton with the Knightley Way at Greens Norton. It follows the Grand Union Canal towpath, and then crosses undulating farmland and passes through the villages of Potterspury, Pury End and Wood Burcote.

Start	Wolverton, Bucks	SP807413
Finish	Greens Norton, Northants	SP671490
On OS maps	152	
Waymark	White circles, black arrows	

Publication(s)
Leaflet: *Grafton Way* (Northamptonshire County Council). 1984\A5\£0.25 (+ 25p).

Grand Union Canal Walk   101

Bucks, Gtr London, Herts, Northants, W Midlands, Warks		225 km / 141 miles

This first national waterways walk was created as part of the celebrations of the 200th anniversary of the creation of the canal companies that later formed the Grand Union Canal between London and Birmingham. Being almost entirely towpath, it is an easy walk with no map-reading problems, and provides much of interest to those interested in canal history.

From the centre of London at Little Venice, the canal heads west to Slough, and then north through Hertfordshire and the Chilterns to Tring. Apart from the stretch through Milton Keynes, the route is then largely rural, passing the Canal Museum at Stoke Bruerne, to Leamington Spa and Warwick. The final stretch is through the suburbs of Birmingham to finish at Gas St Basin.

For anyone wanting a record of their trip, there is a "letterbox" scheme of ten checkpoints, where a special passport can be stamped. For details, contact the project officer at Braunston.

Start	Little Venice,Paddington, Gtr London	TQ260818
Finish	Birmingham, Gas St Basin, W Midlands	SP062867
On OS maps	139, 151, 152, 165, 176	
Waymark	Named posts at regular intervals	

Publication(s)
Looseleaf: *Accommodation Guide* (Grand Union Canal Walk Project Officer). 1993\£1.50.
Softback: *Grand Union Canal Walk* by Anthony Burton and Neil Curtis (Aurum Press). ISBN: 1854102443. 1993\210 x 130\144pp\£9.99.

Grantham Canal   102

Leics, Lincs, Notts	53 km / 33 miles

The Grantham Canal was opened in 1797, and was built to link Grantham with the River Trent at Nottingham. Although the canal is no longer navigable for boats, the towpath provides an excellent opportunity to enjoy some of the most attractive countryside in the East Midlands, running through the heart of the Vale of Belvoir, and passing through many unspoilt villages. Part of the Leicestershire section has been designated an SSSI.

Start	Nottingham, Notts	SK569392
Finish	Grantham, Lincs	SK908355

OS maps   129, 130

Publication(s)
Leaflet: *The Grantham Canal* (Nottinghamshire County Council).
A4/3 \ Free (+ 35p).

Great Glen Way   103

Highland	100 km / 63 miles

A proposed Scottish Long Distance Route to link the west coast and
the end of the W Highland Way at Fort William along the Great
Glen past Loch Ness with the east coast at Inverness. A project
officer at Scottish Natural Heritage's North-West office is currently
evaluating the route and drawing up proposals for consultation.

Until this process is complete in the late 1990s, the cycle route
uses forest tracks, the Caledonian canal towpath, and various
minor roads to provide a route avoiding the busy A82 as much as
possible; it can also be used by walkers.

Start	Fort William, Highland	NN105742
Finish	Inverness, Highland	NH667452
OS maps	26, 34, 35, 41	

Publication(s)
Leaflet: *The Great Glen Cycle Route* (Forest Enterprise N Scotland). 1993 \ A4/3 \ Free.

Greater Manchester Boundary Walk   104

Gtr Man	208 km / 130 miles

Described as a long distance walk for beginners, this route describes a large circle around Manchester, meaning that it is easily
accessible throughout by public transport.

From Woolley Bridge, it runs clockwise thereby starting in the
lowlands, through Wilmslow, the Bollin Valley and over Chat Moss,
and then round to Billinge and Standish. Here it rises to the
moorland section: Winter Hill, the moors north of Bolton, Bury and
Rochdale, before running along the western edge of the Pennines:
Blackstone Edge and Saddleworth Moor.

Start and Finish	Woolley Bridge, Gtr Man	SE008958
OS maps	108, 109, 110	

Publication(s)
Softback: *The Greater Manchester Boundary Walk* by Graham
Phythian (Sigma Leisure). ISBN: 185058284X. 1991 \ 96pp \ £5.95.

Green Chain Walk 105

| Gtr London | 62 km / 39 miles |

An unusual concept, the Green Chain Walk was developed by a consortium of local authorities and provides a link between the river Thames and many of the finest open spaces in South-East London. There are three alternative starting points on the Thames: Thamesmead, Erith or the Thames Barrier at Woolwich, and several variations to the route itself, which passes through Oxleas Wood and Mottingham before terminating at Crystal Palace. Though there is inevitably some street walking, there is a surprising amount of woodland, grassland, park and garden, besides a number of fine viewpoints.

Start	Thamesmead, Gtr London	TQ472813
Finish	Crystal Palace, Gtr London	TQ343705
OS maps	177	

Publication(s)
Booklet: *Green Chain Walk. 1: Thamesmead to Oxleas Wood* (Green Chain Working Party). 1991\100 x 210\24pp\Free (+ 43p A5 SAE).
Booklet: *Green Chain Walk. 2: Thames Barrier to Oxleas Wood* (Green Chain Working Party). 1991\100 x 210\28pp\Free (+ 43p A5 SAE).
Booklet: *Green Chain Walk. 3: Oxleas Wood to Mottingham* (Green Chain Working Party). 1991\100 x 210\20pp\Free (+ 43p A5 SAE).
Booklet: *Green Chain Walk. 4: Mottingham to Crystal Palace* (Green Chain Working Party). 1991\100 x 210\28pp\Free (+ 43p A5 SAE).

Green London Way 106

| Gtr London | 148 km / 93 miles |

An unusual circular urban walk through London suburbs utilising rivers, canals, disused railway lines, alley-ways, parks, commons, woods, and heaths. Most of the route can be used by cyclists as well as walkers.

From Finsbury Park, it descends to the Lea Valley, and thence to East Ham, crossing the river at Woolwich. It passes via Shooters Hill, Crystal Palace, Streatham Common and Richmond Park to Kew. After a brief stretch along the river Brent, it rises to Harrow-on-the-Hill and Hampstead before returning to Finsbury Park.

| Start and Finish | Finsbury Park, Gtr London | TQ315869 |
| OS maps | 176, 177 | |

Publication(s)
Paperback: *Green London Way* by Bob Gilbert (Lawrence and Wishart Ltd). ISBN: 0853157464. 1991\155 x 234\195pp\£9.99.

Greensand Ridge Walk   107

Beds, Bucks, Cambs	64 km / 40 miles

A route suggested by Bedford Rambling Club, which takes in woods and farmlands along the dissected greensand ridge and passes Woburn Abbey and Ampthill Park to finish at Gamlingay in Cambridgeshire.

Start	Leighton Buzzard, Beds	SP915251
Finish	Gamlingay, Cambs	TL226533
On OS maps	152, 153, 165	
Waymark	"GRW" and deer emblem	

Publication(s)
Leaflet: *Greensand Ridge Walk* (Bedfordshire County Council). A4/3\£0.65.

Greensand Way   108

Kent, Surrey	169 km / 106 miles

The initial route through Surrey was devised by the late Geoffrey Hollis and other RA members, and developed by member societies of the Surrey Society. It was later extended through Kent by the RA Kent Area, and adopted by the two county councils. It follows the sandy ridge of the Lower Greensand Formation which runs east-west across the region to the south of the North Downs, and provides firm walking over heath and woodland, with several fine viewpoints.

From Haslemere the Way passes the Devil's Punchbowl and crosses Hascombe Hill and Winterfold Heath to Pitch, Holmbury and Leith Hill. From here, it descends to Dorking and continues eastwards via Reigate Heath, Bletchingley, Tandridge and Limpsfield Chart.

In Kent, it crosses Toy's Hill and Ide Hill before descending through grasslands to Sevenoaks Weald, continues through Knole Park to Ightham Mote, and crosses the Medway floodplain to Yalding. The ridge gradually changes to farmland and the route skirts the south of Ashford to meet the Saxon Shore Way at Hamstreet, near the Royal Military Canal.

Surrey CC's guide also contains five routes linking the Greensand Way to the N Downs Way. These are: Thursley to Farnham (10km), Shamley Green to Guildford (8km), Westcott to Ranmore (3km), Skimmington Castle to Reigate Hill (5km) and Oxted Mill to Oxted Downs (4km).

Start	Haslemere, Surrey	SU898329
Finish	Hamstreet, Kent	TR019349
On OS maps	186, 187, 188, 189	
Waymark	Yellow or blue discs with "GW"	

Publication(s)
Booklet: *Greensand Way in Kent* (Kent County Council). ISBN: 1873010230. 1992\46pp\£2.95.
Folder: *Guide to the Greensand Way (East Kent)* by RA Kent (D & S Stewart). A5\16pp\£1.00 (+ 41p).
Folder: *Guide to the Greensand Way (West Kent)* by RA Kent (D & S Stewart). A5\14pp\£0.75 (+ 41p).
Booklet: *The Greensand Way in Surrey: A Walkers Guide* (Surrey County Council). ISBN: 0946840415. 1989\A5\48pp\£2.50.

Greenway Challenge Walk 109

Essex	51 km / 32 miles

A circular walk around Basildon and Billericay, linking country parks and nature reserves, including Westley Heights, Little Burstead Common and Norsey Wood. The route is used as an annual challenge walk to raise funds for charity.

Start and Finish	Wat Tyler Country Park, Essex	TQ738867
OS maps	178	
Waymark	Standard arrows	

Publication(s)
Leaflet: *Greenway Challenge Walk* (Basildon District Council). 210 x 204\Free.

Gritstone Trail 110

Cheshire, Staffs	29 km / 18 miles

The Trail, developed by Cheshire County Council, follows the gritstone ridge which runs from north to south across the county giving views of the Peak District to the east and the Cheshire Plain to the west. Much of the upland walking is over the 1,000ft contour. From the deer park at Lyme, the Trail climbs to the open moorland of Sponds Hill and then follows an old ridge track over rough pasture and moorland to Tegg's Nose Country Park. A lowland section follows, passing old gritstone farmhouses before climbing to Croker Hill and the crest of The Minns. Finally, the river Dane is crossed to meet the Staffordshire Way at Rushton Spencer.

Start	Lyme Park, Cheshire	SJ962823
Finish	Rushton Spencer, Staffs	SJ935625
On OS maps	109, 118	

Waymark	Black bootmark & yellow "G"

Publication(s)
Booklet: *Gritstone Trail* (Cheshire County Council). 1986\212 x
200\12pp\£1.50 (+ 28p).

Hadrian's Wall Walk   111

Cumbria, Northumb, Tyne & Wear	120 km / 75 miles

Currently the subject of a proposed designation as a National Trail,
the walk runs the length of Hadrian's Wall, constructed under the
direction of that Roman Emperor in AD122. Although there are
rights of way along parts of the total length, including some of the
best-preserved remains of the Wall at Cuddy's Crags and the
milecastles and forts at Housesteads, Great Chesters and Bir-
doswald, until completion of the National Trail, walkers wanting
to follow the entire length from Tyne to Solway have to either resort
to a lot of road-walking to follow the Wall precisely, or deviate from
it using rights of way and minor roads. Mark Richards' guide does
the latter.

Start	Wallsend, Tyne & Wear	NZ304660
Finish	Bowness-on-Solway, Cumbria	NY225628
OS maps	85, 86, 87, 88	

Publication(s)
Paperback: *Guide to Walking Hadrian's Wall* by Graham Mizon
(Hendon Publishing Co). ISBN: 0860670120. 1993\210 x
135\48pp\£2.60.
Paperback: *Hadrian's Wall: Vol I: The Wall Walk* by Mark Richards
(Cicerone Press). ISBN: 1852841281. 1993\116 x 176\216pp\
£7.99.

Haematite Trail   112

Cumbria	29 km / 18 miles

The Trail was devised to explore some of the remains of the iron
mining industry which brought about the industrial expansion of
Furness and the subsequent emergence of Barrow. In its heyday
the Furness mining industry was an equivalent to the American
"Gold Rush", and provided some of the richest iron ore worked in
Britain. The route passes Newton, Little Urswick, Lindal, Marton
and Askam.

Start and Finish	Barrow-in-Furness, Cumbria	SD190688
OS maps	96	
Waymark	Pithead logo and named posts	

Publication(s)
Leaflet: *The Haematite Trail* (Barrow Borough Council).
A4/3 \ Free.

Hangers Way   113

Hants	34 km / 21 miles

This route introduces the walker to the series of steep-sided hills
known as the Hampshire Hangers, which run north from Petersfield. Although many of these are wooded, there is still also some
grassland, both of which habitats are important to wildlife. The
Way passes through the village of Selborne, well known to natu-
ralists as the home of Gilbert White, and his former home is now
a museum. It runs through Petersfield, and meets the South
Downs Way and Staunton Way at its southern end.

Start	Alton, Hants	SU723397
Finish	QE Country Park, Hants	SU718182
On OS maps	186, 197	
Waymark	Tree on hill	

Publication(s)
Leaflet: *Hangers Way* (Hampshire County Council). A4/3 \ Free.

Hanslope Circular Ride   114

Bucks	32 km / 20 miles

A circular bridle route to the north of Milton Keynes, the Ride runs
through open countryside centred on the village of Hanslope, with
its distinctive spire, and gives extensive views over the Ouse and
Tove Valleys.

Start and Finish	Great Linford, Bucks	SP846424
OS maps	152	
Waymark	Named standard discs and posts	

Publication(s)
Leaflet: *Hanslope Circular Ride* (Buckinghamshire County Council). Free (+ SAE).

Harcamlow Way   115

Cambs, Essex, Herts	225 km / 141 miles

A figure-of-eight walk, mainly on tracks and green lanes passing
many places of historic interest open to the public, was devised by
Fred Matthews with the help of RA members to celebrate the tenth
anniversary of the founding of the West Essex Group of the RA and

Footpath 1980 Week. From Harlow it crosses low hills, woods and arable land via Standon and Manuden to meet the cross-over point at Newport. It continues through Saffron Walden and over the low Bartlow Hills to Horseheath and the Fleam Dyke, to enter Cambridge from the north. From the city the return route goes to the west of the outward one, passing through Melbourn and Chrishall and going across flattish farmland to Newport. The Way then continues southwards to the east of the outward route via Debden, Thaxted, Takeley and Hatfield Forest.

Start and Finish	Harlow, Essex	TL445113
On OS maps	153, 154, 166, 167	

Publication(s)
Booklet: *Harcamlow Way* by Fred Matthews and Harry Bitten (Matthews/Bitten Publications). A5 \ 52pp \ £2.50.
Badge (£1.00) available from Matthews/Bitten Publications.

Harrogate Ringway   116

N Yorks	34 km / 21 miles

An easy circular route around the environs of Harrogate, which links with the Knaresborough Round to form a 36-mile route. Adopted by Harrogate Borough Council in 1991, who call it Harrogate & Knaresborough Ringway, it does not go around Knaresborough.

Start and Finish	Pannal, N Yorks	SE307514
On OS maps	104	
Waymark	Named signposts	

Publication(s)
Folder: *Harrogate and Knaresborough Ringway* (Harrogate Borough Council). 1991 \ 6pp \ £1.95 (+ 15p).
Looseleaf: *The Harrogate Ringway* (RA Harrogate Group). A4 \ 1pp \ £0.20 (+ SAE).

Harrogate-Dales Way   117

N Yorks	32 km / 20 miles

A route from Harrogate that links with the Dales Way at Bolton Abbey. It leaves Harrogate via the Valley Gardens to cross Haversh Park and pass a succession of reservoirs along the Washbourn valley before climbing over the open heights of Rocking Moor to Wharfedale.

Start	Harrogate, N Yorks	SE304553
Finish	Bolton Abbey, N Yorks	SE072539
OS maps	104	

User group	Dales Way Association

Publication(s)
Looseleaf: *Harrogate Dalesway* (RA Harrogate Group). A4\10pp\£0.20 (+ SAE).

Haslemere Circular Walk 118

Hants, Surrey, W Sussex	36 km / 23 miles

A circuit around Haslemere, with a large proportion of the route crossing National Trust woodland and heathland, including Gibbet Hill, Blackdown, Marley Common, Waggoners Wells and the Devil's Punchbowl.

Start and Finish	Devil's Punch Bowl, Surrey	SU890358
OS maps	186	

Publication(s)
Looseleaf: *Haslemere Circular Walk* by Elizabeth Pamplin (Elizabeth Pamplin). A4\3pp\Free (+ SAE).

Heart of England Way 119

Glos, Staffs, Warks	160 km / 100 miles

The Way, originally devised by a group of Midland Rambling Clubs and recently extended by the Cotswold Wardens from Chipping Campden to the end of the Oxfordshire Way at Bourton-on-the-Water, follows a curving southerly route across gently undulating farmland and along woodland and riverside paths.

From the sandy heath of Cannock Chase, it crosses farmland to Lichfield. It follows the Birmingham and Fazeley Canal and the other water features of Kingsbury Water Park and Shustoke Reservoir. It continues through the green, well-wooded Arden countryside with lovely English villages and a procession of churches, through Henley-in-Arden to the Roman town of Alcester. Soon after, it enters the flat willowy valley of the Avon, then goes around the northern outliers of the Cotswolds to reach Chipping Campden. After this, the Way heads south through the typical Cotswold villages of Swell and Lower Slaughter through a landscape of clear brooks and green meadows.

Start	Milford, Staffs	SJ975212
Finish	Bourton-on-the-Water, Glos	SP170209
On OS maps	127, 128, 139, 140, 150, 151, 163	
Waymark	Green and white HEW Logo	
User group	Heart of England Way Association	

Publication(s)
Leaflet: *Heart of England Way* (Heart of England Way Association). A4/3 \ Free.
Paperback: *Heart of England Way* by John Roberts (Walkways). ISBN: 0947708235. 1990 \ A5 \ 80pp \ £4.55.
Looseleaf: *Heart of England Way Accommodation List* (Walkways). Free (+ SAE).
Paperback: *Heart of England Way: Chipping Campden–Bourton-on-the-Water* (Cotswold Warden Office). 1992 \ A5 \ 22pp \ £1.25 (+ 25p).

Hereward Way 120

Cambs, Leics, Lincs, Norfolk, Northants, Suffolk	164 km / 103 miles

The Way, developed by Trevor Noyes and members of the Peterborough Group of the RA, links the southern ends of two established long distance routes, the Viking and Peddars Ways. From Oakham it heads in an easterly direction across rolling agricultural country to the old market towns of Stamford and Peterborough. It continues across flat open fenland and past land drainage schemes to Ely, and its cathedral, which is perched on an isolated hill overlooking the former marshes where Hereward the Wake held out for several months against the forces of William the Conqueror. From Ely the Way crosses more fenland to reach the Breckland heaths and forests at Brandon and Thetford.

Start	Oakham, Leics	SK861088
Finish	Harling Road Station, Norfolk	TL978879
On OS maps	141, 142, 143, 144	
Waymark	Named posts in Leics, double sword logo in Cambs, tiger face	

Publication(s)
Leaflet: *Hereward Way* (Cambridgeshire County Council). 1989 \ A5 \ £0.30 (+ 50p).
Leaflet: *Hereward Way* (Leicestershire County Council). A4/3 \ £0.40.
Booklet: *Hereward Way* by Trevor Noyes (RA Peterborough Group). ISBN: 0900613572. 1985 \ A5 \ 72pp \ £1.50 (+ 35p).

Hertfordshire Chain Walk 121

Gtr London, Herts	139 km / 87 miles

A chain of linking circular walks which stretch from near Crews Hill Station in the London Borough of Enfield to Ashwell Station in Cambridgeshire. Though each walk is complete in itself, they can be combined to provide a walk from London to Cambridgeshire and back. The route runs in a generally northerly direction, passing Cuffley, Little Berkhamsted, Hertingfordbury, Watton at Stone, Cottered and Therfield.

Start and Finish	Whitewebbs Park, Gtr London	TQ329998
OS maps	153, 166, 176, 177	

Publication(s)
Paperback: *Hertfordshire Chain Walk* by E Herts Footpath Society (Castlemead Publications). ISBN: 0948555122. 136 x 216\66pp\£2.50.

Hidden Valley Walk   122

Lancs	35 km / 22 miles

This circular walk around Sabden Valley immediately south of Pendle Hill runs east from the centre of Whalley via Nick of Pendle and Newchurch to Blacko, returning via Sabden.

Start and Finish	Whalley, Lancs	SD732362
OS maps	103	

Publication(s)
Booklet: *The Hidden Valley Walk* by David Phipps (Carnegie Press). ISBN: 1874181063. 1994\135 x 214\28pp\£2.75.

High Peak Trail   123

Derby	28 km / 18 miles

The Trail, owned by Derbyshire County Council and the Peak Planning Board, follows the trackbed of the former Cromford and High Peak Railway which was opened in 1830. The first half-mile of the Trail to High Peak Junction is for walkers only; the rest is open to cyclists and horseriders. From the Derwent valley the trackbed climbs in a north-westerly direction to the open limestone countryside of the Peak District, passing several old lead mining villages, old stations and inclines, and the restored engine house at Middleton Top incline.
See also Midshires Way and Tissington Trail.

Start	Cromford, Derby	SK322555
Finish	Dowlow, Derby	SK111674
On OS maps	119	

Publication(s)
Leaflet: *High Peak Trail* (Derbyshire County Council). A4/3\Free.
Leaflet: *Tissington and High Peak Trails* (Peak District National Park). A4/3\Free.
Paperback: *Walking the High Peak Trail* by John Merrill (Trail Crest Publications Ltd). ISBN: 187475411X. 1993\40pp\£3.50.

Badge and certificate (£2.75 / post free) available from Trail Crest Publications Ltd.

High Weald Walk 124

E Sussex, Kent	45 km / 28 miles

A circular route around the town of Tunbridge Wells, developed jointly by Kent and Sussex county councils and opened in June 1994, the Walk passes through the undulating and attractive countryside of the High Weald AONB. There are link routes to the town itself, and the Walk passes through the villages of Southborough, Pembury, Frant, Groombridge and Speldhurst.

Start and Finish	Southborough Common, Kent	TQ574426
OS maps	188	

Publication(s)
Booklet: *High Weald Walk* (Kent County Council). 1994 \ £2.95.

Hillingdon Trail 125

Gtr London	32 km / 20 miles

Brainchild of Phoebe Balk of RA Hillingdon and developed by a working party from various voluntary bodies and the Borough, this route, opened in 1994, spans the London Borough of Hillingdon from south to north via Ruislip and Harefield.

Start	Cranford Park, Gtr London
Finish	Springwell Lock, Gtr London
OS maps	176
Waymark	Fingerposts and trail logo

Publication(s)
Folder: *The Hillingdon Trail* (London Borough of Hillingdon). 1994 \ A5 \ 6pp \.

Holderness Way 126

Humberside	34 km / 21 miles

The Way provides easy walking across the Plain of Holderness, and follows the banks of the river Hull and Leven Canal. It then crosses flat to gently undulating farmland and marshland, where there is abundant wildlife, before reaching the seaside town of Hornsea.

Start	Hull, Humberside	TA097288
Finish	Hornsea, Humberside	TA208479
OS maps	107	

Publication(s)
Folder: *Holderness Explorer* (Humberside County Council).
A5 \ £2.00 (+ 30p).

Holme Valley Circular Walk 127

W Yorks	39 km / 24 miles

A circular walk along the heights around the Holme valley south of Huddersfield. From Berry Brow, the Walk heads east to Castle Hill before heading south through the villages of Farnley Tyas, Thurstonland and Hepworth, passes the farms of Elysium and Hades, and then heads north along the west side of the valley via Upper- and Netherthong and Honley to Berry Brow. There is a variety of scenery including many viewpoints.

Start and Finish	Berry Brow, W Yorks	SE136137
On OS maps	110	

Publication(s)
Paperback: *Holme Valley Circular Walk* by E S Boocock (Holme Valley Civic Society). 135 x 200 \ 32pp \ £1.50.

Hospice Coast to Coast 128

Cumbria, N Yorks	246 km / 154 miles

Set up in March 1991 as an alternative to Wainwright's route, and intended as a sponsored walk for charity, this route visits the three Yorkshire Peaks, Masham, the Hambleton Hills and Dalby Forest. There is no set time limit, but badges and certificates are available for anyone completing the route within 12 months.

Start	Silverdale, Cumbria	SD547718
Finish	Scarborough, N Yorks	TA035897
OS maps	97, 98, 99, 100, 101	

Publication(s)
Booklet: *The Hospice Coast to Coast* by Bill Clapperton (Teesside Hospice Care Foundation). 1991 \ 150 x 210 \ 16pp \ £2.00.

Howdenshire Way 129

Humberside	26 km / 16 miles

A circular route around the village of Howden, the route passes south from Eastrington to Saltmarshe and then west along the Humber to Boothferry. Here it turns north to Asselby and Newsholme, before returning east via Howden Station to the start.

Start and Finish	Eastrington, Humberside	SE786298

OS maps	105
Waymark	Standard arrows with white spot

Publication(s)
Folder: *Boothferry Explorer* (Humberside County Council). 1992\A5\£2.00 (+ 30p).
Looseleaf: *The Howdenshire Way* (Don Sweeting). A4\5pp\Free (+ 9"x4" SAE).
Badge and certificate (£1.20 / - / 6"x4" SAE) available from Don Sweeting.

Hyndburn Way 130

Lancs	56 km / 35 miles

A circular route around the borough (Accrington) which crosses moorland and lowland, rivers and canal. It links Witton Weavers and Burnley Ways, and is largely coincident with the RA's Hyndburn Clog.

Start and Finish	Dean Clough, Lancs	SD706326
OS maps	103	
Waymark	Stylised HW logo	

Publication(s)
Booklet: *The Hyndburn Way* (Hyndburn Borough Council). 1989\A5\36pp\£1.00 (+ 36p).

Icknield Way 131

Beds, Bucks, Cambs, Essex, Herts, Suffolk	165 km / 103 miles

The Way goes along green lanes and farm and forestry tracks, following, as far as possible, the general line of the Icknield Way – the name given to a group of prehistoric trackways which ran along the chalk spine of southern England from the Chilterns to the Norfolk coast. To the east of the Chiltern Hills the trackways, and the Way, run along the middle or lower slopes of the chalk to avoid the heavy clay capping, passing many sites of archaeological interest. From Ivinghoe Beacon the Way heads north-east through Luton, Baldock, Royston, Great Chesterfield and Icklingham to meet the Peddars Way, a Romanised section of the trackway near Thetford.

In 1992 an alternative loop avoiding Dunstable and Luton was created.

Start	Ivinghoe Beacon, Bucks	SP960168
Finish	Knettishall Heath, Suffolk	TL944807
On OS maps	144, 153, 154, 155, 165, 166	
Waymark	Named disc with neolithic flint axe emblem	

User group	Icknield Way Association

Publication(s)
Booklet: *Accommodation List* (Icknield Way Association). £1.00 (+ SAE).
Folder: *Icknield Way* (Bedfordshire County Council). 1992\A4/3\ 3pp\£0.90.
Paperback: *Icknield Way Path* (Icknield Way Association). 1993\210 x 148\£4.50.
Paperback: *The Icknield Way Path* (Wimpole Books). £3.50.

Imber Range Perimeter Path 132

Wilts	48 km / 30 miles

Though most of the area around the village of Imber on Salisbury Plain is a military training area, and therefore closed to visitors, this walk describes a route around the perimeter of the firing range. Walkers should therefore take care not to go past the warning notices into the danger area. The route mainly follows the escarpment, above Westbury White Horse, passing several Iron Age hillforts. It is for the most part open and exposed, meaning there are many fine views, but it does go through Tilshead village where there are pubs and shops.

Start and Finish	Westbury, Wilts	ST893510
OS maps	183, 184	
Waymark	Name of route with cannon logo	

Publication(s)
Looseleaf: *Imber Range Path* (Richard Archard). Free (+ 9"x6" SAE).
Leaflet: *Imber Range Perimeter Path* (Wiltshire County Council). A5\Free.
Badge and certificate (£1.50 / £0.50 / 9"x6" SAE) available from Richard Archard.

Irwell Valley Way 133

Gtr Man, Lancs	48 km / 30 miles

Designed to link the centre of Manchester with the moors above Bacup, this route is one of several following the rivers of Manchester, and was developed as part of efforts to provide "green arteries" for Mancunians.

From Castlefield Urban Heritage Park, the route follows roads through Salford, starting with the river proper by Salford University. At Clifton Junction, it diverts to a disused railway line (now a nature trail) to Radcliffe, follows the former Bolton and Bury canal to Bury, and then follows the river to Ramsbottom, Rawtenstall and Bacup. It ends at Deerplay Inn under Thieveley Pike, where it links with the Rossendale Way.

Start	Manchester (Castlefield), Gtr Man	SJ833976
Finish	Deerplay, Lancs	SD866264
On OS maps	103, 109	
Waymark	Dragonfly	

Publication(s)
Booklet: *The Irwell Valley Way* (Rossendale Borough Council). A4/3\28pp\£0.10.

Isle of Wight Coastal Footpath   134

IOW	104 km / 65 miles

The coastal path completely encircles the island and, with the exception of detours to the west of Thorness Bay and round the Osborne Crown Property at Osborne Bay, stays close to the coast. It is a very varied walk over chalk and sandstone cliffs, through popular holiday resorts and past the less crowded inlets, bays, marshes and saltings.

Start and Finish	Old Castle Point, IOW	SZ510965
On OS maps	196	
Waymark	Coastal footpath	

Publication(s)
Folder: *Isle of Wight Countryside Trails and Coastal Walks* (Isle of Wight County Council). A4/3\11pp\£1.95.
Folder: *Long Distance Trails and Coastal Path* (Isle of Wight County Council). A4/3\12pp\£4.50.
Paperback: *The Isle of Wight Coast Path* by John Merrill (Trail Crest Publications Ltd). ISBN: 0907496687. 56pp\£3.25.
Paperback: *The Isle of Wight Coastal Path* by Alan Charles (Thornhill Press). ISBN: 0946328137. £3.85.
Badge and certificate (£2.75 / post free) available from Trail Crest Publications Ltd.

Itchen Way   135

Hants	43 km / 27 miles

Following the river Itchen from mouth to source, this varied route leads from the urban area of Southampton at the start to the chalk downland at the source. From Southampton, it follows the line of the former Itchen Navigation to the cathedral city of Winchester. From here it follows the stream via water meadows and nature reserves to Alresford and the source on the downs.

Start	Southampton, Hants	SU435102

Finish	New Cheriton, Hants	SU589273
OS maps	185	
Waymark	Named standard arrows	

Publication(s)
Paperback: *Exploring the Itchen Way* by Richard Kenchington (Countryside Books). ISBN: 1853060836. 1990 \ A5 \ 128pp \ £4.95.

Jack Mytton Way 136

Salop	115 km / 72 miles

Billed as Shropshire's long distance bridleway, this route runs across the south of the county from east to west.

From the northern edge of Wyre Forest, it follows a disused railway to Highley and the Severn valley and goes across rolling farmland to Much Wenlock. From here, it follows the escarpment of Wenlock Edge, and descends to Church Stretton. It then climbs to the Long Mynd via the Cardingmill Valley, joining the Port Way to reach Plowden and Clun Forest. It runs for a stretch alongside Offa's Dyke before finishing on the Shropshire/Powys border at Llanfair Waterdine.

Start	Billingsley, Salop	SO715835
Finish	Llanfair Waterdine, Salop	SO246760
OS maps	137, 138	
Waymark	Horseshoe motif with horse and rider	

Publication(s)
Leaflet: *Jack Mytton Way: Shropshire's Long Distance Bridleway* (Shropshire County Council). 1993 \ A5 \ Free.

Jubilee Way 137

Leics, Lincs	25 km / 16 miles

The Way, developed by Leicestershire County Council, was opened in 1977 to mark the Queen's Silver Jubilee. Connecting Melton Mowbray with the Viking Way, it follows a meandering north-easterly course across pasture and woodland and past old ironstone workings near Eaton, before climbing through woods to Belvoir castle from where there are fine views over the Vale of Belvoir.

Start	Melton Mowbray, Leics	SK756191
Finish	Woolsthorpe, Lincs	SK846387
On OS maps	129, 130	
Waymark	Orb, yellow on brown	

Publication(s)
Leaflet: *Jubilee Way* (Leicestershire County Council). A4/3 \ £0.15.

Jubilee Way (Northavon) 138

| Avon | 26 km / 16 miles |

Devised in 1985 as part of the RA's 50th anniversary celebrations, the Way links the Cotswold Way with the Severn Bridge and hence Offa's Dyke Path. Passing from the limestone of the Cotswolds to the alluvial clays of the Severn Vale, the route skirts to the north of Chipping Sodbury and south of Thornbury, following fieldpaths for most of the way.

Start	Old Sodbury, Avon	ST752812
Finish	Severn Bridge, Avon	ST573893
On OS maps	172	
Waymark	RA rucksack logo with "50"	

Publication(s)
Booklet: *Jubilee Way* (Northavon District Council). 1992\100 x 178\28pp\Free.

Jurassic Way 139

| Lincs, Northants, Oxon | 136 km / 85 miles |

Opened in 1994 by Northamptonshire County Council, the Jurassic Way aims to follow the band of Jurassic Limestone that runs along the northern boundary of Northamptonshire. From Banbury it runs first south along the Oxford Canal, and then heads north via Middleton Cheney and Woodford Halse to Braunston on the Grand Union Canal. Here it turns northeast to pass between Market Harborough and Corby, following the Welland Valley to Rockingham with its castle, and the attractive market town of Stamford.

Start	Banbury, Oxon	
Finish	Stamford, Lincs	TF041075
OS maps	141, 151, 152	
Waymark	Ammonite logo	

Publication(s)
None at time of writing.

Kennet and Avon Canal 140

| Avon, Berks, Wilts | 135 km / 84 miles |

Reopened to boat traffic by the Queen in 1990, the Kennet and Avon canal provides a link from the Thames to the Severn, and thus from London to Bristol. Generally, it is given as leaving the Thames at Reading, though strictly speaking whilst following the valley of the river Kennet to Newbury it is the Kennet Navigation. From Newbury, it continues along the Kennet valley to Hungerford, and then crosses to the Vale of Pewsey, which it follows via Devizes to the Avon valley at Trowbridge. It becomes the Avon Waterway at Bath, and the path becomes the Avon Walkway.

Start	Bath, Avon	ST751647
Finish	Reading, Berks	SU731738
OS maps	172, 173, 174, 175	

Publication(s)
Paperback: *Face the Dawn: the Bristol to London Long Distance Path* by Eddie Critchley (Ramblers' Association). ISBN: 0900613556. 1984\A5\50pp\£2.00 (+ 70p).
Paperback: *The Kennet & Avon Walk* by Ray Quinlan (Cicerone Press). ISBN: 1852840900. 1991\116 x 176\200pp\£6.99.

Kerry Ridgeway 141

Powys, Salop	25 km / 16 miles

This route provides comparatively easy, scenic walking along the crest of the Kerry Hills, following the line of a prehistoric ridge track known as the "old road" and passing earthworks, tumuli and a motte and bailey castle at Bishopsmoat.

Start	Kerry Hill, Powys	SJ100840
Finish	Bishop's Castle, Salop	SJ329890
On OS maps	136, 137	

Publication(s)
Leaflet: *Kerry Ridgeway* (Powys County Council). A4/3\£0.10.

Kirklees Way 142

W Yorks	116 km / 73 miles

Devised by the Metropolitan Council as a circuit of the Borough, the Way describes a large circle around the chief town of Huddersfield, and mixes the exposed moorland tops with the industrial towns in the valleys of this part of W Yorkshire.

From Scholes, it crosses the Spen Valley to Oakwell Hall, turns south past Dewsbury to Clayton West, and then west to the Holme Valley and Marsden. It then passes to the west and north of Huddersfield back to Scholes.

Start and Finish	Scholes, W Yorks	SE167259
On OS maps	104, 110	
Waymark	Named discs and blue letter "K"	

Publication(s)
Booklet: *A Stroller's Guide to Walks along the Kirklees Way* by
C Dexter Ellis (C Dexter Ellis). 1991\A5\40pp\£2.70.
Folder: *The Kirklees Way* (Kirklees Metropolitan Council).
12pp\£6.50 (+ 75p).

Knaresborough Round 143

N Yorks	32 km / 20 miles

A circular walk around the town, linking with the Harrogate
Round.

Start and Finish	Knaresborough, N Yorks	SE350564
OS maps	99, 104	

Publication(s)
Leaflet: *Knaresborough Round* (RA Harrogate Group). A4\£0.20 (+
SAE).

Knightley Way 144

Northants	19 km / 12 miles

The Way was opened in 1972 as the first of a series of county paths,
and takes its name from the Knightley family who at one time
owned much of the land over which it passes. It crosses undulating
farm and parkland, and passes through the picturesque ironstone
villages of Foxley, Litchborough, Farthingstone and Fawsley. It
links the Grafton Way at Greens Norton with the Nene Way at
Badby.

Start	Greens Norton, Northants	SP671490
Finish	Badby, Northants	SP560587
On OS maps	152	
Waymark	Black and white circles	

Publication(s)
Leaflet: *Knightley Way* (Northamptonshire County Council).
1983\A5\Free (+ 25p).

Knights' Way 145

Dyfed	14 km / 9 miles

This route links the Pembrokeshire Coast Path at Amroth with the
Daugleddau Trail at Blackpool Mill, and crosses the Landsker
Borderlands Trail. It is named after the Knights Templar and the
Knights Hospitallers of St John, who both have strong associations
with places on the route.

Start	Amroth, Dyfed	SS168071
Finish	Blackpool Mill, Dyfed	SN060145
On OS maps	158	
Waymark	Named disc with Knights Templar cross as logo	

Publication(s)
Leaflet: *The Knights' Way* (Dyfed County Council). A5 \ Free.

Lairig an Laoich 146

Grampian, Highland	51 km / 32 miles

One of the three main north-south passes across the granite massif
of the Cairngorms, providing a challenge for fit walkers, but in bad
or winter conditions it should only be attempted by well-equipped
and experienced hill walkers.

From Braemar, it goes west to Inverey and the Linn of Dee, and
then north to the river Nethy, which it follows to Nethy Bridge.

See also Lairig Ghru, Glen Feshie.

Start	Braemar, Grampian	NJ152915
Finish	Nethy Bridge, Highland	NJ001206
OS maps	34, 36	

Publication(s)
Leaflet: *The Cairngorm Passes* (Scottish Rights of Way Society).
A2 \ £0.25 (+ 25p).

Lairig Ghru 147

Grampian, Highland	45 km / 28 miles

One of the three main north-south passes across the granite massif
of the Cairngorms, providing a challenge for fit walkers, but in bad
or winter conditions it should only be attempted by well-equipped
and experienced hill walkers.

From Braemar, it goes west to Inverey and the Linn of Dee, and
then west and north to Coylumbridge and Aviemore. This is probably the best-known of the three routes.

See also Lairig an Laoich, Glen Feshie.

Start	Braemar, Grampian	NJ152915
Finish	Aviemore, Highland	NH892116
OS maps	34, 36	

Publication(s)
Leaflet: *The Cairngorm Passes* (Scottish Rights of Way Society).
A2 \ £0.25 (+ 25p).

Lakeland Fringe 148

Cumbria	235 km / 147 miles

Basically a circuit around the Lake District National Park, the route aims to take the walker to parts not normally visited by those who concentrate on the main hills in the heart of the Park. It thereby provides an opportunity to explore little-known areas, often with fine views of the fells.

From Newby Bridge at the southern end of Windermere, the route heads north-east to Staveley and Shap. It then turns north-west to Pooley Bridge and Caldbeck, southwest to Bassenthwaite and Cockermouth, and then south to Ennerdale Bridge and Wasdale. It returns to Newby Bridge via Eskdale, Ulpha and the southern tip of Coniston Water.

Start and Finish	Newby Bridge, Cumbria	SD369863
OS maps	89, 90, 91	

Publication(s)
Paperback: *Exploring The Lakeland Fringe* by R H Gambles and B Richardson (A G Publications). ISBN: 0951473204. 1989 \ 210 x 144 \ 190pp \ £3.75 (+ 85p).

Lakes Link 149

Cumbria	196 km / 123 miles

A meandering route over the fells, across passes and along the lakesides, and in several places on long stretches of road, visiting the majority of the Lake District's lakes.

Start and Finish	Ambleside, Cumbria	NY376045
OS maps	90, 97	

Publication(s)
Paperback: *The Lakes Link* by Mike Dixon (Dalesman Publishing Ltd). ISBN: 0852067852. 205 x 135 \ 72pp \ £2.50.

Lambourn Valley Way 150

Berks	35 km / 22 miles

The Lambourn Valley Way runs from the Berkshire Downs near the Uffington White Horse to Newbury along the picturesque valley of the River Lambourn. It thereby connects the Ridgeway with the Kennet valley. The terrain is generally easy-going, though it can be bleak in winter. The route passes through the villages of Lambourn, E Garston, Great Shefford and Boxford.

Start	Uffington Castle, Berks	SU300863

Finish	Newbury, Berks	SU471671
On OS maps	174	
Waymark	Named discs and posts	

Publication(s)
Leaflet: *Lambourn Valley Way* (Berkshire County Council).
1994\A4/3\Free.

Lancashire Coastal Way 151

Lancs	55 km / 34 miles

Eventually, this route will stretch the full length of the Lancashire coastline, linking the Sefton Coast Path from Liverpool with the Cistercian Way and hence the Cumbrian Coast Path all the way to Carlisle.

At present, only the stretch from Lancaster along the Lune to Cockerham, on to the Wyre estuary, and from there through Fleetwood and Blackpool to Freckleton on the Ribble estuary, is open.

Start	Lancaster, Lancs	SD472616
Finish	Freckleton, Lancs	SD437297
On OS maps	97, 102	
Waymark	Gull & wave logo	

Publication(s)
Folder: *Lancashire Coastal Way* (Lancashire County Council).
1992\A5\Free.

Lancashire Trail 152

Gtr Man, Lancs, Merseyside, N Yorks	113 km / 71 miles

A route linking industrial Lancashire with the Pennine Way, devised by St Helens and District CHA/HF Rambling Club to commemorate their Golden Jubilee in 1978. From St Helens the Trail heads north-east to Billinge, Abbey Lakes and the viewpoints of Ashurst Beacon and Harrock Hill. It continues along the ridge to Coppull Moor, Blackrod and Rivington Pike. A relatively low-lying section follows via Abbey village and Mellor, before reaching Whalley and the climb to Pendle Hill, from where the route descends to Barley and Thornton-in-Craven.

In addition to the main trail, link routes have been developed from the centres of Wigan, Bolton and Burnley, to and from the Ribble Way at Sawley, and to the Sandstone Trail.

Start	St Helens, Merseyside	SJ512956
Finish	Thornton-in-Craven, N Yorks	SD906484

OS maps   102, 103, 108, 109

Publication(s)
Paperback: *The Lancashire Trail* (A Richmond). 1990 \
A5 \ 28pp \ £2.75.

Lancashire Way   153

Cumbria, Gtr Man, Lancs	193 km / 121 miles

A tour through Lancashire with a mixture of moorland, farmland, canal, riverside and coastal walking, passing Wycoller Country Park, Barley, Pendle Hill, and Lancaster Castle. As well as busy town centres like Bolton, Burnley and Lancaster, the route includes miles of scenic footpaths, for example over Pendle Hill and Salter Fell.

Start	Bolton, Gtr Man	SD719087
Finish	Arnside, Cumbria	SD461788
OS maps	97, 103, 109	

Publication(s)
Looseleaf: *The Lancs Way Footpath* (Frank Hodson). A4 \ 3pp \ Free (+ SAE).
Certificate (£0.50 / SAE) available from Frank Hodson.

Lancaster Canal   154

Cumbria, Lancs	91 km / 57 miles

Though not open to boat traffic in its entirety, the towpath is fully walkable from Preston to Kendal, and therefore provides an easy link from the Ribble across the Fylde and through Lancaster and Carnforth to the Lake District.

Start	Preston, Lancs	SD526303
Finish	Kendal, Cumbria	SD520931
OS maps	97, 102	

Publication(s)
Paperback: *A Walker's Guide to the Lancaster Canal* by Robert Swain (Cicerone Press). ISBN: 1852840552. 1990 \ 116 x 176 \ 116pp \ £5.50.
Leaflet: *The Lancaster Canal (Lancaster to Kendal)* (South Lakeland District Council). A4/3 \ Free.
Paperback: *Walking the Lancaster Canal* by Gay Quilter (Gay Quilter). £5.90.

Lanchester Valley Walk   155

Durham   19 km / 12 miles

One of a series of railway-lines bought by local authorities, and developed for use by walkers and cyclists; horseriders may use them with a permit. The Lanchester Valley Walk links the Deerness Valley and Brandon/Bishop Auckland Walks on the western edge of Durham City to Lanchester, and a planned extension will connect with the Waskerley Way, Derwent Walk and Consett and Sunderland Railway Path.

Start	Broompark, Durham	NZ254415
Finish	Hownes Gill, Durham	NZ099495
On OS maps	88	

Publication(s)
Folder: *Railway Walks in County Durham* (Durham County Council). 1990\A5\10pp\£0.99 (+ 75p).
Folder: *Railway Walks in Derwentside* (Derwentside District Council). A4/3\4pp\£0.80.

Landsker Borderlands Trail   156

Dyfed   96 km / 60 miles

Landsker is an old Norse word meaning "frontier", and this route explores the rural area on the Pembrokeshire/Carmarthenshire border. Developed by a partnership of 42 rural communities in South Pembrokeshire, it reaches from Llanboidy and Efailwen in the north via Canaston Bridge on the Daugleddau (where it crosses the Knights Way and Daugleddau Trail) to Landshipping and Lawrenny in the south, returning to Whitland via Reynalton and Ludchurch.

Start and Finish	Canaston Bridge, Dyfed	SN067152
On OS maps	158	
Waymark	Named disc with Celtic design for logo	

Publication(s)
Leaflet: *The Landsker Borderlands Trail* (SPARC). 1993\A5\Free.

Langbaurgh Loop   157

Cleveland   61 km / 38 miles

This circular walk was designed to take the walker over some of the most diverse and beautiful countryside in the north-east of England. The route goes along sandy coastland paths; high cliff edges; rich agricultural land; high rugged moors, thick with heather; dense pine forests; and ancient woods. Parts of the route are over little-used footpaths and rights of way, and some knowledge of map reading is required.

Start and Finish	Saltburn-by-the-Sea, Cleveland	NZ668216
OS maps	93, 94	
Waymark	Ellipse and callipers	

Publication(s)
Leaflet: *Langbaurgh Loop* (Langbaurgh Loop). A4/3 \ Free (+ 9"x4" SAE).
Badge and certificate (£2.50 / - / SAE) available from Langbaurgh Loop.

Lark Valley Path   158

| Suffolk | | 20 km / 13 miles |

Developed by the Brecks Countryside Project of Suffolk County Council, this route links Bury St Edmunds with the Icknield Way at Icklingham. It runs along a river valley with woodland, heath and arable fields.

Start	Bury St Edmunds, Suffolk	TL848664
Finish	Mildenhall, Suffolk	TL711744
OS maps	143, 154, 155	
Waymark	Named discs and posts with lark logo	

Publication(s)
Leaflet: *The Lark Valley Path* (Suffolk County Council). 1994 \ A4/3 \ Free.

Lea Valley Walk   159

| Beds, Gtr London, Herts | | 80 km / 50 miles |

A route on riverside paths, linking London's Docklands with Dunstable Downs and the Icknield Way, and following the course of the river, which is variously spelt Lee and Lea. It incorporates the Lee Navigation towpath, and the Upper Lea Valley Walk, and also uses the Cole Green Way west of Hertford.

From Bow Locks (from where the Limehouse Cut provides a link to the Thames), it passes north past the numerous reservoirs that line the valley through North London. At Hoddesdon, the Stort Navigation branches off to Harlow and Bishop's Stortford (14 miles). At Ware, the river turns west to Hertford, passes between Hatfield and Welwyn Garden City before heading north-west to Harpenden and Luton. An urban stretch through Luton finishes on the Icknield Way.

| Start | Bow Locks, Gtr London | TQ382828 |
| Finish | Luton, Beds | TL061249 |

OS maps	166, 177
Waymark	Named discs with swan logo

Publication(s)
Leaflet: *Cole Green Way: Natural History* (Hertfordshire County Council). A4/3\Free.
Folder: *Lea Valley Walk* (Hertfordshire County Council). 1994\A5\2pp\Free.
Folder: *Lea Valley Walk* (Lee Valley Regional Park Authority). 1993\A5\2pp\Free (+ SAE).
Leaflet: *The Lea Valley Walk: An Introductory Leaflet* (Hertfordshire County Council). A4/3\Free.
Leaflet: *The Upper Lea Valley Walk in Bedfordshire* (Bedfordshire County Council). A4/3\£0.30 (+ 18p).

Leeds and Liverpool Canal 160

Gtr Man, Lancs, Merseyside, N Yorks, W Yorks	203 km / 127 miles

The canal linking Leeds and Liverpool, Yorkshire and Lancashire, is the longest single canal in Britain. Starting in 1770, it took 46 years to complete, and there is now a walkable towpath for almost all its length. Though it passes through and links many well-known industrial towns, there is a wide variety of scenery.

From the centre of Liverpool near the Stanley Dock, it meanders north and east to Wigan where it turns north past Chorley to Blackburn, before heading north-east through Burnley, Nelson and Colne. It crosses the Pennine watershed near Barnoldswick, where it is briefly used by the Pennine Way. Reaching Airedale, it turns right, south-east, passing via Skipton, Keighley and Shipley to Leeds where it joins the Aire and Calder Navigation in the centre of the city.

Start	Liverpool Stanley Dock, Merseyside	SJ343921
Finish	Leeds, W Yorks	SE293351
OS maps	103, 104, 108, 109	

Publication(s)
Paperback: *Aerofilms Guide: The Leeds-Liverpool Canal* by Colin Speakman (Ian Allan Publishing). ISBN: 071102135X. 1993\286 x 140\144pp\£9.99.
Leaflet: *Wigan-Burscough Canal Path* (British Waterways Board). A4/3\Free.

Leeds Country Way 161

W Yorks	96 km / 60 miles

A circular route around Leeds some 5-6 miles from the city centre. Much of the route is over green belt land and there are 25 access points to public transport. From Golden Acre Park the Way heads eastwards through the Harewood estate and Bardsey, and swings south past Thorner, Barwick in Elmet, Rothwell and the outskirts of Wakefield. It then heads west, going north of Dewsbury to Birstall before following a meandering northerly route back to Golden Acre Park via Thornbury, Hornforth and Cookridge.

Start and Finish	Golden Acre Park, W Yorks	SE267417
On OS maps	104, 105	
Waymark	Yellow owl and "LCW" on olive green plaque	

Publication(s)
Folder: *Leeds Country Way* (Leeds Metropolitan Borough Council). A5\5pp\Free.

Leeds-Dales Way 162

W Yorks	32 km / 20 miles

A link from Leeds' Marsden monument to the Dales Way at Ilkley, through the city's parks across rolling countryside to meet and follow the Ebor Way through Bramhope and over the Chevin and Ilkley Moor.

Start	Leeds, W Yorks	SE293351
Finish	Ilkley, W Yorks	SE117476
OS maps	104	
User group	Dales Way Association	

Publication(s)
Booklet: *Dales Way Route Guide* by Arthur Gemmell and Colin Speakman (Stile Publications). ISBN: 0906886538. 1991\197 x 120\44pp\£2.80.

Leicestershire Round 163

Leics	161 km / 101 miles

A walk around the county devised by the Leicestershire Footpath Association. From Burrough Hill it heads southwards across the open pastures and through the villages of the east Leicestershire hills via Launde Abbey, Hallaton and Thorpe to Foxton Locks on the Grand Union Canal. From here it heads west and then north over mixed farmland, river- and canalside and some urban paths via Ashby Magna, Hinckley and Market Bosworth.

Start and Finish	Burrough Hill, Leics	SK766115
On OS maps	128, 129, 130, 140, 141	
Waymark	Circle of brown arrows on standard waymarks	

Publication(s)
Paperback: *Leicestershire Round: 1 – Burrough Hill to Foxton Locks* by Leicestershire Footpath Assn (Leicestershire Libraries & Information). ISBN: 0850221056. 1981\210 x 149\24pp\£0.75 (+ 75p).
Paperback: *Leicestershire Round: 2 – Foxton Locks to Market Bosworth* by Leicestershire Footpath Assn (Leicestershire Libraries & Information). ISBN: 0850221234. 1983\210 x 149\24pp\£0.75 (+ 75p).
Paperback: *Leicestershire Round: 3 – Market Bosworth to Burrough Hill* by Leicestershire Footpath Assn (Leicestershire Libraries & Information). ISBN: 0850221358. 1983\210 x 149\28pp\£0.75 (+ 75p).

Leland Trail 164

Somerset   61 km / 38 miles

An easy path through the rolling hills of Somerset from near Stourhead to near Stoke-sub-Hamdon following the route traversed by John Leland during his survey of Britain made in the 1530s.

Start	Alfred's Tower, Somerset	ST745352
Finish	Ham Hill, Somerset	ST478172
On OS maps	183, 184, 193	
Waymark	Bust of John Leland	

Publication(s)
Folder: *Leland Trail* (South Somerset District Council). 1990\A5\14pp\£3.25.

Liberty Trail 165

Dorset, Somerset   45 km / 28 miles

Linking the Leland Trail with the Dorset Coast Path, this route, a joint development between South Somerset District Council and Dorset County Council, follows the footsteps of people who, in 1685, walked to join the protestant Monmouth rebellion at Lyme.

From Ham Hill, the Trail proceeds south over farm and rolling downland to Crewkerne and Forde Abbey with its beautiful gardens. For the last stretch through Dorset into Lyme Regis via the Iron Age hillforts of Lamberts and Coneys Castles, it is coincident with the Wessex Ridgeway.

Start	Ham Hill, Somerset	ST478172
Finish	Lyme Regis, Dorset	SY347922
OS maps	193	
Waymark	Bird logo	

Publication(s)
Leaflet: *An Introduction to the Liberty Trail* (South Somerset District Council). 1993\210 x 150\Free.
Folder: *The Liberty Trail* (South Somerset District Council). 1993\160 x 210\£4.25 (+ 35p).

Limestone Link   166

Cumbria	21 km / 13 miles

The Link runs from west to east across the limestone country of South Cumbria with its nationally important flora, through the low wooded hills of the Arnside area, across the flat open mosses between Hale and Holme, and over the rocky fells of Clawthorpe and Hutton Roof.

Start	Arnside, Cumbria	SD461788
Finish	Kirkby Lonsdale, Cumbria	SD611789
On OS maps	97	

Publication(s)
Leaflet: *The Limestone Link* (South Lakeland District Council). 1994\A4/3\Free.

Limestone Link Path   167

Avon, Somerset	58 km / 36 miles

This route, from where it joins the Cotswold Way at Cold Ashton, goes south through the St Catherine's valley to the north-east of Bath, then along the Kennet and Avon Canal. Leaving the towpath at Dundas Aqueduct, which is also one end of the Avon Walkway, the route then meanders south-west to the northern Mendip escarpment at Compton Martin. It goes past Burrington Combe and Dolebury Warren to reach Shipham, where it joins the West Mendip Way.

Start	Cold Ashton, Avon	ST751728
Finish	Shipham, Somerset	ST443572
On OS maps	172, 182	
Waymark	Ammonite logo	

Publication(s)
Booklet: *The Limestone Link* (Yatton Ramblers). ISBN: 0951134248. 1989\145 x 205\66pp\£1.95.

Limestone Way   168

Derby   44 km / 28 miles

An easy walk devised and sponsored by the Rotary Club of Matlock
in association with Derbyshire Dales District Council. From the
start it climbs quickly over Masson Hill, as far as Bonsall, following
tracks used by generations of lead miners. It crosses Bonsall Moor
to Wyn's Tor, after which a prehistoric track known as the Portway
climbs between Robin Hood's Stride and Cratcliff Rocks. The route
then passes through woodland and fields to Monyash, Miller's Dale
and the river Wye. Here it ascends to follow a grassy track to Monks
Dale, Dry Peter Dale and Hay Dale, before reaching Old Moor, the
highest point on the route. It goes past the remains of lead mines,
then descends steeply down Cave Dale into Castleton.
    Though deliberately not part of the route, Castleton can easily
be linked to the Pennine Way at Edale via Hollins Cross.

Start	Matlock, Derby	SK298603
Finish	Castleton, Derby	SK150829
On OS maps	110, 119	
Waymark	Derby ram	

Publication(s)
Looseleaf: *The Limestone Way* (Derbyshire Dales District Council).
A4 \ 1pp \ Free.
Badge (£1.00) available from Derbyshire Dales District Council.

Limey Way   169

Derby   64 km / 40 miles

A meandering north-to-south traverse of the limestone countryside
of the White Peak area of the Peak District National Park, visiting
twenty dales. From Castleton, Cave Dale is followed before climbing Old Moor and following Dam, Hay, Peter, Monks, Millers,
Monsal and Deep Dales to Monyash. From here Bagshaw, Ricklow,
Lathkill, Bradford and Gratton Dales are followed to Biggin. Then
the Way heads due south along Biggin, Wolfscote, Mill, Dove and
Lin Dales to the village of Thorpe.

Start	Castleton, Derby	SK150829
Finish	Thorpe, Derby	SK157504
OS maps	110, 119	

Publication(s)
Paperback: *Limey Way* by J N Merrill (Trail Crest Publications
Ltd). ISBN: 0907496830. 1979 \ 185 x 122 \ 48pp \ £2.95.
Badge and certificate (£2.75 / post free) available from Trail Crest
Publications Ltd.

Lindsey Loop 170

Humberside, Lincs	160 km / 100 miles

A figure-of-eight loop, devised by the Lincoln Group of the RA, over the rounded chalk hills of the Lincolnshire Wolds and lowland farmland. It links the six market towns in East and West Lindsey: Market Rasen, Spilsby, Alford, Caistor, Horncastle and Louth.

Start and Finish	Market Rasen, Lincs	TF111897
OS maps	113, 121, 122	

Publication(s)
Folder: *Lindsey Loop* by Brett Collier (RA Lincs and S Humberside Area). A4 \ 9pp \ Free (+ SAE).
Badge available from RA Lincs and S Humberside Area.

Lipchis Way 171

Hants, W Sussex	42 km / 26 miles

A scenic route, devised by Liphook Rambling Club, across the heaths, woods and farmland of the western Weald. It goes over Older Hill and Woolbeding Common to Midhurst and Heyshott, and across the South Downs via The Trundle to Lavant and Chichester.

Start	Liphook, Hants	SU842309
Finish	Chichester, W Sussex	SU858043
OS maps	186, 197	

Publication(s)
Leaflet: *The Lipchis Way* (Liphook Rambling Club). 1985 \ A4/3 \ £0.50.

London Countryway 172

Berks, Bucks, Essex, Gtr London, Kent, Surrey	330 km / 206 miles

The route, devised by Keith Chesterton and developed with the help of other LDWA members, describes a complete circuit around London and keeps from between 13 to 31 miles from the centre. From Box Hill the Way heads north-west over the wood-, farm- and heathlands of Surrey and Berkshire, and along canal towpaths to Windsor, from where the river Thames is followed to Maidenhead and Marlow. Here it turns northwards across the wood- and farmlands of the Chiltern hills to West Wycombe and Great Missenden, and then follows a meandering easterly route to Kings Langley and crosses gently undulating countryside to St Albans, Broxbourne, the Lea valley, Epping Forest and Theydon Bois. The Countryway goes south-east to Brentwood and over the Essex fens to cross the

Thames via the Tilbury-to-Gravesend ferry, before heading south and then west along the sandstone and chalk hills of Kent and Surrey.

Start and Finish	Box Hill, Surrey	TQ173513
OS maps	165, 166, 167, 175, 176, 177, 186, 187, 188	

Publication(s)
Softback: *Guide to the London Countryway* by Keith Chesterton (Constable and Co Ltd). ISBN: 0094639604. 1981\171 x 114\ 280pp\£5.95.

Longster Trail   173

Cheshire	18 km / 11 miles

One of a series of four interlinked, waymarked walks developed by the Mid-Cheshire Footpath Society. From Helsby Hill, south of the M56, the Trail loops south-west across farmland to finish to the east of Chester.

Start	Helsby, Cheshire	SJ493753
Finish	Pipers Ash, Cheshire	SJ435677
On OS maps	117	
Waymark	Standard arrows with red spot	

Publication(s)
Booklet: *Longer Trails in Vale Royal* by Carl Rogers (Vale Royal Borough Council). 1993\A5\76pp\£1.95.
Booklet: *Waymarked Walks in Central Cheshire* (Mid-Cheshire Footpath Society). 100 x 223\16pp\£0.75.

Lune Valley Ramble   174

Cumbria, Lancs	26 km / 16 miles

An easy walk along the riverbank, the Ramble links at Lancaster with the Lancashire Coastal Path. Robert Swain's book describes a longer route from source to mouth via Newbiggin, Tebay and Sedbergh.

Start	Lancaster, Lancs	SD472616
Finish	Kirkby Lonsdale, Cumbria	SD611789
OS maps	97	
Waymark	Named signposts	

Publication(s)
Booklet: *The Lune Valley Ramble* (Lancaster City Council). A5\12pp\Free.
Paperback: *Walking Down The Lune* by Robert Swain (Cicerone Press). ISBN: 1852841036. 1992\116 x 176\152pp\£6.99.

Macmillan Way   175

Avon, Dorset, Glos, Leics, Northants, Oxon, Somerset, Warks, Wilts	363 km / 227 miles

Being developed in aid of the Macmillan Nurse Appeal, a charity funding cancer care nurses in hospitals, the route runs along the Oolitic limestone belt that runs south and west from the end of the Viking Way at Oakham in Rutland through the Cotswolds and Somerset to the south coast. Designed not to duplicate the Jurassic or Cotswold Ways, it passes Stow-on-the-Wold, Cirencester, Bradford-upon-Avon and Sherborne.

Start	Oakham, Leics	SK861088
Finish	Abbotsbury, Dorset	SY572849
OS maps	141, 151, 152, 162, 163, 173, 183, 194	

Publication(s)
None at time of writing.

Maelor Way   176

Cheshire, Clwyd, Salop	38 km / 24 miles

Devised by the late Jack Baker to link the Sandstone Trail with Offa's Dyke Path at Chirk, the route crosses farmland to Hanmer Mere and Overton, where it follows the rivers Dee and Ceiriog to Chirk.

Start	Grindley Brook, Salop	SJ522433
Finish	Bronygarth, Clwyd	SJ263375
OS maps	117, 126	
Waymark	"MW" monogram as arrow	

Publication(s)
Paperback: *Guide to the Maelor Way* by Gordon Emery (Gordon Emery). ISBN: 1872265987. 1991\A5\126pp\£5.95.
Leaflet: *Introducing the Maelor Way* (Wrexham Maelor Borough Council). 1991\A4/3\Free.

Maldon Millennium   177

Essex	35 km / 22 miles

Inaugurated as part of the celebrations for the millennium of the town of Maldon in 1991, the Way is a circular around the town at the head of the Blackwater estuary. It visits the site of the battle of Maldon in 991 at the end of the causeway to Northey Island (a nature reserve now owned by the National Trust), and also the villages of Woodham Mortimer, Woodham Walter, Langford, Great and Little Totham, and Heybridge.

Start and Finish	Maldon, Essex	TL853072
OS maps	168	

Publication(s)
Folder: *Walking in and around Maldon* (RA Chelmer & Blackwater Group). 1992\£2.00.

Malvern Link   178

Heref & Worc		64 km / 40 miles

This route links the North Worcestershire Path with the Worcestershire Way, making a round of about a hundred miles. It provides a blend of fieldpaths, country lanes, woodland, parkland, canal and riverside scenery.

Start	Forhill, Heref & Worc	SP055755
Finish	Cowleigh Park Farm, Heref & Worc	SO766476
OS maps	139, 150	

Publication(s)
Looseleaf: *Malvern Link* by Dave Irons (Dave Irons). 1992\A4\2pp\Free (+ SAE).

Marches Way   179

Cheshire, Gwent, Heref & Worc, S Glam, Salop		326 km / 204 miles

A walk through the borderland between England and Wales, characterised by rich farming country, castles and small towns and villages. At first a riverside walk along the Dee, the walk is designed for use with public transport, and mainly follows the course of the railway line from Whitchurch to Newport, and then over hills to Tongwynlais and Cardiff. It visits all the main towns and villages en route, including Wem, Shrewsbury, Church Stretton, Ludlow, Leominster, Hereford, Abergavenny, Pontypool and Caerleon. It thereby also links the two main Roman forts built to guard the Welsh border: Chester and Caerleon.

Start	Chester, Cheshire	SJ413670
Finish	Cardiff, S Glam	ST180765
OS maps	117, 126, 138, 149, 161, 171	
Waymark	Named discs in Cheshire only	

Publication(s)
Softback: *The Marches Way* by Les Lumsdon (Sigma Leisure). ISBN: 1850582696. 1992\A5\164pp\£6.95.

Marriott's Way   180

Norfolk	34 km / 21 miles

Named after a former chief engineer and manager of the Midland and Great Northern Railway, the Way is a route for walkers, horse-riders and cyclists along two disused railway lines. From the end of the 5-mile Norwich Riverside Walk at Hellesdon, the Way goes northwest via Drayton and Attlebridge to the village of Themelthorpe; from here it curves eastwards to Reepham and Aylsham, where it meets another converted railway line, the 9-mile Bure Valley Walk, which runs to Hoveton. Although mainly over arable land, the Way also passes through woods and water-meadows, and is a haven for wildlife. Between Cawston and Aylsham, there is a link path to the Weavers Way.

Start	Hellesdon Bridge, Norfolk	TG198000
Finish	Aylsham, Norfolk	TG195265
On OS maps	133, 134	

Publication(s)
Leaflet: *Marriott's Way* (Norfolk County Council). 1991 \ A4/3 \ Free (+ SAE).

Medlock Valley Way   181

Gtr Man	20 km / 13 miles

One of several routes developed along Manchester's rivers, the Medlock Valley Way runs from Ducie Street near Piccadilly Station via Clayton Vale, Daisy Nook and Strines Dale to finish at Bishop Park NE of Oldham. The landscape varies from canal stretches through reclaimed areas to clough woodland and open country near the finish.

Start	Manchester (Ducie St), Gtr Man	SJ848981
Finish	Bishop Park, Gtr Man	SD962084
On OS maps	109	
Waymark	Named discs with valley logo	

Publication(s)
Folder: *The Medlock Valley Way* (Medlock Valley Warden Service). A5 \ 13pp \ £1.50.

Mersey Way   182

Cheshire, Merseyside	48 km / 30 miles

Eventually it is hoped to have a Merseyside footpath all the way from the centre of Liverpool to Greater Manchester, but much of the route will take a long time to develop as the riverside land itself is redeveloped. At present, there are paths along the seafront at Otterspool, from Garston to Hale, around Pickering's Pasture, along the former St Helens Canal from Widnes to Warrington, and from Warrington to Woolston Eyes. Though there is still much industry along the river, there are also many sites of interest to birdwatchers and botanists, and good views across to the Wirral peninsula and northwest Cheshire.

Parts of this route are being used by the Trans Pennine Trail.

Start	Liverpool, Merseyside
Finish	Warrington, Cheshire
On OS maps	108, 109
Waymark	Signposts + standard waymarks

Publication(s)
Leaflet: *Walk the Mersey Way* (Mersey Valley Partnership). A4/3 \ Free.

Mid Suffolk Footpath 183

Suffolk	32 km / 20 miles

The path, opened in 1994, connects the end of the Gipping Valley Path at Stowmarket with the Angles Way on the river Waveney at Hoxne, and runs north-south across the District. It broadly follows the valleys of the rivers Dove and Gipping via Eye, Thorndon and Mendlesham.

Start	Hoxne, Suffolk	TM184782
Finish	Stowmarket Greens Meadow, Suffolk	TM042599
OS maps	155, 156	
Waymark	Named discs with poppy logo	

Publication(s)
Leaflet: *The Mid Suffolk Footpath* (Mid Suffolk District Council). 1994 \ A5 \ Free.

Mid Sussex Link 184

E Sussex, W Sussex	61 km / 38 miles

Part of the Sussex Border Path, the Mid Sussex Link follows the administrative boundary between West and East Sussex. Leaving the main route at East Grinstead, it runs south through Ashdown Forest by Weir Wood Reservoir, Horsted Keynes and east of Burgess Hill to Ditchling (south of which it crosses the S Downs Way). At Patcham it turns west for a downland walk to Mile Oak on the northern edge of Shoreham.

Start	East Grinstead, W Sussex	TQ388382
Finish	Mile Oak, W Sussex	TQ250065

On OS maps	187, 198
Waymark	Martlet

Publication(s)
Folder: *The Sussex Border Path* by Ben Perkins and Aeneas Mackintosh (Dr Ben Perkins). 1991 \ A5 \ 9pp \ £3.50 (+ 34p).

Middlesex Greenway 185

Essex, Gtr London, Surrey	69 km / 43 miles

A route that travels almost the whole of the former county, from the south-west to the north-east, and passing West Drayton, Uxbridge, Ruislip, Pinner, Mill Hill, Finchley and Enfield. It was designed to heighten public awareness of the county and to help safeguard the Green Belt.

Start	Staines, Surrey	TQ032725
Finish	Waltham Abbey, Essex	TL376005
OS maps	166, 176, 177	

Publication(s)
Looseleaf: *The Middlesex Greenway* by Stephen J. Collins (Stephen J Collins). 1990 \ A4 \ 16pp \ £1.00 (+ SAE).

Middy Railway Footpath 186

Suffolk	32 km / 20 miles

Running as it did far from much habitation or industry, the Mid Suffolk Light Railway was never a commercial success, and was dismantled long ago. This path, being developed by Mid Suffolk District Council, follows as closely as possible the line of the railway, running through agricultural land to the north of Stowmarket and Framlingham. The first stage, from Haughley Junction to Brockford, is scheduled to open in Autumn 1994; the second, on to Laxfield, is scheduled for Summer 1995.

Start	Haughley Junction, Suffolk
Finish	Laxfield, Suffolk
OS maps	155, 156
Waymark	Named discs with steam engine logo

Publication(s)
None at time of writing.

Midshires Way 187

Bucks, Derby, Gtr Man, Leics, Northants, Notts	360 km / 225 miles

Originally proposed by the East Midlands Sports Council as a multi-use bridleway linking the Ridgeway with the Pennine Bridleway, it was later developed by the five county councils concerned, together with the Peak District National Park and Stockport Borough Council, and extended through the Peak District National Park to the Goyt Valley and the Trans Pennine Trail to Stockport.

Opened in June 1994, it uses the Swans Way through Buckinghamshire, running to the west and north of Northampton to pick up the 14-mile Brampton Valley Way to Market Harborough. Continuing north through Leicestershire to the west of Melton Mowbray, it skirts to the south and west of Derby, uses the High Peak Trail through the White Peak, the 3-mile Sett Valley Trail, finishing via the Goyt and Etherow valleys to Stockport. The route is multi-use and braided to Kegworth on the Leicestershire/Nottinghamshire border, and from there north to the High Peak Trail for walkers only.

Start	Bledlow, Bucks	SP770012
Finish	Stockport, Gtr Man	SJ893903
OS maps	109, 110, 119, 128, 129, 141, 152, 165	
Waymark	Named discs with "MW" in linked acorn form	

Publication(s)
Folder: *The Midshires Way* (Leicestershire County Council). 1994\A5\12pp\£3.00.

Millennium Way 188

IOM	45 km / 28 miles

This, the Isle of Man's first long distance footpath, was developed to celebrate the Manx Millennium, the 1000th anniversary in 1979 of the establishment of Tynwald, the island's parliament. The route is based on the Royal Way, an ancient high-level route between Ramsey, at one time a favoured landing place, and the former capital, Castletown. The Way crosses the island in a south-westerly direction, climbing to open heather moorland on the western slopes of Snaefell (the highest point on the island) to reach the Way's highest point at 1,500ft. From here it descends to Crosby, and follows lowland paths, roads and the banks of the Silverburn river through Ballasalla to the medieval castle of Rushen, which guards Castletown Harbour. The upland parts of the Way can be difficult to follow in bad weather and should only be attempted by walkers with navigational skills and suitable equipment.

Start	Sky Hill, IOM	SC432945

Finish	Castletown, IOM	SC265675
OS maps	95	
Waymark	Disc waymark with arrow	

Publication(s)
Paperback: *Isle of Man Coastal Walk: Raad ny Foillan* by Aileen Evans (Cicerone Press). ISBN: 0902363956. 1988\116 x 176\ 144pp\£5.99.
Folder: *Millennium Way* (Isle of Man Dept of Tourism & Transp't). Free.

Milton Keynes Boundary Walk   189

Bucks	96 km / 60 miles

As its name suggests, the Walk follows the town boundary through lowland farmland in the valleys of the Rivers Tove and Ouse. The landscape includes canal towpath, deciduous and pine forest, and arable and pasture land, with stone and thatched cottages.

From Stony Stratford, the route heads north to Salcey Forest (end of the Swan's Way), east through Yardley Chase to Turvey, where it turns south to Woburn Sands. Apsley Heath is crossed, after which the route turns north again to Stony Stratford.

Start and Finish	Stony Stratford, Bucks	SP788396
OS maps	152, 153, 165	

Publication(s)
Leaflet: *Milton Keynes Boundary Walk* (Milton Keynes Borough Council). Free.

Minster Way   190

Humberside, N Yorks	80 km / 50 miles

The Way, linking the two famous medieval minsters at Beverley and York, crosses farmland and the rounded chalk hills of the Yorkshire Wolds. It follows the Wolds Way across Sylan Dale before diverting to Millington, Bishop Wilton and Stamford Bridge. Here the river Derwent and the Derwent Way are followed for 3 miles before the Plain of York is crossed on field and woodland paths to meet and follow the river Ouse to the centre of York.

Start	Beverley, Humberside	TA038393
Finish	York, N Yorks	SE603522
On OS maps	105, 106, 107	
Waymark	"MW" on standard waymarks plus named signposts	

Publication(s)
Paperback: *The Minster Way* by Ray Wallis (Ray Wallis). ISBN: 0905490126. 1980\A5\72pp\£2.75.

Badge (£1.25 / SAE) available from Ray Wallis.

Montgomery Canal 191

Powys, Salop	56 km / 35 miles

This partially restored canal runs north to south from a junction with the busy Llangollen Canal to Newtown. The northern section crosses the North Shropshire Plain and the southern section goes through the Severn valley. Although work is progressing to fully restore the canal, some parts are still dry, and others are unnavigable because of lowered bridges. The walk is a very pastoral one, rich in wildlife, and a large section has been designated as a Site of Special Scientific Interest (SSSI).

Start	Frankton Junction, Salop	SJ371318
Finish	Newtown, Powys	SO135925
OS maps	126, 136	

Publication(s)
Leaflet: *The Montgomery Canal* (Montgomery Waterway Restoration Trust). A4/3\Free.

Morecambe Bay Shoreline 192

Cumbria, Lancs	80 km / 50 miles

Eventually, the coast of Morecambe Bay will form part of the Lancashire Coast Path; until then, this leaflet describes a route around the shore from Heysham via Carnforth, the limestone AONB of Silverdale and Arnside, genteel Grange-over-Sands, and the Furness peninsula to finish at Roa or Foulney Island. The train can be caught across the Kent and Leven estuaries, for, although a sand crossing is possible, it is highly dangerous and should only be attempted in the company of the sand pilot.

Start	Heysham, Lancs	SD412617
Finish	Barrow-in-Furness, Cumbria	SD190688
OS maps	96, 97	

Publication(s)
Leaflet: *Walking Round The Bay* (Paddy Dillon). 1990\A3/9\£0.40.

Moyle Way 193

Antrim	29 km / 18 miles

This is a tough day's walk, starting easily enough on the Antrim coast at Ballycastle before heading inland to cross the boggy Antrim Mountains. After going round the forested slopes of Knocklayd the route follows Glenshesk River upstream, then makes an ascent of Slieveanorra (508m). Boggy moorland slopes and forest paths follow, then the route crosses a boggy shoulder of Trostan before dropping down to Glenariff Forest Park.

The route requires OSNI maps 5 and 9.

Start	Ballycastle, Antrim	IJ115407
Finish	Glenariff, Antrim	IJ200208
OS maps	See text above	
Waymark	Wooden markers with yellow arrows	

Publication(s)
Leaflet: *The Moyle Way* (Sports Council for Northern Ireland). A5 \ Free.

Navigation Way   194

W Midlands	160 km / 100 miles

A meandering towpath walk which passes through a mixture of urban and rural areas and follows sections of the many canals in the area. The first loop follows towpaths to the south-east of Birmingham – the Birmingham and Fazeley, Grand Union, Stratford-upon-Avon, and Worcester and Birmingham Canals – before returning to Gas Street basin. A second loop goes along towpaths to the west of the city and follows parts of the Birmingham, Dudley, Stourbridge, Staffordshire and Worcestershire, and Tame Valley Canals. The final section heads north to Chasewater along the Rushall and Wyrley and Essington ("Curley Wyrley") canals.

Start	Birmingham, Gas St Basin, W Midlands	SP062867
Finish	Chasewater, W Midlands	SK040070
OS maps	138, 139	

Publication(s)
Paperback: *The Navigation Way* by Peter Groves and Trevor Antill (Meridian Books). ISBN: 1869922190. 1993 \ A5 \ 40pp \ £4.95.

Nene Way   195

Cambs, Lincs, Northants	176 km / 110 miles

A joint development by three local authorities, this is an easy route through the gentle countryside of the Nene valley, and latterly along the canalised riverbank. En route, it passes through the towns of Northampton, Wellingborough, Oundle, Peterborough and Wisbech. At Badby it connects with the Knightley Way, and at Sutton Bridge with the Wash Coast Path/Peter Scott Walk. Information on possible flooding can be obtained from the National Rivers Authority in Peterborough (0733 371811).

Start	Badby, Northants	SP560587

Finish	Sutton Bridge, Lincs	TF482210
On OS maps	131, 141, 142, 143, 152, 153	
Waymark	Named signposts	

Publication(s)
Paperback: *Exploring the Nene Way* by Mia Butler (Countryside Books). ISBN: 185306176X. 210 x 150 \ 128pp \ £4.95.
Leaflet: *Nene Way: A Cambridgeshire Country Walk* (Cambridgeshire County Council). A5 \ £0.30 (+ 50p).
Folder: *Nene Way: A Northamptonshire County Path* (Northamptonshire County Council). 1990 \ A5 \ £1.75 (+ 45p).
Leaflet: *Nene Way: A Peterborough Country Walk* (Peterborough City Council). A5 \ Free.

Nev Cole Way 196

Humberside, Lincs	92 km / 58 miles

Created by the Grimsby-based Wanderlust Rambling Club in memory of the club's founder, the Way passes from the Jurassic scarp overlooking the River Trent at Burton-upon-Stather via the south bank of the Humber past the Humber bridge at Barton to Immingham and Grimsby, which it skirts on the southern side. Here it turns inland into the gently sloping Lincolnshire Wolds, passing through several villages to Nettleton near Caistor. Here it meets the Viking Way, and this could be used to return north to Barton-upon-Humber. The route is notable for its bird and plant life, particularly near the coastal paths and clay pits.

Start	Burton upon Stather, Humberside	SE870178
Finish	Nettleton, Lincs	TA112001
OS maps	112, 113	
Waymark	Named discs	

Publication(s)
Booklet: *Nev Cole Way* (Wanderlust Rambling Club). ISBN: 0951109227. 1991 \ 147 x 206 \ 40pp \ £2.00.

Nidderdale Way 197

N Yorks	85 km / 53 miles

A tour of Nidderdale from the lowland pastures to the open fells near the Nidd's source. From Hampsthwaite the Way follows the northern side of the dale upstream, first going over Brimham Moor and past the fantastic gritstone outcrops of Brimham Rocks (NT) high above the dale, and the old lead mill at Smelthouses, before following paths close to the Nidd from Pateley Bridge to Lofthouse. Here the Way loops round the head of the valley to Scar House Reservoir, passing swallow holes where limestone and gritstone meet under the shadow of Little Whernside. The route returns along the south side of the dale, looping away from the Nidd to visit Merryfield Mines and Heyshaw Moor before returning to Hampsthwaite.

Start and Finish	Hampsthwaite, N Yorks	SE259587
On OS maps	99, 104	
Waymark	Named signposts	

Publication(s)
Paperback: *Nidderdale Way* by J.K.E. Piggin (Dalesman Publishing Ltd). ISBN: 1855680025. 205 x 135\48pp\£1.95.

North Bowland Traverse   198

Lancs, N Yorks	50 km / 31 miles

This is a low-level walk over the fine countryside of the Bowland Forest. The route follows rights of way across farmland and meadow land, but apart from the occasional farm there are no places to obtain refreshments, so walkers are advised to take all they need with them. Although it is a fairly easy walk, it is best to go well-prepared, as much of the route is well away from any good roads and conditions can change rapidly.

Start	Slaidburn, Lancs	SD712524
Finish	Stainforth, N Yorks	SD822673
OS maps	97, 98, 103	

Publication(s)
Paperback: *North Bowland Traverse* by David Johnson (Hillside Publications). ISBN: 1870141016. 1987\167 x 111\56pp\£3.75. Badge and certificate (£1.20 / - / 9"x4" SAE) available from David Johnson.

North Buckinghamshire Way   199

Bucks	56 km / 35 miles

This walk through the quiet and secluded countryside of Buckinghamshire links one of Britain's oldest highways, the Chiltern Ridgeway, with the newest of Britain's cities, Milton Keynes. From the start at Chequers Knapp, the route heads north-west through the historic village of Great Kimble before turning north to cross the Vale of Aylesbury. It passes through a number of attractive villages, including Bishopstone, Quainton and Great Horwood. There is a choice of finishing in Milton Keynes or at Wolverton, where the Way joins the Grafton Way.

Start	Great Kimble, Bucks	SP830053
Finish	Wolverton, Bucks	SP807413
On OS maps	152, 165	

Waymark	Orange arrows

Publication(s)
Leaflet: *North Bucks Way* (Buckinghamshire County Council).
A4/3 \ Free (+ SAE).

North Downs Way   200

Kent, Surrey	227 km / 142 miles

The North Downs Way was opened in 1978, and broadly follows
the historic Pilgrims Way along the Downs to Canterbury.

From Farnham the first 14 miles are not along the narrow chalk
ridge but over sandy countryside to the south: the Downs are first
reached at Newlands Corner, east of Guildford. From there on, the
Way mainly follows the crest of the southern escarpment of the
North Downs, or footpaths and tracks along their lower slopes.
There are fine views over the Weald to the South Downs and
several steepish ascents where the ridge is cut by valleys, notably
those of the Mole at Box Hill, the Darent at Otford, the Medway at
Rochester, and the Stour near Wye.

Generally, the route provides comparatively easy walking
through woods, over chalk grassland and, especially in Kent,
through orchards and farmland. At Boughton Lees there is a choice
of routes. The direct one goes through Wye, over the Downs to
Folkestone and along the cliffs to Dover. The alternative follows
hills to the west of the river Stour and passes through orchards
and the picturesque village of Chilham to Canterbury. From the
cathedral city it heads south-east via Barham Downs, Shepherd-
swell and Waldershare Park to Dover.

The main route is 112 miles long, the Canterbury loop an extra
30 miles. For the five link routes to the Greensand Way, see
Greensand Way.

In 1994, the London to Paris Walk was inaugurated. This uses
the North Downs Way and the system of GR paths in France to
provide a route between the two cities. It links the Thames to the
North Downs Way via the Green Chain Walk, the Cray and Shuttle
Riverways, and the Darent Valley Path. Details from Kent County
Council.

Start	Farnham, Surrey	SU844468
Finish	Shakespeare Cliff, Kent	TR308399
On OS maps	178, 179, 186, 187, 188, 189	
Waymark	National Trail Acorn	

Publication(s)
Paperback: *Discovering the North Downs Way* by David J Allen and
Patrick R Imrie (Shire Publications). ISBN: 0852638841. £2.95.
Softback: *Guide to the Pilgrims' Way and North Downs Way* by
Christopher John Wright (Constable and Co Ltd). ISBN:
0094722307. 1993 \ 171 x 114 \ 316pp \ £10.95.

Softback: *North Downs Way* by Neil Curtis (Aurum Press). ISBN: 1854101870. 210 x 130\£8.99.
Leaflet: *North Downs Way* (Countryside Commission Postal Sales). 1992\A4/3\Free.
Booklet: *The North Downs Way: A Users Guide* (Kent County Council). ISBN: 1873010249. A5\44pp\£1.00.

North Wales Coastal Footpath 201

Clwyd, Gwynedd	116 km / 73 miles

At the time of writing, this route across North Wales, developed by Gwynedd and Clwyd County Councils, is scheduled for opening in 1995.

Start	Prestatyn, Clwyd	SJ081838
Finish	Caernarvon, Gwynedd	
OS maps	115, 116	

Publication(s)
None at time of writing.

North Worcestershire Hills Marathon 202

Heref & Worc	42 km / 26 miles

From Bromsgrove High Street, the route runs via Burcot, Linthurst and Lickey Beacon to the Clent Hills, and returns via Belbroughton, Pepper Wood, Dogford, Park Gate and Sanger Park.

Start and Finish	Bromsgrove, Heref & Worc	SO960707
OS maps	139	

Publication(s)
Looseleaf: *North Worcestershire Hills Marathon* (Dave Irons). Free (+ 9"x4" SAE).

North Worcestershire Path 203

Heref & Worc	42 km / 26 miles

An easy route linking four country parks in north-east Worcestershire, which crosses woods and fields and provides contrasting views of Birmingham and the Black Country to the north, and the Vale of Worcester with the Severn Valley to the south.
From Kingsford Country Park on Kinver Edge, where it meets the Staffordshire and Worcestershire Ways, it passes over the Stour valley to the Clent Hills, Waseley Hills and Lickey Hills. It then continues via Upper Bittell Reservoir and Forhill to finish at Major's Green near Shirley. There are steep climbs up and down the Clent Hills.

Start	Kingsford, Heref & Worc	SO836821
Finish	Major's Green, Heref & Worc	SP101782
On OS maps	138, 139	
Waymark	Named discs and marker posts	

Publication(s)
Leaflet: *North Worcestershire Path* (Hereford and Worcester County Council). 1992\A4/3\Free.

North York Moors 204

N Yorks	156 km / 98 miles

Using mostly well-walked paths, this walk takes in most of the best and well-known beauty spots on the North York Moors. From the start on the Esk Valley Railway, the route goes to Danby Rigg, Rosedale Abbey, Urra Moor, Hasty Bank, Great Broughton, Mount Grace Priory, Osmotherly, along the Hambleton Drove Road and on to Rievaulx Abbey. It then goes on to Kirk Dale, Kirkbymoorside, Hutton-le-Hole and Lastingham to reach the Cawthorn Roman camps. From here it continues to Newton-on-Rawcliffe, Levisham and Hole of Horcum through Cropton Forest on to the Wheeldale Moor Roman road and to the finish at Goathland, where the North Yorkshire Moors Railway can connect the walker with the Esk Valley Railway.

Start	Danby, N Yorks	NZ707084
Finish	Goathland, N Yorks	NZ838014
OS maps	93, 94, 99, 100	

Publication(s)
Paperback: *Footpath Touring: North York Moors* by Ken Ward (Footpath Touring). ISBN: 0711704260. 221 x 114\64pp\£3.50.

Northumbrian Coastline 205

Northumb, Tyne & Wear	96 km / 60 miles

A scenic coastal route with many interesting features en route including Berwick fortifications, Holy Island, Bamburgh Castle, Farne Islands, Dunstanburgh Castle, Warkworth Castle, Cambois power station and Tynemouth Castle and Priory.

Start	Berwick-upon-Tweed, Northumb	NT994534
Finish	North Shields, Tyne & Wear	NZ356678
OS maps	75, 81, 88	

Publication(s)
Paperback: *Northumbrian Coastline* by Ian Smith (Sandhill Press Ltd). ISBN: 0946098328. 175 x 125\£3.95 (+ 60p).

Offa's Dyke Path 206

Clwyd, Glos, Gwent, Heref & Worc, Powys, Salop	285 km / 178 miles

This was the fourth National Trail to be completed and is now run jointly by the Countryside Commission and the Countryside Council for Wales; it was opened in 1971. For over 60 miles the route runs along or close to the Dyke, an impressive earthwork constructed in the eighth century AD under the direction of Offa, King of Mercia, following his 150-mile frontier with the Welsh. Some 80 miles of the dyke are extant today, but in places the Path either leaves its course or is diverted because of lack of access agreements. This is a very varied route, and, in addition to the Dyke itself, many historical sites are passed.

From Chepstow the Path meanders along the east side of the Wye valley to Monmouth, and then crosses lowland farmland to Pandy. Hatterrall Ridge, the most easterly of the high ridges of the Black Mountains, is followed to Hay-on-Wye. The Radnorshire Hills are crossed to reach Knighton, the largest town directly on the route and the headquarters of the Offa's Dyke Association. From here the Path crosses the open hill country of the Clun district of Shropshire, following some of the most impresssive and best-preserved sections of the Dyke to Brompton Hall. The next part of the route provides easier walking across the plain of Montgomery, along the Severn valley, past another impressive section of the Dyke by Chirk Castle and across the vale of Llangollen. Finally, the Clwydian Hills are crossed to reach the sea-front at Prestatyn.

Start	Sedbury Cliffs, Glos	ST552927
Finish	Prestatyn, Clwyd	SJ081838
On OS maps	116, 117, 126, 137, 148, 161, 162	
Waymark	National Trail Acorn	
User group	Offa's Dyke Association	

Publication(s)
Paperback: *Aerofilms Guide: Offa's Dyke (South) and River Wye Valley* by Des Hannigan (Ian Allan Publishing). ISBN: 0711021341. 1993\286 x 140\128pp\£9.99.
Softback: *Guide to Offa's Dyke Path* by Christopher John Wright (Constable and Co Ltd). ISBN: 0094691401. 1990\171 x 114\320pp\£8.95.
Folder: *Offa's Dyke Path* (Offa's Dyke Association). £2.00.
Booklet: *Offa's Dyke Path Accommodation Guide* (Offa's Dyke Association). 1994\A6\£1.00.
Softback: *Offa's Dyke Path North* by Ernie Kay and Kathy Kay (Aurum Press). ISBN: 1854100165. 1989\210 x 130\144pp\£8.99.
Softback: *Offa's Dyke Path South* by Ernie Kay and Kathy Kay (Aurum Press). ISBN: 1854100173. 1989\210 x 130\144pp\£8.99.
Leaflet: *Offa's Dyke Path, Chepstow to Monmouth* (Wye Valley AONB Joint Advisory Cttee). A4/3\Free.

Folder: *Strip Maps of Offa's Dyke Path* by Tony Drake and Allan Russell (Offa's Dyke Association). £2.50.
Leaflet: *The Offa's Dyke Path / Llwybr Clawdd Offa* (Countryside Council for Wales). 1991\A4/3\Free.
Paperback: *Through Welsh Border Country* by Mark Richards (Thornhill Press). ISBN: 0904110532. 1976\210pp\£4.50.
Badge and certificate (£1.60 / 40p / £1.35 / 35p) available from Offa's Dyke Association.

Offa's Dyke Path Castles Alternative 207

Gwent, Heref & Worc, Powys	50 km / 31 miles

This route, developed by the Offa's Dyke Association and utilising existing rights of way, provides an interesting alternative to the official route across the Plain of Monmouth and the Black Mountains. It follows higher terrain than the official Path, and passes the medieval castles of Pembridge, Skenfrith, Grosmont and Longtown before crossing the Black Mountains along the Cat's Back ridge to meet the official route near Pen-y-Beacon.

Start	Monmouth, Gwent	SO505129
Finish	Hay-on-Wye, Powys	SO229425
OS maps	161, 162	

Publication(s)
Paperback: *Offa's Dyke Path Accommodation Guide* (Offa's Dyke Association). 1994\A6\£1.00.
Paperback: *Offa's Dyke Path Castles Alternative* (Offa's Dyke Association). 1987\A5\24pp\£0.80.
Paperback: *Through Welsh Border Country* by Mark Richards (Thornhill Press). ISBN: 0904110532. 1976\210pp\£4.50.

Ogwr Ridgeway Walk 208

Mid Glam	21 km / 13 miles

Part of a long ridge walk across SW Wales, the Ogwr Ridgeway links the Taff-Ely Ridgeway Walk (Ffordd y Bryniau) with the Coed Morgannwg Way. It largely follows the tops of the southern Lower Pennant Sandstone ridge from Mynydd y Gaer and Bryn y Wrach, to Mynydd Baeden and Mynydd Margam, taking in the valleys of the Ogwr Fawr and Fach, Garw and Llynfi. The scenery varies from windswept heights with fine views to the woodlands and arable farms of the valley sides and floors.

Start	Mynydd Margam, Mid Glam	SS835880
Finish	Mynydd y Gaer, Mid Glam	ST156853
On OS maps	170	
Waymark	Arrows with named hill logo	

Publication(s)
Leaflet: *Ogwr Ridgeway Walk* (Ogwr Borough Council). 1991\
A4/3\Free.

Oldham Way 209

Gtr Man	64 km / 40 miles

A circular walk around the borough, the Oldham Way's landscape varies from moorland to urban canal. It starts at Dove Stone Reservoir near Greenfield, and continues over Saddleworth Moor to Diggle and Castleshaw Moor to Denshaw. It then skirts the north of Shaw and Royton to meet the Rochdale Canal at Chadderton Hall Park. It follows the canal south through Chadderton to Failsworth, after which it joins the Medlock Valley to Daisy Nook and Park Bridge before climbing over Hartshead Pike to Quick and the start at Greenfield.

Start and Finish	Dove Stone, Gtr Man	SE002036
On OS maps	109, 110	
Waymark	Owl	

Publication(s)
Folder: *The Oldham Way* (Oldham Metropolitan District Council). 1992\A4/3\7pp\Free.

Ouse Valley Way 210

Cambs	41 km / 26 miles

The Way follows the river Great Ouse from Eaton Socon via the old and attractive towns of St Neots, Godmanchester and St Ives to Earith. Much of the route is low-lying and liable to flooding, but this means there are significant areas of meadowland which hold considerable botanical interest. There are also many sites of ornithological and entomological interest, e.g. Little Paxton Pits, an SSSI. North of Holywell, the banks are mainly elevated, affording open views over the landscape.

Start	Eaton Socon, Cambs	TL173587
Finish	Earith, Cambs	TL394746
On OS maps	142, 153, 154	
Waymark	Standard waymarks with swan, water and tree logo	

Publication(s)
Folder: *Ouse Valley Way* (Huntingdon District Council). A4/3\ 7pp\£1.00.

Ox Drove Way   211

Hants   40 km / 25 miles

The Ox Drove itself is part of an old cross-country route on the
Downs to the northeast of Winchester called the Lunway, a name
recalled in the Lunways Inn at Itchen Wood. This bridle route
forms a figure of eight using the Ox Drove, starting at Abbotstone
Down, and passing Preston Down, Bentworth, Upper Wield, and
Old Alresford.

Start and Finish	Abbotstone Down, Hants	SU585361
On OS maps	185	
Waymark	Standard arrows with ox logo	

Publication(s)
Leaflet: *The Ox Drove Way* (Hampshire County Council).
A4/3 \ Free.

Oxfordshire Trek   212

Oxon   103 km / 64 miles

The Trek makes a fine circular walk around the city of Oxford. It
can be completed in stages, as there are several places where the
route links with public transport. Starting at Bladon, the site of
Sir Winston Churchill's grave, the route passes Blenheim Palace
and Dorchester Abbey. It crosses both the Oxford Canal and the
river Thames, where the towpaths contrast with Wittenham
Clumps and Jarn Mound.

Start and Finish	Bladon, Oxon	SP449149
OS maps	164	

Publication(s)
Paperback: *Guide to the Oxfordshire Trek* by Laurence Main (Kittiwake Press). ISBN: 0702809152. 1989 \ 210 x 120 \ 64pp \ £3.95 (+
57p).

Oxfordshire Way   213

Glos, Oxon   104 km / 65 miles

The Way, a traverse of Oxfordshire from the Cotswolds to the
Chilterns, was devised by members of the Oxfordshire branch of
the Council for the Protection of Rural England and was developed
by the county council. From the tourist village of Bourton-on-the-
Water, the Way heads eastwards across the rolling limestone
countryside of the Cotswold Hills, passing through Shipton-under-
Wychwood, Charlbury and other attractive villages before crossing
Otmoor to Studley, north of Oxford. Here it turns south-east to

Tetsworth and Pyrton, and crosses the open farmland and woods of the chalk hills of the Chilterns to reach Henley-on-Thames.

Start	Bourton-on-the-Water, Glos	SP170209
Finish	Henley-on-Thames, Oxon	SU757833
On OS maps	163, 164, 165, 175	
Waymark	"OW" on standard waymarks	

Publication(s)
Paperback: *The Oxfordshire Way* by Faith Cooke and Keith Wheal (Alan Sutton Publishing Ltd). ISBN: 0750903562. 1993\A5\ 90pp\£5.99 (+ 50p).

Painters Way   214

Essex, Suffolk	45 km / 28 miles

The Way crosses meadow- and arable land, follows the hills flanking the river Stour and its tributaries, and passes many places associated with the painters Thomas Gainsborough and John Constable, who lived and worked in the Stour valley. From Sudbury, where Gainsborough's house can be visited, the Way passes through Bures, Nayland and Stratford St Mary. A short diversion from the direct route takes in Dedham Mill and East Bergholt, Constable's birthplace, before passing Flatford Mill to reach Manningtree.

Start	Sudbury, Suffolk	TL877410
Finish	Manningtree, Essex	TM094322
OS maps	155, 168	

Publication(s)
Booklet: *A Guide to The Painters Way* by Hugh R P Turner (Peddar Publications). 1992\A5\12pp\£1.25.

Peak District High Level Route   215

Derby, S Yorks, Staffs	145 km / 91 miles

A circular walk around the Peak National Park. This is a particularly strenuous route that includes some of the toughest country in the Peak. From Matlock it crosses the limestone plateau to Dove Dale and heads north to the Roaches and Shining Tor before swinging eastwards over Chinley Churn and the southern edge of Kinder to the Ladybower reservoir. It then heads south along the whole of the eastern gritstone edges from Stanage to Beeley before following the Derwent valley to Matlock.

Start and Finish	Matlock, Derby	SK298603
OS maps	110, 119	

Publication(s)
Paperback: *The Peak District High Level Route* by John Merrill
(Trail Crest Publications Ltd). ISBN: 0907496555. 60pp \ £2.75.
Badge and certificate (£2.75 / post free) available from Trail Crest
Publications Ltd.

Peakland Way   216

Derby   155 km / 97 miles

A circular walk through the Peak National Park. The itinerary
includes limestone dales and high moorland gritstone. From Ashbourne the route runs north-east and north to Ilam, Longnor and
Blackwell, passes over Mam Tor to Kinder Scout and the Snake
Pass. It then turns southeast to Win Hill and Hathersage, returning via Chatsworth, Birchover and Tissington, where it joins the
Tissington Trail into Ashbourne.

Start and Finish	Ashbourne, Derby	SK178469
OS maps	110, 119	

Publication(s)
Paperback: *The Peakland Way* by John Merrill (Trail Crest Publi-
cations Ltd). ISBN: 0907496520. 1989 \ 130 x 210 \ 64pp \ £3.50.
Badge and certificate (£2.75 / post free) available from Trail Crest
Publications Ltd.

Peddars Way & Norfolk Coast Path   217

Norfolk, Suffolk   151 km / 94 miles

Officially approved by the Countryside Commission in 1982, the
first part of this National Trail follows tracks, footpaths and minor
roads along, or as near as possible to, the Peddars Way – a
Romanised section of the prehistoric Icknield Way, the extant
sections of which are a scheduled ancient monument. From its
start in the wooded, sandy Breckland, it passes Castle Acre and
the ruins of its priory and castle, and crosses remote, open and
gently undulating farmland to reach the north Norfolk coast at
Holme-next-the-Sea. Here a short section of the Coast Path leads
west to Hunstanton, while the main path heads east along or near
to the shoreline over low cliffs, sand dunes, coastal defences enclos-
ing marshes and mud flats, and past woodland, bird sanctuaries
and harbours to the resort of Cromer.
   Although actually two paths, this route is almost always referred
to as one.

Start	Knettishall Heath, Suffolk	TL944807
Finish	Cromer, Norfolk	TG215420
On OS maps	132, 133, 144	
Waymark	National Trail Acorn	

User group	Peddars Way Association

Publication(s)
Softback: *Peddars Way and Norfolk Coast Path* by Bruce Robinson (Aurum Press). ISBN: 1854101889. 210 x 130 \ £8.99.
Leaflet: *Peddars Way and Norfolk Coast Path* (Countryside Commission Postal Sales). 1991 \ A4/3 \ Free.
Booklet: *Peddars Way Guide and Accommodation List* (Peddars Way Association). 1994 \ A5 \ 24pp \ £1.80 (+ 25p).
Paperback: *The Peddars Way and Norfolk Coast Path* by D C Haiselden (Countryside Books). ISBN: 0723228337. 198 x 130 \ 96pp \ £2.95.

Pembrokeshire Coast Path 218

Dyfed	292 km / 183 miles

This was the third National Trail to be completed, and was officially opened by Wynford Vaughan-Thomas in May 1970. It is now run by the Countryside Council for Wales. With the exception of Milford Haven and several MOD establishments, the route from Amroth follows the coastline around the old county of Pembrokeshire and the Pembrokeshire Coast National Park, and once the popular resort of Tenby, Pembroke and Milford Haven have been passed, only small settlements and relatively few obstrusive holiday developments are encountered. The walking along an ever undulating cliff path can be strenuous, but the scenery is magnificent and provides an interesting contrast between the softer sedimentary rocks of the south coast, with its fine beaches, and the more resistant igneous and metamorphic rocks of the rugged northern coast. The area is rich in prehistoric remains and is noted for its sea birds and seals.

Start	Amroth, Dyfed	SS168071
Finish	St Dogmaels, Dyfed	SN163469
On OS maps	145, 157, 158	
Waymark	National Trail Acorn	

Publication(s)
Leaflet: *Coast Path Accommodation Guide* (Pembrokeshire Coast National Park). £1.50 (+ 36p).
Folder: *Coast Path Cards* (Pembrokeshire Coast National Park). 10pp \ £2.50 (+ 43p).
Leaflet: *Coast Path Mileage Chart* (Pembrokeshire Coast National Park). £0.10 (+ 29p).
Booklet: *Flowers along the Coast Path* (Pembrokeshire Coast National Park). £0.95 (+ 36p).
Softback: *Guide to the Pembrokeshire Coast Path* by Christopher John Wright (Constable and Co Ltd). ISBN: 0094692602. 1990 \ 171 x 114 \ 391pp \ £8.95.

Leaflet: *Llwybr Arfordir Sir Benfro / The Pembrokeshire Coast Path* (Countryside Council for Wales). 1992\A4/3\Free.
Softback: *Pembrokeshire Coast Path* by Brian John (Aurum Press). ISBN: 1854100238. 1990\210 x 130\168pp\£8.99.
Paperback: *The Pembrokeshire Coast Path* by John Merrill (Trail Crest Publications Ltd). ISBN: 0907496695. 1993\84pp\£4.50.
Paperback: *Walking the Pembrokeshire Coast Path* by Patrick Stark (Gomer Press). ISBN: 0863836860. 1990\84pp\£2.75.

Pendle Way 219

Lancs	72 km / 45 miles

A circular route through contrasting scenery, ranging from moorland to river valleys. The latter part of the route has associations with George Fox and the Pendle witches. From the Pendle Heritage Centre at Barrowford, the route heads north to Barnoldswick and Thornton-in-Craven before heading south-east to Wycoller. It then circles west to Reedley, north to Newchurch, and climbs Pendle Hill before returning to Barrowford via Barley.

Start and Finish	Barrowford, Lancs	SD863398
On OS maps	103	
Waymark	Black witch	

Publication(s)
Folder: *The Pendle Way* (Pendle Borough Council). 1987\A4/3\9pp\£2.50 (+ 50p).

Pennine Bridleway 220

Cumbria, Durham, N Yorks, Northumb, W Yorks	500 km / 313 miles

The Pennine Bridleway was originally proposed in 1986 as an alternative for horseriders to the Pennine Way. The original proposal was for a route from Ashbourne through the Peak District, Yorkshire Dales, and North Pennines to Hexham in the Tyne valley. This was later amended to a route starting in the Matlock area. At the time of writing, the proposal is still awaiting ministerial decision, though even if the go-ahead is given, it will still be at least 6 years before the route is complete.

Start	Hexham, Cumbria	NY937639
Finish	Matlock, Derby	SK298603
OS maps	86, 87, 91, 92, 98, 99, 103, 104	

Publication(s)
Leaflet: *Pennine Bridleway* (Countryside Commission Postal Sales). 1989\A4/3\Free.

Pennine Way   221

Borders, Cumbria, Derby, Durham, Gtr Man, N Yorks, Northumb, W Yorks	402 km / 251 miles

This first and most famous National Trail was formally opened in 1965 after a 30-year campaign led by Tom Stephenson of the RA. It follows the central upland spine of England from Derbyshire to the Scottish Borders, crossing a wide variety of terrain.

From Edale the Way crosses the peaty expanse of the gritstone moorlands of the Kinder Plateau to Marsden, Stoodley Pike and the Bronte country around Haworth to reach the predominantly limestone areas of the Yorkshire Dales National Park. This is traversed via Malham Cove and Malham Tarn, Pen-y-ghent, Hawes in Wensleydale, Great Shunner Fell, Keld and the Tan Hill Inn. The Way descends from the high fells to cross the river Greta and reach Middleton-in-Teesdale, from where the river Tees is followed past High Force and Cauldron Snout waterfalls. It then crosses the fells to High Cup, the village of Dufton, Great Dunfell and Cross Fell, and descends to Alston to reach the Northumberland National Park and Hadrian's Wall. The Wall is followed for several miles to Housesteads Fort before turning north across the Kielder Forest to Redesdale and the often boggy uplands of the Cheviot Hills. Here the Pennine Way follows the English-Scottish border fence before gradually descending to Kirk Yetholm.

Start	Edale, Derby	SK125858
Finish	Kirk Yetholm, Borders	NT827282
On OS maps	74, 75, 80, 86, 87, 91, 92, 98, 103, 109, 110, 119	
Waymark	National Trail Acorn	
User group	Pennine Way Association	

Publication(s)

Paperback: *Great Northern Walks: Where to Stay* by John Morrison (Leading Edge Press and Publishing). ISBN: 0948135247. 1991\188 x 105\160pp\£3.25.

Softback: *Guide to the Pennine Way* by Christopher John Wright (Constable and Co Ltd). ISBN: 0094706409. 1991\171 x 114\240pp\£8.95.

Booklet: *Pennine Way Association Accommodation and Camping Guide* (Pennine Way Association). 1994\£0.90 (+ SAE).

Booklet: *Pennine Way Bureau* (YHA Northern Region). 1993\A5\24pp\£2.00.

Hardback: *Pennine Way Companion* by A Wainwright (Michael Joseph). ISBN: 0717140710. 1994\175 x 117\224pp\£9.99.

Softback: *Pennine Way North* by Tony Hopkins (Aurum Press). ISBN: 1854100181. 1989\210 x 130\168pp\£8.99.

Softback: *Pennine Way South* by Tony Hopkins (Aurum Press). ISBN: 185410022X. 1990\210 x 130\£8.99.

Leaflet: *The Pennine Way* (Countryside Commission Postal Sales). 1992\A4/3\Free.

Stripmap: *The Pennine Way, Part One: Edale to Teesdale* (Footprint). £2.95.
Stripmap: *The Pennine Way, Part Two: Teesdale to Kirk Yetholm* (Footprint). £2.95.
Hardback: *Wainwright on the Pennine Way* by A Wainwright (Michael Joseph). ISBN: 0718124294. 1985\250 x 215\224pp\£16.99.
Paperback: *Wainwright on the Pennine Way* by A Wainwright (Michael Joseph). ISBN: 0718128389. 1987\250 x 215\224pp\£12.99.
Badge and certificate (£2.75 / post free) available from Trail Crest Publications Ltd.

Plogsland Round   222

Lincs, Notts	72 km / 45 miles

A circular walk around Lincoln, with the cathedral staying in view for much of the route. It links many of the interesting villages around the city and follows paths and green lanes across the flat, drained arable land and along the banks of the river Witham.

Start and Finish	Fiskerton, Lincs	TF058715
OS maps	121	

Publication(s)
Folder: *The Plogsland Round* by Brett Collier (Lincolnshire Fieldpath Association). 5pp\£1.00.
Badge and certificate available from Lincolnshire Fieldpath Association.

Raad ny Foillan/Gulls Road   223

IOM	145 km / 91 miles

The Isle of Man coast path. Circuits the island and, with a few exceptions, stays close to the shoreline and along the clifftops which provide spectacular views and nesting sites for a rich variety of birdlife. Contrasting sections follow roads and promenades through the harbour and resort towns.

Start and Finish	Douglas, IOM	SC379754
OS maps	95	
Waymark	White gull and lettering on blue background	

Publication(s)
Paperback: *Isle of Man Coastal Walk: Raad ny Foillan* by Aileen Evans (Cicerone Press). ISBN: 0902363956. 1988\116 x 176\144pp\£5.99.
Looseleaf: *Raad ny Foillan: Coastal Footpath* (Isle of Man Government). A4\4pp\Free.

Ramblers Route   224

Berks	42 km / 26 miles

A figure-of-eight route allowing circuits of 18.5 or 11.5 miles to be walked, designed by Robin Mosses, and developed by Bracknell District Council in conjunction with the Ramblers' Association and Bracknell District Council's Community Programme. The Route passes open farmland, heaths and coniferous forests as well as passing through several country parks as it follows footpaths, tracks and roads around and to the south of Bracknell new town.

Start and Finish	Bracknell Look Out, Berks	SU875661
OS maps	175	
Waymark	Black arrow on named white disc	

Publication(s)
Leaflet: *Ramblers Route – Around the borough of Bracknell Forest* (Bracknell Forest District Council). A4/3 \ Free.

Ramblers Way   225

Derby, S Yorks	61 km / 38 miles

The walk was designed as a tribute to the ramblers who earlier this century were involved in the fight for access to the hills and moors, and links some of the places associated with its history, including the now legendary mass trespass on the slopes of Kinder Scout in 1932. The route involves over 5,000ft of climbing and should not be walked without a map and compass.

From Castleton it goes over Mam Tor to Edale and crosses the peaty, gritstone uplands of the southern edge of the Kinder Plateau to Hayfield, where it turns north-east across the northern side of the Plateau to the Snake Pass. From here it continues its meandering route to Hathersage via Win Hill, Yorkshire Bridge, Moscar and Stanage Edge.

Start	Castleton, Derby	SK150829
Finish	Hathersage, Derby	SK232815
OS maps	110	

Publication(s)
Booklet: *Ramblers Way* by Andrew Newton and Paul Summers (Mountain Peaks Climbing Club). A5 \ 36pp \ £2.60 (+ 30p).
Badge (£1.00 / 6"x4" SAE) available from Mountain Peaks Climbing Club.

Recedham Way 226

Gtr Man, W Yorks 80 km / 50 miles

Circular walk following the former boundary of the parish of Rochdale. Runs to the south of Rochdale via Thornham Fold and Jubilee to meet the Pennine Way at White Hill; this it follows north to Warland Reservoir before dropping down to Todmorden. It then crosses Todmorden Moor to Bacup, and goes south to Knowl Moor and the western edge of Rochdale. Landscape ranges from moorland to deep wooded valleys.

Start and Finish	Marland, Rochdale, Gtr Man
OS maps	103, 109

Publication(s)
Looseleaf: *Recedham Way* by Les Hardman (Les Hardman). A5 \
5pp \ Free (+ SAE).

Red Rose Walk 227

Cumbria, Gtr Man, Lancs 187 km / 117 miles

This is a route through the old and new counties of Lancashire, using footpaths, old packhorse routes, bridleways and Roman roads, and passing on a meandering and generally northwesterly course through Rossendale and the Forest of Bowland, via Wardle, Holcombe Brook, Whalley, Sawley, Slaidburn and Hornby.

Start	Uppermill, Gtr Man	SD997057
Finish	Arnside, Cumbria	SD461788
OS maps	97, 102, 109	

Publication(s)
Paperback: *The Red Rose Walk* by Tom Schofield (Sigma Leisure). ISBN: 1850583420. 1993 \ A5 \ 90pp \ £6.95.

Reivers Way 228

Northumb 240 km / 150 miles

A meandering route across Northumberland, starting in the Tyne Valley west of Newcastle, going west to the finest remains of Hadrian's Wall, and then heading northwest to Rothbury, over the Cheviots to Wooler, and finishing with the coast path from Budle Bay to Alnmouth.

Start	Corbridge Station, Northumb	NZ989635
Finish	Alnmouth, Northumb	NU248108
OS maps	75, 80, 81, 87	

Publication(s)
Paperback: *The Reiver's Way* by James Roberts (Cicerone Press).
ISBN: 1852841303. 1993\116 x 176\112pp\£5.99.

Rhymney Valley Ridgeway Walk   229

Mid Glam	45 km / 28 miles

The Ridgeway Walk is a large circular route around the Rhymney Valley with its towns of Ystrad Mynach and Caerphilly with its castle. Its highest point is Mynydd Machen at 362m. The scenery changes from hedged lanes to beech woodlands to hill tops with panoramic views. In the east, the Walk is partly coincident with the Sirhowy Valley Walk, and in the west it meets with the end of the Taff-Ely Ridgeway Walk.

Start and Finish	Gelligaer, Mid Glam	ST137969
On OS maps	171	
Waymark	Ridgeway Walk logo and standard arrows	

Publication(s)
Leaflet: *Rhymney Valley Ridgeway Walk* (Caerphilly Mountain Countryside Servce). 1993\A4/3\Free.

Ribble Way   230

Lancs, N Yorks	116 km / 73 miles

The Way follows the valley of the river Ribble from its mouth at Longton Marsh to the Yorkshire Dales National Park and the source of the river near the Pennine Way on Gayle Moor.

From the flat tidal marshes of Longton, the route passes Preston, Ribchester and Clitheroe, with its castle perched above the valley and views of Pendle Hill, to Gisburn and the Yorkshire Dales National Park. It then passes Settle and Horton-in-Ribblesdale to follow moorland paths to the river's source.

Start	Longton, Lancs	SD458255
Finish	Gayle Moor, N Yorks	SD813832
On OS maps	98, 102, 103	
Waymark	Blue and white "RW" wave logo	

Publication(s)
Softback: *The Ribble Way* by Gladys Sellers (Cicerone Press).
ISBN: 1852841079. 1992\116 x 176\112pp\£5.99.
Booklet: *The Ribble Way* (Lancashire County Council). 1988\A5\32pp\£0.90.

Ridgeway Path 231

Berks, Bucks, Herts, Oxon, Wilts	136 km / 85 miles

The western half of the Ridgeway Path National Trail largely follows the route of a prehistoric ridge track running along the crest of the North Wessex Downs and passing many prehistoric sites, including Barbury and Uffington Castles (hill forts), Uffington White Horse and Wayland's Smithy (long barrow). Much of the Way is along a broad, rutted track. At Streatley the route crosses and then follows the river Thames, leaving the line of the trackway. The Path continues over the Chiltern Hills, mainly along their north-western escarpment. The walking on this eastern half is far more varied: along tracks and paths, across open downland, and through farm and woodland, passing Nuffield, Swyncombe, Princes Risborough, Wendover and Pitstone.

Start	Overton Hill, Wilts	SU118681
Finish	Ivinghoe Beacon, Bucks	SP960168
On OS maps	165, 173, 174, 175	
Waymark	National Trail Acorn	
User group	Friends of The Ridgeway	

Publication(s)
Paperback: *Discovering the Ridgeway* by Vera Burden (Shire Publications). ISBN: 0852639902. 1981\112 x 177\£1.95.
Softback: *Exploring The Ridgeway* by Alan Charles (Countryside Books). ISBN: 1853060097. 1988\210 x 150\96pp\£4.95.
Booklet: *Ridgeway Information and Accommodation Guide* (Ridgeway Officer). 1994\A5\40pp\£1.00 (+ 40p).
Softback: *The Ridgeway* by Neil Curtis (Aurum Press). ISBN: 185410019X. 1989\210 x 130\144pp\£8.99.
Leaflet: *The Ridgeway* (Countryside Commission Postal Sales). 1994\A4/3\Free.
Stripmap: *The Ridgeway* (Footprint). £2.95.
Booklet: *The Ridgeway Public Transport Guide* (Ridgeway Officer). 1994\A5\36pp\Free (+ SAE).

Rivers Way 232

Derby	64 km / 40 miles

A meandering route through the Peak District National Park, the Way links the five principal rivers – the Noe, Derwent, Wye, Dove and Manifold – and passes the villages of Hope, Grindleford, Baslow, Bakewell, Flagg, Hartington and Wetton.

Start	Edale, Derby	SK125858
Finish	Ilam, Derby	SK135508
OS maps	119	

Publication(s)
Paperback: *The Rivers Way* by John Merrill (Trail Crest Publications Ltd). ISBN: 0907496415. 1988\140 x 210\36pp\£2.50.
Badge and certificate (£2.75 / post free) available from Trail Crest Publications Ltd.

Robin Hood Way 233

Notts	142 km / 89 miles

The Way, officially opened in 1985, has been developed by Nottingham Wayfarers Rambling Club in conjunction with Nottinghamshire County Council. Areas of Nottingham associated with the legendary figure of Robin Hood and his exploits are linked by this walk which crosses lowland farmland and heathland. It visits the great houses and parks of the Dukeries, and forests created by former owners of the houses and the Forestry Commission, including Sherwood Forest, and finishes at Edwinstowe Church, where Maid Marion and Robin Hood were said to have been married. This is an easy-going, meandering route which takes in some of the best of the countryside around Nottingham.

Start	Nottingham, Notts	SK569392
Finish	Edwinstowe, Notts	SK626669
On OS maps	120, 129	
Waymark	Bow and arrow, green on white	

Publication(s)
Paperback: *The Robin Hood Walks* (Cordee Ltd). ISBN: 1871890020. 1994\156pp\£5.45.

Rossendale Way 234

Lancs	72 km / 45 miles

A high-level route around Bacup, Rawtenstall, Haslingden and Whitworth in the Rossendale valley, crossing the open moors and farmland of the south Pennines. This is a circular route which roughly follows the Rossendale borough boundary; although it is easy to follow, it does need care in poor conditions and in winter is subject to cold winds.

Start and Finish	Sharneyford, Lancs	SD889246
On OS maps	103, 109	
Waymark	"RW"	

Publication(s)
Paperback: *Rossendale Rambles* by Ian Goldthorpe (Rossendale Groundwork Trust Ltd). ISBN: 0947738150. 1985\210 x 149\160pp\£3.75.

Folder: *Rossendale Way* (Rossendale Borough Council). 1982\A4/3\9pp\£2.00.

Rotherham Round Walk 235

S Yorks	40 km / 25 miles

A walk combining the beautiful wooded areas of Wentworth with the industrialised sectors of town centre and motorway zones. Starting in the town centre the route heads north-west to the parkland, woods, lakes and architectural monuments of Wentworth, returning south-east by fields to the steelworks area of Parkgate and via suburbs and woods towards the Wickersley area. A southern arc is then followed through fields, woods and motorway areas back into the town centre.

Start and Finish	Rotherham, S Yorks	SK428928
OS maps	111	
Waymark	Named discs with Chantry Bridge logo	

Publication(s)
Leaflet: *Rotherham Roundwalk* (Rotherham Metropolitan Borough Council). A4/3\Free.

Round Fetlar Walk 236

Shetland	50 km / 31 miles

The third in a series of walks around the islands of Shetland, this route describes Fetlar, the "fertile island" with its crofting communities and bird sanctuaries, Pictish brochs and ponies. Starting where the ferry from Gutcher lands at Oddsta, the route follows the coastline clockwise as near as possible via Gruting, The Snap and Tresta.

Start and Finish	Oddsta, Shetland	HU582943
OS maps	1	

Publication(s)
Paperback: *Walking the Coastline of Shetland: 3 – Island of Fetlar* by Peter Guy (The Shetland Times Ltd). ISBN: 0951584510. 1991\210 x 149\70pp\£3.00.

Round Northmavine Trek 237

Shetland	200 km / 125 miles

This walk around the largest parish in Shetland excels in wild rock scenery. Although part of Mainland, Shetland's largest island, Northmavine is almost an island itself as the neck of land connecting it is only 100 yards across.

The route includes Shetland's highest hill, Ronas Hill (1,486ft), and runs clockwise around the peninsula via Urafirth, Hillswick, Stenness, Hamnavoe, Swinister, Lang Clodie Wick, Sandvoe, North Roe and Ollaberry.

Start and Finish	Mavis Grind, Shetland	HU340683
OS maps	1, 2, 3	

Publication(s)
Paperback: *Walking the Coastline of Shetland: 4 – Northmavine* by Peter Guy (The Shetland Times Ltd). ISBN: 0952002604. 1993 \ 210 x149 \ 112pp \ £4.00.

Round Preston Walk 238

Lancs	37 km / 23 miles

Created by the Ramblers' Association group in 1970, this route runs in a circle around the town, the southern section along the river Ribble (partly coincident with the Ribble Way), and then passing through farmland to Grimsargh, Broughton, Woodplumpton and Lea. A new section through the recently revitalised docks completes the walk back to the river at Penwortham Bridge.

Start and Finish	Penwortham Bridge, Lancs	SD527288
OS maps	102	
Waymark	Preston Guild logo (cross-bearing lamb)	

Publication(s)
Booklet: *The Round Preston Walk* (RA Preston Group). 1991 \ 32pp \ £1.50.

Round Unst Trek 239

Shetland	100 km / 63 miles

The second in a series of walks around the coastline of the islands of Shetland, this one describes the third largest and northernmost, Unst, and offers the walker a magnificent variety of scenery as well as the opportunity to look at many historical sites. Like other Shetland walks, this one is notable for its bird and other wildlife, for its cliff scenery, and for its sheep.

From the ferry port of Belmont, the route heads clockwise via Westing, Woodwick, Burrafirth, Norwick, Haroldswick, Baltasound, Muness and Uyeasound.

Start and Finish	Belmont, Shetland	HP566004
OS maps	1	

Publication(s)
Paperback: *Walking the Coastline of Shetland: 2 – Unst* by P N Guy
(The Shetland Times Ltd). ISBN: 0951584502. 1994\210 x
149\80pp\£4.00.

Round Yell Trek   240

Shetland	161 km / 101 miles

The first in a series of walks around the coastline of the islands of
Shetland, this one describes the second largest, Yell. With its
plentiful bird and other wildlife, cliff scenery and historical remains, the walk provides much for those looking for peace and
quiet. Note that walkers are supposed to give way to sheep and
ponies.

From the Ferry Booking Office at Ulsta, the route goes clockwise
via West Sandwick, Windhouse, Gloup, Cullivoe, Gutcher, Sel-
lafirth, Mid Yell, Otterswick, Burravoe and Bridge of Arisdale.

Start and Finish	Ulsta, Shetland	HU463795
OS maps	1, 2	

Publication(s)
Paperback: *Walking the Coastline of Shetland: 1 – Yell* by P N Guy
(The Shetland Times Ltd). ISBN: 0951202502. 1989\210 x
149\50pp\£3.00.

Saints Way/Forth an Syns   241

Cornwall	42 km / 26 miles

As the name suggests, this Way follows the route thought to have
been taken by the ancient Cornish and Welsh saints. The walk
should be thought of as a series of linking parish walks through
the attractive but little-known area of mid-Cornwall. From Padstow Parish Church in the north, the Way crosses St Breock Downs
to reach Lanivet, continues on to Helman Tor and then goes via
either St Samsons or St Blazey to the finish at Fowey, on the south
coast.

Start	Padstow, Cornwall	SW920754
Finish	Fowey, Cornwall	SX127522
On OS maps	200, 204	
Waymark	Celtic cross	

Publication(s)
Paperback: *The Saints Way: Forth an Syns* (Cornwall County
Council). 1991\A5\32pp\£2.50.

Salter's Way 242

Cheshire	38 km / 24 miles

The Way follows an old salt track across lowland Cheshire from the salt area around Northwich to the moors above Macclesfield. It passes still-working brine pumps, as well as such varied features as Jodrell Bank and the raised lowland bog of Danes Moss.

Start	Broken Cross, Cheshire	SJ682732
Finish	Salterford, Cheshire	SJ983763
OS maps	118	

Publication(s)
Softback: *The Salter's Way* by John N Merrill (Trail Crest Publications Ltd). ISBN: 0907496970. 1991\132 x 210\32pp\£2.95.
Badge and certificate (£2.75 / post free) available from Trail Crest Publications Ltd.

Sandstone Trail 243

Cheshire, Salop	51 km / 32 miles

The Trail, developed by Cheshire County Council, follows the dissected central Cheshire sandstone ridge which runs in a north-south direction, rising to heights of over 700ft from the low-lying Cheshire Plain. From Frodsham the route heads south through Delamere Forest and across the farmlands of the Beeston Gap to pass Beeston Castle and climb the wooded Peckforton Hills, passing rocky outcrops near Rawhead, which at 746ft is the highest point on the route. The heather-clad Bickerton Hills are crossed before the descent to farmland and the route along the Shropshire Union Canal to Grindley Brook.

Start	Frodsham (Beacon Hill), Cheshire	SJ517767
Finish	Grindley Brook, Salop	SJ522433
On OS maps	117	
Waymark	Black bootmark and yellow "S"	

Publication(s)
Booklet: *Longer Trails in Vale Royal* by Carl Rogers (Vale Royal Borough Council). 1993\A5\76pp\£1.95.
Booklet: *Sandstone Trail* (Cheshire County Council). ISBN: 0906759005. 1986\212 x 200\16pp\£1.50 (+ 28p).

Sarn Helen 244

Dyfed, Gwynedd	256 km / 160 miles

The origin of the phrase "Sarn Helen" is somewhat obscure, but it generally refers to Roman roads. This route traces the line of one of these Roman roads through West Wales, connecting various places with Roman remains. In places the old road is clearly visible, but in others it is a matter of conjecture.

From the Roman fort at Caerhun south of Conwy, the route heads south along the edge of Snowdonia to the Swallow Falls and Dolwyddelan, skirts to the east of Ffestiniog to Trawsfynydd, and continues south to Dolgellau and Machynlleth. After crossing the Rheidol valley, the route becomes less wild and more agricultural, continuing to Bronant, Lampeter, and Carmarthen. Although the route does not go over the highest hills and the southern part is mainly lowland valleys, the northern part crosses wild and remote moors, and it is essential that walkers are properly equipped, and able to use a map and compass.

Start	Caerhun, Gwynedd	SH775704
Finish	Carmarthen, Dyfed	SN400210
OS maps	115, 124, 135, 146, 159	

Publication(s)
Paperback: *Sarn Helen: Walking a Roman Road through Wales* by John Cantrell and Arthur Rylance (Cicerone Press). ISBN: 185284101X. 1992\116 x 176\240pp\£8.99.

Saxon Shore Way 245

E Sussex, Kent   225 km / 141 miles

The Way, developed by the now disbanded Kent Rights of Way Council, was conceived as a long distance history and natural history trail; it follows a route approximating to the coastline as it was in Roman times. It passes the Roman forts of Reculver, Richborough, Dover (with its lighthouse), and Lympne; these formed part of a chain of coastal defences erected against Saxon raiders. It avoids the industrial areas of the Thames and Medway Estuaries and the coastal resorts of Thanet and Romney Marsh, and follows or crosses sea walls, marshes, woods, farmland, old cliff-faces now some way inland, nature reserves and many sites of historic interest.

East Sussex County Council plans to extend the route to Hastings by 1996.

Start	Gravesend, Kent	TQ647744
Finish	Rye, E Sussex	TQ918205
On OS maps	177, 178, 179, 189	
Waymark	Red Viking helmet; red arrows on yellow background	

Publication(s)
Folder: *Saxon Shore Way* by RA Kent (Peter Miller). A5\10pp\ £6.55.

Scarborough and Whitby Trailway 246

N Yorks	32 km / 20 miles

When it was the Scarborough and Whitby Railway, this route via Ravenscar and Robin Hood's Bay was formerly considered one of the most scenic in Britain. It passes through varied countryside, offering extensive views of North Yorkshire's coastline scenery.

Start	Scarborough, N Yorks	TA035897
Finish	Whitby, N Yorks	NZ900117
OS maps	94, 101	

Publication(s)
Leaflet: *The Scarborough and Whitby Trailway 1885–1985* (Scarborough Borough Council). 1985\A4/3\£0.25.

Sefton Coastal Footpath 247

Merseyside	35 km / 22 miles

Originally opened as a 15-mile route from Blundellsands to Birkdale, the Footpath has now been extended along the coast of Sefton Borough Council, and will eventually link Liverpool with the Lancashire Coastal Way.

From the northern outskirts of Liverpool, the route goes north primarily through dunes, but also along the promenade at Crosby and Southport, and through marshes at the northern end. It is of great interest botanically, passing through the National Nature Reserve at Ainsdale and the National Trust reserve at Formby, and ornithologically at the mouth of the Ribble at its northern end. It is also easily accessible from Merseyrail's Liverpool-Southport line.

Start	Waterloo Station, Merseyside	SJ321981
Finish	Crossens, Merseyside	SD374205
On OS maps	102, 108	
Waymark	Natterjack toad logo	

Publication(s)
Leaflet: *Sefton Coastal Footpath* (Metropolitan Borough of Sefton). A4\Free.

Settle to Carlisle Walk 248

Cumbria, W Yorks	240 km / 150 miles

Designed for both walkers and railway buffs and providing easy access using the railway, the walk follows the line of the track through the Ribblesdale valley, passing to the east of both Ingleborough and Whernside. It continues north along the shoulder of

Mallerstang Edge to Kirkby Stephen and the Eden Valley, passing through Appleby-in-Westmorland to Carlisle.

Start	Leeds, W Yorks	SE293351
Finish	Carlisle, Cumbria	NY400554
OS maps	85, 86, 90, 91, 97, 98, 103, 104	

Publication(s)
Paperback: *Great Northern Walks: Where to Stay* by John Morrison (Leading Edge Press and Publishing). ISBN: 0948135247. 1991\188 x 105\160pp\£3.25.
Softback: *Settle-Carlisle Country* by Colin Speakman and John Morrison (Leading Edge Press and Publishing). ISBN: 0948135166. 1990\137 x 210\160pp\£5.95.

Severn Way   249

Avon, Glos	105 km / 66 miles

A route along the east bank of the river Severn and the Gloucester and Sharpness Canal, overlooked by the Cotswold escarpment on the east and the Forest of Dean on the west.

From Tewkesbury with its abbey and Battle Trail (commemorating the Battle of Tewkesbury in 1471), it passes the cathedral city of Gloucester, the Wildfowl Trust headquarters at Slimbridge, Berkeley nuclear power station, the Severn Bridge (and thence the southern end of Offa's Dyke Path) before reaching Avonmouth. Here it goes inland to the northern outskirts of Bristol before descending to the end of the Avon Walkway at Pill.

An extension from here to join the coastal footpath to Portishead and Clevedon is planned for end 1994, and the National Rivers Authority also plan to continue upstream from Tewkesbury through Worcerstershire and Shropshire to Shrewsbury in 1995.

Start	Tewkesbury, Glos	SO891324
Finish	Pill, Avon	ST525759
On OS maps	150, 162, 172	
Waymark	Severn Trow signposts and arrow waymarks	

Publication(s)
Paperback: *Guide to the Severn Way: East Bank* by Stanley Gidman (Gloucestershire County Council). 1989\£3.95.
Booklet: *The Severn Way* (Northavon District Council). 1994\100 x 180\Free.
Leaflet: *The Severn Way East Bank* (Gloucestershire County Council). 1989\148 x 210\Free.

Shipley-Dales Way 250

W Yorks	11 km / 7 miles

A well-walked route from Shipley north of Bradford to the start of the Dales Way at Ilkley via Baildon Moor, Dick Hudson's Inn, and Bingley and Ilkley Moors.

Start	Shipley, W Yorks	SE149376
Finish	Ilkley, W Yorks	SE117476
OS maps	104	
User group	Dales Way Association	

Publication(s)
Booklet: *Dales Way Route Guide* by Arthur Gemmell and Colin Speakman (Stile Publications). ISBN: 0906886538. 1991\197 x 120\44pp\£2.80.

Shropshire Union Canal 251

Cheshire, Staffs, W Midlands	60 km / 38 miles

The Birmingham and Liverpool Junction Canal opened in 1835 and later formed part of the Shropshire Union. It was Thomas Telford's last great engineering challenge, and was constructed at a time when most saw the future of transport in railways rather than waterways.

From Autherley near Wolverhampton on the edge of the Black Country, it passes through rural Shropshire via Gnosall, Norbury, Market Drayton and Audlem to Nantwich in Cheshire. The canal itself, though not the book listed, continues via Chester to Ellesmere Port.

Start	Autherley Junction, W Midlands	SJ902020
Finish	Nantwich, Cheshire	SJ640530
OS maps	118, 127	

Publication(s)
Paperback: *The Shropshire Union Canal* by Jonathan Morris (Management Update Ltd). ISBN: 0946679436. 1991\128pp\ £5.99 (+ £1).

Shropshire Way 252

Salop	224 km / 140 miles

A varied route developed by a group of Shropshire rambling clubs, crossing lowland farmland and many of Shropshire's more notable hills, and passing a rich variety of historic houses and picturesque villages. From Wem the Way loops south to Shrewsbury, the county town, and over the Stiperstones to Bishops Castle, Clun, Hopesay

Hill, Stokesay Castle and Ludlow, the most southerly point. It
returns to Wem via the Clee Hills, the limestone ridge of Wenlock
Edge, Ironbridge on the river Severn with its several industrial
museums, and the Wrekin, to complete the 140-mile route. An
11-mile spur runs north from Wem to meet the Sandstone Trail,
Marches, Maelor and South Cheshire Ways at Grindley Brook. A
13-mile shortcut leaves the main route at Bridges and runs over
the open moorland of the Long Mynd ridge to meet the main route
on Hopesay Hill.

Start and Finish	Wem, Salop	SJ513289
OS maps	117, 126, 127, 137, 138	
Waymark	Buzzard	

Publication(s)
Paperback: *Rambler's Guide to the Shropshire Way* by RA Shropshire (Management Update Ltd). ISBN: 0946679428.
1991 \ A5 \ 76pp \ £5.99 (+ £1).

Sirhowy Valley Walk   253

Gwent, Mid Glam	42 km / 26 miles

Starting from one of the finest country houses in Wales, Tredegar
House, the route follows a challenging route from the built-up
fringes of Newport to the hill ridges of Mynyddd Machen and
Mynydd Manmoel. It passes lowland and upland farms, woodlands
and riverside parks, many sites of historical interest, including an
Iron Age hill fort, an old mill and a canal centre, before finishing
near Tredegar, the birthplace of the Labour MP, Aneurin Bevan.

Start	Newport, Gwent	ST310879
Finish	Tredegar, Mid Glam	SO151105
On OS maps	161, 171	
Waymark	"S" on standard waymarks	

Publication(s)
Folder: *The Sirhowy Valley Walk* (Gwent County Council). 175 x
240 \ 14pp \ £2.50 (+ 50p).

Snowdonia to the Gower   254

Dyfed, Gwynedd, Powys, W Glam	355 km / 222 miles

This coast-to-coast route from north to south Wales was primarily
designed for the backpacker. Starting at Llanfairfechan in Conwy
Bay, the walk climbs to cross the peaks of the Carneddau and the
Glyders before dropping down through the Pass of Llanberis, then
climbing up and over Snowdon. The walk continues south over the
Moelwyns, climbs over the Rhinogs, Cadair Idris and the Tarrens
and then descends into the Dyfi valley and Machynlleth.

Becoming more wild and remote, the walk passes Bwlch Hyddgen (where the forces of Henry IV were slaughtered by Owain Glyndwr in 1401). Once over Plynlimon, the source of the rivers Severn, Wye and Rheidol, the walk enters the Elan valley with its great reservoirs and continues south through the Tywi valley. The Carmarthen Fan and the Black Mountain on the western end of the Brecon Beacons are climbed to give splendid views. The walk continues over the softer Lliw Hills to pass to the west of Swansea and onto the Gower, through Bishopston valley, then along the coast path to Three Cliffs Bay and the end of the walk.

Start	Llanfairfechan, Gwynedd	SH680750
Finish	Parkmill, W Glam	SS545892
OS maps	115, 124, 135, 136, 147, 159, 160	

Publication(s)
Hardback. *Snowdonia to the Gower* by J Gillham (Diadem Books). 225 x 272 \ 100pp \ £14.95.
Paperback: *Snowdonia to the Gower: Route Text* by J Gillham (Cordee Ltd). 225 x 272 \ 24pp \ £1.00.

Solent Way   255

Hants	96 km / 60 miles

The route was developed by Hampshire County Council and opened in 1982. From Milford on Sea it crosses coastal marshes, heading eastwards to Lymington, before going inland past the heaths, woods and villages of the New Forest and visiting the tourist areas of Bucklers Hard and Beaulieu to reach Hythe on the Test Estuary. The ferry is taken to Southampton, from where the Way follows the Solent shoreline, crossing the river Hamble (a popular yachting area) and continuing eastwards to reach Portsmouth via the Gosport ferry. It continues along the historic waterfront of Portsmouth and Southsea, and passes the coastal marshes and quays around Langstone Harbour to reach Emsworth, north of Hayling Island.

Start	Milford-on-Sea, Hants	SZ292918
Finish	Emsworth, Hants	SU753055
On OS maps	195, 196, 197	
Waymark	Dark blue bird on light blue ground	

Publication(s)
Leaflet: *The Solent Way* (Hampshire County Council). A4/3 \ Free.

South Bucks Way 256

Bucks	37 km / 23 miles

An easy route from the Ridgeway Path at Wendover via Chequers Knap, where it connects with the North Buckinghamshire Way, to the towpath of the Grand Union Canal. The route crosses the chalk hills of the Chilterns.

Start	Coombe Hill, Bucks	SP849067
Finish	Denham, Bucks	TQ053862
On OS maps	165, 176	
Waymark	Standard waymark with name	

Publication(s)
Leaflet: *South Bucks Way* (Buckinghamshire County Council). A4/3\Free (+ SAE).

South Cheshire Way 257

Cheshire, Salop	50 km / 31 miles

From the southern end of the Sandstone Trail the way runs north-east over lowland farmland past Marbury Mere, and skirting Crewe and Alsager, before passing by the half-timbered Little Moreton Hall (NT) and climbing to Mow Cop at the western end of the Staffordshire Way.

Start	Grindley Brook, Salop	SJ522433
Finish	Mow Cop, Cheshire	SJ856573
On OS maps	117, 118	
Waymark	"SCW" on standard waymarks	

Publication(s)
Booklet: *Guide to the South Cheshire Way* by Justin McCarthy (Mid-Cheshire Footpath Society). 1988\145 x 203\20pp\£0.75.

South Downs Way 258

E Sussex, Hants, W Sussex	162 km / 101 miles

The South Downs Way, opened in 1972, was the first National Trail to be designed as a bridleway. Originally terminating at Buriton on the Hampshire/Sussex border, it has now been extended west to Winchester for walkers, though the official opening of this extension as a bridleway is scheduled for 1995. It follows the northern escarpment of the chalk Downs from where there are extensive views across the Weald to the north and over the rounded hills and dry valleys to the sea to the south.

Apart from several steep ascents when crossing the valleys of the rivers Cuckmere at Alfriston, Ouse at Southease, Adur south of Bramber and Arun at Amberley, the Way provides relatively easy walking (although the flinty tracks can be hard on the feet, and the route can be surprisingly exposed, the majority of it being over 600ft, often with very little shelter). The route also passes several iron-age hillforts and barrows.

From Eastbourne the bridleway goes over the Downs to Jevington and Alfriston; there is an alternative footpath which runs along the clifftops to Beachy Head and the Seven Sisters, which turns inland at Cuckmere Haven along the Cuckmere valley to join the bridleway at Alfriston.

Start	Eastbourne (Holywell), E Sussex	TV600972
Finish	Winchester, Hants	SU483293
On OS maps	185, 197, 198, 199	
Waymark	National Trail Acorn	

Publication(s)

Leaflet: *Accommodation Guide to the South Downs Way* (South Downs Way Officer). Free.

Paperback: *Aerofilms Guide: The South Downs Way* by John Godfrey (Ian Allan Publishing). ISBN: 0711020426. 286 x 140\132pp\ £8.99.

Paperback: *Along the South Downs Way to Winchester* (Society of Sussex Downsmen). £5.00.

Hardback: *Guide to the South Downs Way* by Miles Jebb (Constable and Co Ltd). ISBN: 0094711704. 171 x 114\336pp\ £10.95.

Softback: *South Downs Way* by Paul Millmore (Aurum Press). ISBN: 1854100998. 1990\210 x 130\168pp\£8.99.

Leaflet: *South Downs Way* (Countryside Commission Postal Sales). 1991\A4/3\Free.

Paperback: *The South Downs Way and Downs Link* by Kev Reynolds (Cicerone Press). ISBN: 1852840234. 116 x 176\136pp\ £5.99.

South West Coast Path   259

Cornwall, Devon, Dorset, Somerset	960 km / 600 miles

Britain's longest National Trail, also known as the South West Peninsula Coast Path, or simply the South West Way, it was designed to form a continuous right of way around the peninsula, and for much of the route it does just that, going along undulating cliffs from where there are extensive views, and passing remote coves, beaches, harbours, coastal routes and ports. However, some sections of the Way have been diverted away from the coast.

The Path was formerly split into four sections, and is often still referred to in those terms.

a) **Somerset and North Devon**
From Minehead the Path goes through the Exmoor National Park to Lynton and continues along the coast through the North Devon AONB to Ilfracombe, Barnstaple and Bideford, then on to Marsland Mouth.

b) **Cornwall**
From Marsland Mouth the route passes through Bude and then along some of the wildest and most rugged areas on the path to Tintagel. It continues along the north coast to round Land's End and Lizard Point, the most western and southern tips respectively of Britain, and then along the south coast through the holiday villages of St Austell and Fowey to Cremyll.

c) **South Devon**
From Plymouth, a ferry ride away from Cremyll, the walking becomes easier as the Coast Path continues through Salcombe, Dartmouth and Brixham and the busy holiday resorts around Tor Bay and Babbacombe Bay to Sidmouth and Lyme Regis.

d) **Dorset**
The Coast Path passes Bridport and follows Chesil Beach to the busy port of Weymouth, from where it goes along the cliffs of the heritage coast, famous for its fossils and varied geology. There are two firing ranges along this beautiful coast, one at Tidmore Point, and the other at Lulworth where the Coast Path is only open at weekends and holiday periods – the inland route should be followed whenever the red flags are flying.

Start	Minehead, Somerset	SS972467
Finish	South Haven Point, Dorset	SZ036866
On OS maps	180, 181, 190, 192, 193, 194, 195, 200, 201, 202, 203, 204	
Waymark	National Trail Acorn	
User group	South West Way Association	

Publication(s)
Paperback: *Aerofilms Guide: The South Devon Coast Path* by Des Hannigan (Ian Allan Publishing). ISBN: 0711020418. 286 x 140\144pp\£8.99.
Paperback: *Exploring the Dorset Coast Path* by Leigh Hatts (Countryside Books). ISBN: 1853062243. 1993\210 x 150\128pp\£4.95.
Paperback: *Footpath Touring: Land's End and the Lizard* by Ken Ward (Footpath Touring). ISBN: 0711701938. 1985\224 x 114\64pp\£3.50.
Softback: *South West Coast Path: Exmouth to Poole* by Roland Tarr (Aurum Press). ISBN: 1854100203. 1989\210 x 130\168pp\£8.99.
Softback: *South West Coast Path: Falmouth to Exmouth* by Brian le Messurier (Aurum Press). ISBN: 1854100963. 1990\210 x 130\168pp\£8.99.

Softback: *South West Coast Path: Minehead to Padstow* by Roland Tarr (Aurum Press). ISBN: 1854100971. 1990\210 x 130\168pp\£8.99.

Softback: *South West Coast Path: Padstow to Falmouth* by John Macadam (Aurum Press). ISBN: 185410098X. 1990\210 x 130\£8.99.

Paperback: *The Dorset Coast Path* by Mike Power (Power Publications). ISBN: 0951450239. 210 x 150\40pp\£2.95.

Leaflet: *The South West Coast Path* (Countryside Commission Postal Sales). 1992\A4/3\Free.

Softback: *The South West Way* (South West Way Association). ISBN: 187264015X. 1994\A5\88pp\£3.95.

Paperback: *The South West Way Vol 1: Minehead to Penzance* by Martin Collins (Cicerone Press). ISBN: 1852840250. 1989\116 x 176\184pp\£8.99.

Paperback: *The South West Way Vol 2: Penzance to Poole* by Martin Collins (Cicerone Press). ISBN: 1852840269. 1989\116 x 176\198pp\£8.99.

Softback: *Walk the Cornish Coastal Path* by John H N Mason (Bartholomew & Times Books). ISBN: 0702809020. 210 x 148\£5.99.

Southern Coast to Coast Walk 260

Avon, Hants, Kent, Somerset, Surrey, Wilts	453 km / 283 miles

Written as Southern England's response to Wainwright's famous Coast to Coast Walk, this route connects the Bristol and English Channels. Apart from a couple of connecting sections in Wiltshire along the Wylye valley and Hampshire from New Alresford via Selborne and Ludshott Common to Haslemere, it mainly uses other waymarked routes: the West and East Mendip Ways, the Imber Range Perimeter Path, Clarendon Way, Itchen Way, Greensand Way and Saxon Shore Path.

Start	Weston-super-Mare, Avon	ST317614
Finish	Dover (Castle), Kent	TR324419
OS maps	179, 182, 183, 184, 185, 186, 187, 188, 189	

Publication(s)
Paperback: *The Southern Coast-to-Coast Walk* by Ray Quinlan (Cicerone Press). ISBN: 1852841176. 1993\116 x 176\200pp\£6.99.

Southern Upland Way 261

Borders, Dum & Gall, Strathclyde	340 km / 213 miles

Officially opened in 1984, this route provides a relatively safe route across varied and often sparsely populated terrain, avoiding the high tops. From Portpatrick it heads north-east across the Rhinns of Galloway and Glen Trool Forest Park to Sanquhar and the open, heather-clad Lowther Hills, and reaches St Mary's Loch near Broad Law, the highest point in the southern uplands. From here the Way passes through Melrose and Lauder, and over the foothills of the Lammermuir Hills to reach the east coast at Cockburnspath.

Start	Portpatrick, Dum & Gall	NW998542
Finish	Cockburnspath, Borders	NT774709
On OS maps	67, 73, 74, 77, 78, 79, 82	
Waymark	Spannered thistle	

Publication(s)
Softback: *Guide to the Southern Upland Way* by David Williams (Constable and Co Ltd). ISBN: 009467910X. 1989\171 x 114\333pp\£8.95.
Leaflet: *Southern Upland Way* (Scottish Natural Heritage). 1993\A4/3\Free.
Leaflet: *The Southern Upland Way* (Dumfries and Galloway Regional Council). 1994\A4/3\Free.
Folder: *The Southern Upland Way* by Roger Smith (HMSO Scotland). ISBN: 0114951705. 1994\220 x 135\208pp\£17.50.

Spen Way Heritage Trail   262

W Yorks	34 km / 21 miles

A circuit of the former borough of Spenborough and the Spen, a tributary of the river Calder. The Way concentrates on the history of this old textile manufacturing area, visiting Scholes, East Bierley and Gomersal as it follows through a varied mixture of urban areas, parkland and farmland.

Start and Finish	Cleckheaton, W Yorks	SE246199
On OS maps	104	
Waymark	"HT" on standard waymarks	

Publication(s)
Leaflet: *Spen Valley Leisure & Heritage Guide* by Spen Valley Civic Society (Kirklees Metropolitan Council). 1990\A5\£1.25 (+ 65p).

Speyside Way   263

Grampian	77 km / 48 miles

Approved by the Secretary of State for Scotland in 1978, the first part of this route from Tugnet on Spey Bay on the Moray Firth to Ballindalloch was opened in 1981 and is an easy 30-mile walk following the valley of the river Spey. The Way passes numerous whisky distilleries, and at Tamdhu the station has been opened as a distillery visitor centre. At Craigellachie there is a short spur track along the disued railway to Dufftown and the Glenfiddich distillery.

The section from Ballindalloch was opened in 1988, and climbs over Carn Daimh, where there are magnificent views of the Grampians, and the Feithmusach peat bog to Tomintoul, the highest village in Moray at 1,100ft.

It is hoped eventually to extend the Way from Ballindalloch to Glen More and Aviemore.

Start	Spey Bay, Grampian	NJ350653
Finish	Tomintoul, Grampian	NJ165195
On OS maps	28, 36	
Waymark	Spannered thistle	

Publication(s)
Leaflet: *Speyside Way* (Moray District Council). A4/3 \ £0.50.

St Edmund Way 264

Essex, Suffolk	140 km / 88 miles

A south-north route across Suffolk, the Way uses the Stour Valley Path to Sudbury and Long Melford, then heads north via Lavenham and Little Welnetham to Bury St Edmunds (hence the name), then along the Lark Valley Path to the Icknield Way at West Stow before striking over the Brecks to Thetford and the Hereward Way to finish at Brandon.

Start	Manningtree, Essex	TM094322
Finish	Brandon, Suffolk	TL784866
OS maps	143, 144, 155, 168	

Publication(s)
Paperback: *The St Edmund Way – A Walk across Suffolk* by John and Jean Andrews (Suffolk County Council). 1994 \ 208 x 146 \ 66pp \ £3.75.

St Peter's Way 265

Essex	72 km / 45 miles

From Chipping Ongar the Way heads east across the open agricultural land of Essex, past Hanningfield Reservoir and inlets of the Blackwater Estuary (both rich in birdlife), and reaches the coast to the east of Tillingham. The sea wall, from where there are extensive views across the Essex marshes, is followed northwards to reach St Peter's Chapel.

Start	Chipping Ongar, Essex	TL551036
Finish	St Peter's Flat, Essex	TM032082
On OS maps	167, 168, 177	

Publication(s)
Booklet: *The St Peter's Way* by Fred Matthews and Harry Bitten (Matthews/Bitten Publications). 1985\A5\25pp\£1.20.

Staffordshire Way 266

Cheshire, Derby, Staffs	148 km / 93 miles

From the 18th century folly, Mow Cop Castle, the Way, at this point coincident with Cheshire County Council's 9-mile Mow Cop Trail, heads north-east along Congleton Edge to The Cloud before turning south-east to meet the southern end of the Gritstone Trail and pass to the west of Rudyard Reservoir. The towpath of the Caldon Canal is followed past Cheddleton Flint Mill and along the Churnet valley before crossing woodland and pasture to Rocester. Here the Way turns due south and follows the river Dove to Uttoxeter and then crosses farmland to Abbots Bromley and the Trent and Mersey Canal, which is followed to Shugborough Hall (NT), before climbing to the wooded heights of Cannock Chase. It continues in a south-easterly direction to Penkridge and the old village of Brewood and across farmland to Codsall and Highgate Common, from where it crosses a series of wooded hills and valleys to finish on the sandstone heights of Kinver Edge.

Start	Mow Cop, Cheshire	SJ856573
Finish	Kinver Edge, Staffs	SO829822
On OS maps	118, 119, 127, 128, 138, 139	
Waymark	Staffordshire knot	

Publication(s)
Paperback: *Staffordshire Way* (Staffordshire County Council). £3.00 (+ 40p).
Softback: *The Staffordshire Way* by Les Lusdon and Chris Rushton (Sigma Leisure). ISBN: 1850583153. 1993\A5\120pp\£6.95.
Leaflet: *The Staffordshire Way* (Staffordshire County Council). 147 x 210\Free.

Staunton Way 267

Hants	20 km / 13 miles

Named after Sir George Staunton, a 19th-century MP who owned the estate which is now the Staunton country park, the way links the Hangers Way at the Queen Elizabeth country park at Butser Hill on the South Downs Way with the Solent Way and Wayfarers Walk at Langstone Harbour. It roughly follows the Hampshire/Sussex border, passing through the villages of Chalton and Finchdean, and following a stream through Havant.

Start	QE Country Park, Hants	SU718182
Finish	Broadmarsh, Hants	SZ700057

On OS maps	197
Waymark	Brown deer's head on standard arrows

Publication(s)
Leaflet: *Staunton Way* (Hampshire County Council). 1993\A4/3\
Free.

Stort Valley Way 268

Essex, Herts	51 km / 32 miles

A circular walk around the town of Harlow opened in 1994 by
Hertfordshire and Essex County Councils, this route runs firstly
in Hertfordshire via Hunsdon, Widford, Gilston and High Wych
to Sawbridgeworth; then into Essex via Sheering, Hatfield
Heath, Matching, Magdalen Laver, North Weald Bassett, Epping Upland and Nazeing. There are link paths connecting to
Harlow.

Start and Finish	Roydon, Essex
OS maps	167

Publication(s)
None at time of writing.

Stour Valley Path 269

Cambs, Essex, Suffolk	96 km / 60 miles

The Path, developed by Suffolk County Council, follows the river
valley downstream and links the Icknield Way Path, which it
crosses at Stetchworth, with Sudbury and the Essex Way at
Manningtree. It follows the meandering course of the river,
which for much of its length forms the Suffolk/Essex border, and
passes through some of the most attractive country in East
Anglia, including Constable country towards the end around
East Bergholt.
  Long term, it is planned to extend the route east along the Stour
and Orwell estuaries to Ipswich and the Suffolk Coast Path at
Felixstowe.

Start	Newmarket, Suffolk	TL646636
Finish	Cattawade, Suffolk	TM101332
OS maps	154, 155, 168, 169	
Waymark	Named discs and posts with stylised river and dragonfly logo	

Publication(s)
Folder: *Stour Valley Path* (Suffolk County Council). 1994\A5\
10pp\£1.80.

Stour Valley Walk 270

Kent	61 km / 38 miles

An easy route along the valley of the Great Stour in East Kent, the Walk passes through agricultural land with views of the North Downs to Canterbury. East of here it reaches Fordwich, the medieval limit of the navigable section of the river, from where it traces the old Saxon shoreline of the Wantsum Channel to the important Roman site at Richborough and the ancient Cinque Port of Sandwich.

Start	Ashford, Kent	TR035448
Finish	Sandwich, Kent	TR332582
On OS maps	179, 189	
Waymark	Heron	

Publication(s)
Booklet: *Stour Valley Walk* (Kent County Council). ISBN: 1873010028. 1990\210 x 210\28pp\£2.45.

Stour Valley Way 271

Dorset	50 km / 31 miles

Currently under development by Dorset County Council, this route along the river Stour to the north of Bournemouth and via Wimborne Minster is due to open end 1994.

Start	Christchurch, Dorset	SZ160925
Finish	Blandford Forum, Dorset	ST888067
OS maps	194, 195	

Publication(s)
None at time of writing.

Suffolk Coast Path 272

Suffolk	80 km / 50 miles

The Path, developed by Suffolk County Council, follows rights of way and permissive paths along the Suffolk Heritage Coast on river and sea walls, and across marsh, heath, foreshore and low cliffs to link two ports. From Felixstowe it heads north via the foot ferry to Bawdsey, and follows the river wall along the large shingle spit of Orford Ness to meet the river Alde at Snape Maltings and regain the coast at the festival town of Aldeburgh. From here it follows the coast to Lowestoft Harbour past Sizewell, Minsmere Bird Reserve, the remnants of the medieval port of Dunwich, and Southwold.

Start	Felixstowe, Suffolk	TM324364
Finish	Lowestoft, Suffolk	TM548926
On OS maps	134, 156, 169	
Waymark	"Coast Path" and standard waymarks on brown background	

Publication(s)
Leaflet: *Suffolk Coast Path* (Suffolk County Council). A4/3 \ £0.20
(+ SAE).

Suffolk Way   273

Suffolk	170 km / 106 miles

The Suffolk Way is a meandering route across the county from the
south-west to the north-east, and it is hoped that eventually it can
be adopted by the local authorities and given official status. It
starts at the famous Flatford Mill, and proceeds north-west to
Lavenham with its fine half-timbered buildings. From here it
meanders across the county to Framlingham and Halesworth,
where it turns east along the river Blyth to the coast at Walber-
swick. From here it follows the coast north to Southwold and the
finish at Lowestoft.

Start	Flatford, Suffolk	TM076332
Finish	Lowestoft, Suffolk	TM548926
OS maps	134, 155, 156, 169	

Publication(s)
Booklet: *Suffolk Way* by Ian St John (Footpath Guides).
1993 \ A5 \ 36pp \ £2.50.

Sussex Border Path   274

E Sussex, Hants, Kent, Surrey, W Sussex	243 km / 152 miles

The Path follows rights of way approximating to the Sussex border
with Hampshire, Surrey and Kent, and crosses undulating weal-
den wood-, farm- and heathland. From Emsworth the Path first
follows a 9-mile circuit around Thorney Island, and then heads
north across the South Downs to South Harting and Liphook,
before heading east to Gospel Green, Rudgwick, Gatwick and East
Grinstead. Here the Mid Sussex Link branches off along the line
of the administrative boundary between East and West Sussex.
The main Border Path heads south-east through Ashurst, Wad-
hurst and Bodiam to Rye.

Start	Emsworth, Hants	SU753055
Finish	Rye, E Sussex	TQ918205
On OS maps	186, 187, 188, 189, 197, 198, 199	

Waymark	Martlet on green plaques or wooden signposts

Publication(s)
Folder: *The Sussex Border Path* by Ben Perkins and Aeneas Mackintosh (Dr Ben Perkins). 1991 \ A5 \ 9pp \ £3.50 (+ 34p).

Swan's Way 275

Bucks, Oxon	108 km / 68 miles

A bridleway route through Buckinghamshire, the Swan's Way starts on the Northants border, runs through Milton Keynes, and crosses the Vale of Aylesbury to meet the Ridgeway near Princes Risborough. It then follows the Ridgeway along the chalk slopes of the Chilterns to the Thames at Goring. See also Midshires Way.

Start	Salcey Forest, Bucks	SP811509
Finish	Goring-on-Thames, Oxon	SU600810
On OS maps	152, 164, 165, 174, 175	
Waymark	Swan's head in horseshoe	

Publication(s)
Leaflet: *Swan's Way* (Buckinghamshire County Council). A4/3 \ Free (+ SAE).

Tabular Hills Link Walk 276

N Yorks	76 km / 48 miles

A walk along the southern boundary of the North York Moors, passing through the limestone Tabular Hills via Hutton-le-Hole and Dalby Forest. It is designed to link the start and end of the Cleveland Way, and can therefore be combined with it to form a circular walk around the National Park. Not the same as the "Missing Link".

Start	Helmsley, N Yorks	SE611839
Finish	Scalby Ness, N Yorks	TA032915
OS maps	100, 101	
Waymark	Stylised arrows with "Link"	

Publication(s)
Booklet: *Regional Routes Accommodation Guide* (North York Moors National Park). 1993 \ 120 x 170 \ 12pp \ Free (+ SAE).
Booklet: *The Link Through the Tabular Hills Walk* (North York Moors National Park). ISBN: 0907480446. 1993 \ 120 x 170 \ 44pp \ £3.95.

Taff Trail 277

Mid Glam, Powys, S Glam		88 km / 55 miles

A route designed for both walkers and cyclists, the Taff Trail is mainly converted railway lines with former canals and forestry tracks, so is an easy walk. It runs from the centre of Cardiff north along the Taff valley to the cathedral city of Llandaff, Pontypridd and Merthyr Tydfil. From here the main route circles to the east of the Brecon Beacons via Talybont and Pencelli to Brecon, though another route via Neuadd reservoir enables a circular route between Merthyr and Brecon.

Start	Cardiff, S Glam	ST180765
Finish	Brecon, Powys	SO043286
On OS maps	160, 161, 170, 171	
Waymark	Stylised viaduct in yellow arrow on black background	

Publication(s)
Paperback: *The Taff Trail* by Jeff Vinter (Alan Sutton Publishing Ltd). ISBN: 0750903414. 1993\219 x 154\128pp\£6.99.
Booklet: *The Taff Trail for Walkers and Cyclists* (Merthyr and Cynon Valley Groundwork). A5\16pp\Free (+ SAE).

Taff-Ely Ridgeway Walk 278

Mid Glam		32 km / 20 miles

The Walk, also known simply as Ridgeway Walk or Ffordd y Bryniau, was developed by the Borough Council and, together with the Ogwr Ridgeway Walk and the Rhymney Valley Ridgeway Walk, is based on an ancient east-west ridgeway which follows the dissected ridge of Pennant sandstone, bounding the southern outcrop of the south Wales coalfield. It gives views of the former mining valleys to the north and the coastal plain to the south, and passes through Llantrisant Forest and the old hill town of Llantrisant. Besides climbing hilltops, it crosses the Ely and Taff valleys to finish on Caerphilly Common.

Start	Heol-y-Cyw, Mid Glam	SS969862
Finish	Caerphilly, Mid Glam	ST155852
On OS maps	170, 171	
Waymark	Yellow/black disc with hills motif	

Publication(s)
Leaflet: *Ridgeway Walk / Ffordd y Bryniau* (Taff Ely Borough Council). A4/3\Free.

Tame Valley Way   279

| Gtr Man | 40 km / 25 miles |

One of a series of routes following Greater Manchester's rivers, the Tame Valley Way runs from central Stockport to Reddish Vale and Hyde. From here canal towpaths are followed through Ashton-under-Lyne, Stalybridge and Mossley. From Uppermill, the route leaves the canal, following riverside paths to Delph and Denshaw. In spite of being through densely populated areas, the route is surprisingly attractive, with much woodland besides the attractions of the waterside route.

Start	Stockport, Gtr Man	SJ893903
Finish	Denshaw, Gtr Man	SD975105
OS maps	109	

Publication(s)
Looseleaf: *The Tame Valley* (Tameside Leisure Services). A4 \ 11pp \ £1.10.

Tameside Trail   280

| Gtr Man | 64 km / 40 miles |

A circular walk, opened in 1994, roughly following the borough boundary. From Broadbottom, it runs clockwise along the Etherow Valley Way and Tame Valley Way to Stockport, where it turns north through Audenshaw and Droylsden. Here it picks up the Medlock Valley Way which it follows north-east to Park Bridge, where it turns east to Mossley. It returns south to Broadbottom via the Swineshaw Valley and Hollingworth.

Start and Finish	Broadbottom, Gtr Man	SJ996936
OS maps	109	
Waymark	Named discs	

Publication(s)
Folder: *The Tameside Trail* (Tameside Leisure Services). ISBN: 1871324114. 1994.

Tarka Trail   281

| Devon, Somerset | 290 km / 181 miles |

The Trail is the centrepiece of Devon County Council's Tarka Project, which promotes conservation and tourism in North Devon, relating the scenery and the modern landscape to that depicted in Henry Williamson's classic "Tarka the Otter". Varying from coastal cliffs to disused railway lines, the route is a large figure of eight centred around Barnstaple. The northern loop runs over Exmoor via Exe Head to Lynton, and then follows the coast path round via Ilfracombe to Braunton and Barnstaple. The southern loop follows a former railway line to Bideford, Torrington and Meeth, and continues along the Okement valley to Okehampton and Sticklepath. Here it turns north along the Taw valley to Eggesford, where the Tarka Line train returns the walker to Barnstaple.

Start and Finish	Barnstaple, Devon	SS558331
On OS maps	180, 191	
Waymark	Otter pawmark	

Publication(s)
Paperback: *Tarka Trail – A Walker's Guide* by Richard Williamson (Tarka Project Officer). ISBN: 0861148770. 1989\£3.95.
Booklet: *The Tarka Trail: an introductory guide* (Tarka Project Officer). 1990\A4/3\12pp\Free.

Teesdale Way 282

Cleveland, Durham	230 km / 144 miles

Open in summer 1994, the Way largely follows the banks of the river, thereby connecting industrial Teesside with the Pennines and the Pennine Way at Middleton, and passing through Barnard Castle and to the south of Darlington.

Start	Middleton-in-Teesdale, Durham
Finish	Middlesborough, Cleveland
OS maps	92, 93
Waymark	Named discs with dipper logo in Durham and fish in Cleveland

Publication(s)
Leaflet: *The Teesdale Way – in Cleveland* (Cleveland County Council). A4\Free.

Templer Way 283

Devon	24 km / 15 miles

Named after the Templer family who constructed the Stover Canal and Tramway to bring granite quarried at Haytor to the coast at Teignmouth, the Way is still under development, but open sections provide interest for ecological reasons as well as for the locks and buildings. The terrain ranges from open moor to woodland and estuary foreshore.

Start	Haytor Quarry, Devon	SX750778
Finish	Shaldon, Devon	SX931724
On OS maps	191, 192	

Waymark	White logo on brown

Publication(s)
Leaflet: *Templer Way Guide for the Walker* (Devon County Council).
A4/3 \ Free.

Test Way   284

Berks, Hants, Wilts	74 km / 46 miles

The Way follows the Test valley from the outskirts of Southampton, northwards along lowland farmland and woodland paths. It continues along a disused railway line past Romsey, Mottisfont Abbey (NT), Stockbridge, Wherwell and St Mary Bourne, before gradually climbing to Inkpen Beacon on the crest of the chalk downs.

Start	Totton, Hants	SU360140
Finish	Inkpen Beacon, Berks	SU365622
On OS maps	174, 185, 196	
Waymark	Green "TW" on white ground	

Publication(s)
Leaflet: *Test & Clarendon Way* (Hampshire County Council).
1986 \ A4/3 \ Free.
Paperback: *The Test Way and The Clarendon Way* by Barry Shurlock (Hampshire County Council). ISBN: 0948176032. 210 x 125 \ 128pp \ £3.95.

Thame Valley Walk   285

Bucks, Oxon	26 km / 16 miles

A path along the river Thame, created by the RA and later adopted by Aylesbury Vale DC. The route described by the RA is slightly longer than the waymarked route which runs from the N Bucks Way north of Hartwell to the Oxfordshire Way near Albury, east of Wheatley.

Start	Wheatley, Oxon	SP611052
Finish	Hartwell, Bucks	SP794122
On OS maps	165	
Waymark	Named discs with stylised river logo	

Publication(s)
Booklet: *Thame Valley Walk* (Aylesbury Vale District Council).
1993 \ A4/3 \ 20pp \ Free (+ SAE).
Paperback: *Vale of Aylesbury Walker* by Peter Gulland and Diana Gulland (RA Buckinghamshire). ISBN: 090061367X. A5 \ 140pp \ £3.00.

Thames Path 286

Berks, Bucks, Glos, Gtr London, Oxon, Surrey, Wilts   341 km / 213 miles

Although designated as a National Trail in 1989, a route the length of the river was first proposed in 1981, surveyed by the Ramblers' Association in conjunction with the River Thames Society, and published by the RA as the "Thames Walk". This route basically followed the towpath from Putney to Lechlade, and then footpaths to the source, though diversions had to be made to cope with defunct ferries and, in places, private estates.

The National Trail, the only one to follow a river, was originally due to open officially in 1994, though this has now been postponed to 1996. It starts in central London, goes upstream via Putney, Richmond, Windsor, Abingdon, Oxford, Cricklade and Lechlade, and finishes at the official source near Kemble. As this is just over an hour by train from Paddington, the whole of the path can be easily accessed by public transport from London. It is easy to follow, and provides level walking, and designation as a National Trail has enabled new lengths of path to be created, and footbridges constructed to replace the defunct ferries.

Start	Thames Source, Glos	ST980994
Finish	Thames Barrier, Gtr London	TQ417794
On OS maps	163, 164, 174, 175, 176	
Waymark	National Trail Acorn	

Publication(s)
Paperback: *Aerofilms Guide: The Thames Path* by Helen Livingstone (Ian Allan Publishing). ISBN: 0711021333. 1993\286 x 140\176pp\£9.99.
Paperback: *Face the Dawn: the Bristol to London Long Distance Path* by Eddie Critchley (Ramblers' Association). ISBN: 0900613556. 1984\A5\50pp\£2.00 (+ 70p).
Softback: *Guide to the Thames Path* by Miles Jebb (Constable and Co Ltd). ISBN: 0094669503. 1988\171 x 114\336pp\£8.95.
Leaflet: *Thames Path* (Countryside Commission Postal Sales). 1991\A4/3\Free.
Paperback: *The Kennet & Avon Walk* by Ray Quinlan (Cicerone Press). ISBN: 1852840900. 1991\116 x 176\200pp\£6.99.
Paperback: *The Thames Walk* by David Sharp (Ramblers' Association). £2.95 (+ 50p).
Paperback: *Walks along the Thames Path* by Leigh Hatts (Patrick Stephens Ltd). ISBN: 1852602074. 216 x 135\192pp\£6.99.

Thirlmere Way 287

Cumbria, Gtr Man, Lancs   208 km / 130 miles

An unusual concept, this walk follows (in reverse) the route of Manchester's water supply from Thirlmere reservoir in the Lake

District to Manchester. It thus provides a walking link from the Greater Manchester conurbation through Lancashire to Cumbria. Following a much more meandering route than the pipeline itself in order to keep to public footpaths and pass places for overnight stops, it visits Hulton, Abbey Village, Longridge, Dolphinholme, Caton, Kirkby Lonsdale, Kendal, Windermere and Grasmere.

Start	Heaton Park, Gtr Man	SD834044
Finish	Thirlmere, Cumbria	NY310190
OS maps	90, 97, 102, 109	

Publication(s)
Softback: *The Thirlmere Way* by Tim Cappelli (Sigma Leisure). ISBN: 1850582882. 1992\A5\130pp\£6.95.

Three Castles Path   288

Berks, Hants	96 km / 60 miles

The idea for this route was inspired by the 13th-century journeys of King John between Windsor and Winchester via the Castle he built near Odiham, roughly half-way along. Though much has changed since then, the route passes through a variety of scenery – parkland and forest, heath and downland, past quiet streams and picturesque villages.

From Windsor, the route passes through the Great Park to Ascot and Bracknell, and then to the Blackwater valley near Sandhurst. The Basingstoke canal is followed through Odiham, and the downs crossed via Preston and Abbotstone, before the route descends to the river Itchen at Itchen Abbas which it follows into the cathedral city of Winchester.

Start	Windsor, Berks	SU968770
Finish	Winchester, Hants	SU483293
On OS maps	175, 185, 186	

Publication(s)
Booklet: *The Three Castles Path* by David Bounds (RA E Berkshire Group). ISBN: 1874258015. 1992\128 x 210\48pp\£2.50.

Three Castles Walk   289

Gwent	29 km / 18 miles

A circular route connecting the three Norman fortresses of Skenfrith, White Castle and Grosmont, the Walk passes through undulating countryside, with hidden valleys and secluded and historic farmhouses. The landscape is still that of mixed farming, and most of the hedgerows have survived, as have the characteristic small woods, making this area rich in wildlife.

Start and Finish	Skenfrith, Gwent	SO457202

On OS maps	161

Waymark	Named yellow arrows on white background

Publication(s)
Booklet: *Three Castles Walk* (Gwent County Council). 1991\A5\
14pp\£1.00 (+ 50p).

Three Forests Way 290

Essex, Herts	96 km / 60 miles

A circular route devised by the West Essex Group of the RA to
commemorate Queen Elizabeth's Silver Jubilee in 1977. Footpaths, tracks and lanes across gently undulating agricultural land
are followed to link three Essex forests, although only eight miles
of the Way are through them. From Harlow the Way visits Hatfield
Forest and then turns south through White Roding and Abbess
Roding to Fyfield, and along the Roding valley to Chipping Ongar
and Abridge where it passses through Hainault Forest to
Loughton. Here it heads north through Epping Forest and over
farmland to Roydon, from where it follows the Stort valley back to
Harlow.

Start and Finish	Harlow, Essex	TL445113

On OS maps	166, 167, 177

Publication(s)
Booklet: *Three Forests Way* by Fred Matthews and Harry Bitten
(Matthews/Bitten Publications). 1986\A5\20pp\.
Badge (£1.00) available from Matthews/Bitten Publications.

Three Shires Way 291

Beds, Bucks, Cambs, Northants	57 km / 36 miles

A long distance bridleway that runs through a quiet rural landscape with historic villages, remnants of ancient woodland, and
many fine viewpoints. From Tathall End, where it links with the
Swans Way, the Way runs to Olney, home of poet William Cowper,
the boundary of Bucks, Beds and Northants at Threeshire Wood,
Yielden with its motte and bailey castle, and Covington before
finishing with the circular ride around Grafham Water. Note that
much of the route is over clay, so the track may get muddy in wet
conditions.

Start	Tathall End, Bucks	SP821467
Finish	Grafham Water, Cambs	TL146695
OS maps	152, 153	
Waymark	Triple-linked horseshoes	

Publication(s)
Leaflet: *Three Shires Way* (Cambridgeshire County Council). 1990\A4/3\Free (+ 50p).

Tinners Way 292

Cornwall	29 km / 18 miles

The Way traces as closely as possible the ancient paths along which tin and copper were transported by people, sledges and pack animals from the mineral-rich area around St Just to the sheltered anchorage of St Ives Bay. It passes over 20 prehistoric and early Christian sites, from stone circles and cairns to quoits and menhirs. From Cape Cornwall/St Just, it uses an inland route parallel to the coast, via Woon Gumpus and Towednack.

Start	Cape Cornwall, Cornwall	SW349318
Finish	St Ives, Cornwall	SW521412
OS maps	203	

Publication(s)
Paperback: *Guide to the Tinners Way and Nearby Ancient Sites* by Ian Cooke (Men-an-Tol Studio). ISBN: 0951237152. 1991\A5\48pp\£2.60.

Tissington Trail 293

Derby	21 km / 13 miles

The Trail, owned by the Peak Park Planning Board and open to cyclists and horseriders, follows the trackbed of the former Buxton to Ashbourne Railway through the limestone countryside of the White Peak. Although not as steep as the High Peak Trail and lacking its inclines, it climbs to 1,250ft. At Hartington the old signal box has been converted into a Peak Park Information Centre and is open on summer weekends.

Start	Ashbourne, Derby	SK178469
Finish	Parsley Hay, Derby	SK147636
On OS maps	119, 128	
Waymark	Name boards	

Publication(s)
Leaflet: *Tissington and High Peak Trails* (Peak District National Park). A4/3\Free.
Paperback: *Walking the Tissington Trail* by John Merrill (Trail Crest Publications Ltd). ISBN: 1874754101. 1993\32pp\£3.50.
Badge and certificate (£2.75 / post free) available from Trail Crest Publications Ltd.

Trans Pennine Trail   294

Cheshire, Derby, Gtr Man, Humberside, Merseyside, N Yorks, S Yorks	320 km / 200 miles

Designed originally as an off-road coast-to-coast route across northern England for cyclists, the idea has developed into a multi-use trail for cyclists, walkers, and where possible horseriders. Following disused railway lines, canal towpaths, and other water-side routes that can be adapted for multi-use, it links the urban areas of Hull, Doncaster, Barnsley, Greater Manchester and Merseyside, and is more or less open for walkers, though it will not be open for cyclists in its entirety for quite some time. In spite of being in part urban, long stretches of the route in the east are far from much habitation, and other sections pass through attractive country in the Pennines and Greater Manchester. The route is being coordinated with land rehabilitation and redevelopment in several former industrial areas, and additional spurs are open or planned from Selby to York, to Wakefield and Leeds, and via Sheffield to Chesterfield.

Other paths (all converted railway lines) that now form part of the Trans Pennine Trail are the Cheshire Lines Path (a Sustrans route from Ainsdale to Lydiate), the Liverpool Loop Line (a Sustrans route from Aintree to Halewood), the Longdendale Trail (a NW Water route from Hadfield to Woodhead Tunnel), the Dove Valley Trail (a Barnsley Council route from Silkstone to Wombwell), the Hornsea Rail Trail (a Humberside County Council route from Hull to Hornsea) and the York and Selby Railway Path (a Sustrans route linking York to the TPT).

It is planned that the section from Hull to Merseyside will form part of the E8 European long distance path.

Start	Southport, Merseyside	SD338172
Finish	Hornsea, Humberside	TA208479
OS maps	105, 106, 107, 108, 109, 110, 111	
Waymark	Named discs with trail logo	

Publication(s)
Looseleaf: *Trans Pennine Trail Accommodation List* (Trans Pennine Trail Officer). 1993\A4\17pp\Free.
Booklet: *Trans Pennine Trail: Walking the Trail* (Trans Pennine Trail Officer). 1993\A5\12pp\Free.

Trans Pennine Walk   295

Gtr Man, Lancs, W Yorks	87 km / 54 miles

A route of high scenic value that links the western extremity of the Lancashire Pennines with the Bronte country of Yorkshire. From the start at Adlington on the west side of the Pennines, the walk heads north-east across Rivington Pike, and over open moorland

and intervening lowland sections, passing several of the towers and reservoirs which are a characteristic feature of the area. It skirts Rochdale to meet and follow the Pennine Way to Stoodley Pike. The route then continues through Hebden Bridge, Heptonstall and Hardcastle Crags to rejoin the Pennine Way at Top Withins. The Walk passes Bronte Bridge and Peristone Hill to finish at Haworth on the east side of the Pennines. An easy route for the most part, but it does require some map reading skill, and it can be difficult in poor weather conditions.

Start	Adlington, Lancs	SD610130
Finish	Haworth, W Yorks	SE030372
OS maps	103, 104, 109	

Publication(s)
Paperback: *Trans Pennine Walk* by R. Mackrory (Dalesman Publishing Ltd). ISBN: 0852067461. 205 x 135 \ 48pp \ £1.10.

Trent Valley Way 296

Derby, Notts	135 km / 84 miles

Opened in 1989 to celebrate the Centenary of Notts County Council, the Way follows the river Trent through Nottinghamshire, from either Long Eaton or Thrumpton in the west to West Stockwith where the Chesterfield Canal enters the Trent. Though sticking close to the river for the most part, it sometimes leaves it to explore various interesting features in the wider valley. The route passes through Nottingham and Newark, both with castles, besides numerous smaller places with many interesting churches, water- and windmills. There are also many valuable wildlife habitats.

Start	Long Eaton, Derby	SK507326
Finish	West Stockwith, Notts	SK791949
On OS maps	112, 120, 121, 129	
Waymark	Wavy blue symbol	

Publication(s)
Paperback: *Trent Valley Way* (Nottinghamshire County Council). 1989 \ 212 x 150 \ 88pp \ £2.75 (+ 35p).

Two Moors Way 297

Devon, Somerset	166 km / 104 miles

Connecting the two National Parks in southwest England, this route runs north from Ivybridge across Dartmoor, climbing to Ugborough Moor and crossing exposed moorland to Holne and Grimspound (one of the many prehistoric sites passed) to reach Teigncombe. From here the river Teign is followed to Chagford and Castle Drogo (NT). North of Drewsteignton the Dartmoor National

Park is left behind, and roads and paths are followed across farmland to reach Exmoor National Park and the river Barle at Tarr Steps. From here the Way climbs to Exe Head before passing through Cheriton and following paths high above the East Lyn to Lynmouth on the North Devon coast.

Start	Ivybridge, Devon	SX636563
Finish	Lynmouth, Devon	SS724494
On OS maps	180, 181, 191, 202	
Waymark	"MW" on standard waymarks	

Publication(s)
Leaflet: *Two Moors Way* (Devon County Council). A4/3 \ Free.
Paperback: *Two Moors Way* (RA Devon Area). £3.20.
Looseleaf: *Two Moors Way Accommodation List* (RA Devon Area). £0.25 (+ SAE).

Two Ridges Link   298

Bucks	13 km / 8 miles

This is a linear walk which connects the Ridgeway Path at Ivinghoe Beacon with the Greensand Ridge Walk at Leighton Buzzard. From the start at Ivinghoe, where there are good views over the Downs, the route passes through peaceful countryside with good views of the Chilterns, and eventually follows the Grand Union Canal towpath to end in the heart of Linslade, near Leighton Buzzard.

Start	Ivinghoe Beacon, Bucks	SP960168
Finish	Leighton Buzzard, Beds	SP915251
On OS maps	165	
Waymark	Two Ridges Link signs and waymarking arrows	

Publication(s)
Leaflet: *Two Ridges Link* (Buckinghamshire County Council). A4/3 \ Free (+ SAE).

Two Rivers Way   299

Avon	32 km / 20 miles

Created in 1987 by Yatton Ramblers, this route follows the river Yeo from Congresbury upstream, and then the river Chew downstream to its confluence with the Avon at Keynsham, where the route meets the Avon Walkway. It passes through farmland and historic villages, such as Chew Stoke, Chew Magna and Compton Dando.

Start	Congresbury, Avon	ST438639
Finish	Keynsham, Avon	ST659690

On OS maps	172
Waymark	Named discs with wave motif

Publication(s)
Leaflet: *2 Rivers Congresbury to Keynsham* (Avon County Council). 1994\A4/3\Free.
Booklet: *The Two Rivers Way* by Marian Barraclough (Yatton Ramblers). ISBN: 0951134264. 1992\42pp\£1.50.

Two Roses Way 300

Lancs, W Yorks	158 km / 99 miles

Described as six days of hill walks, this is a circular route around the Ribble valley and upper reaches of Airedale on the Lancashire/Yorkshire border, passing via Gisburn, Skipton, Malham, Settle, Slaidburn and Chipping.

Start and Finish	Whalley, Lancs	SD732362
OS maps	98, 103	

Publication(s)
Softback: *The Two Roses Way* by Peter Billington and others (Sigma Leisure). ISBN: 1850583382. 1993\A5\130pp\£6.95.

Two Seasons Way 301

Essex, Herts	48 km / 30 miles

The route was surveyed in 1985 to mark the RA Golden Jubilee and is so named because it links the villages of Cold Christmas and Good Easter, though the route was later extended to the stations at Hertford and Helmsford. It is written as a series of 15 interlocking circular walks which can be linked to form a walk with a different return route, and passes Thundridge, Widford, Sawbridgeworth, Matching and Roxwell.

At the time of writing, a book is about to be published by Matthews/Bitten Publications.

Start	Hertford, Herts
Finish	Chelmsford, Essex
OS maps	166, 167

Publication(s)
None at time of writing.

Ulster Way 302

Antrim, Armagh, Down, Fermanagh, Londonderry, Tyrone	912 km / 570 miles

The Ulster Way was created under the direction of the Sports Council for Northern Ireland and implemented by the District Councils and Forest Service. It encircles the province and has links with trails in the Republic of Ireland. The route is divided into five sections: North East; North West; South West; South; and South East. Donegal County Council has responsibility for a 69-mile spur which traverses mountainous country in Co. Donegal.

The route visits most of the Areas of Outstanding Natural Beauty in Northern Ireland and links these together using paths, forest tracks and minor roads. Starting from Belfast the route goes through the Lagan Valley AONB, crosses the Belfast Hills, Antrim Coast & Glens AONB, Causeway Coast AONB and North Derry AONB. Turning inland, accommodation becomes sparse through the Sperrin AONB, Erne Lakeland AONB and Fermanagh Caveland AONB. Lengthy road walks have to be endured through South Tyrone and North Armagh, then the towpath of the Newry Canal leads to the Mourne AONB. After passing the mountains the Lecale Coast AONB and Strangford AONB are visited on the way back to Belfast.

Within each of the five sections of the Ulster Way there are individually named trails – including the North Antrim Coast Path, Big Dog Trail, Mourne Trail, St Patrick's Trail, etc. – which offer scope for shorter weekend walks. Most of the Ulster Way is now waymarked, with the exception of the the Belfast Hills, North East Antrim, South Tyrone and the Newry Canal towpath. Trails branching off into the Republic of Ireland are also waymarked. In upland areas where waymarking is sparse, navigational skills are required.

The following OSNI maps are needed: 4, 5, 7, 8, 9, 12, 13, 15, 17, 18, 19, 21, 26, 27, 29 – though the route is wrongly depicted on these in places.

Start and Finish	Belfast Castle, Antrim	IJ290745
OS maps	See text above	
Waymark	Walker with rucksack and stick, plus orange-coloured arrows	

Publication(s)

Leaflet: *An Information Guide to Walking* (Northern Ireland Tourist Board). 1993\A5\Free.

Paperback: *On Foot in Ulster* by Alan Warner (The Appletree Press Ltd). ISBN: 0862811104. 1989\210 x 143\128pp\£3.95.

Booklet: *The Ulster Way* by Paddy Dillon (Walking World Ireland). 1994\A5\48pp\Free.

Leaflet: *The Ulster Way: Accommodation for Walkers* (Northern Ireland Tourist Board). 1994\A5\Free.

Upper Tas Valley Walk 303

Norfolk	30 km / 19 miles

Situated to the south-west of Norwich, the Walk runs along a valley of rich botanical interest past several SSSIs with orchids and other rarities. It runs through the villages of Swardeston, Mulbarton, Flordon, Hapton, Forncett and Aslacton, past many interesting churches.

Start	Hethersett, Norfolk	TG158048
Finish	New Buckenham, Norfolk	TM090906
On OS maps	134	
Waymark	Named discs	

Publication(s)
Folder: *Upper Tas Valley Walk* (South Norfolk District Council). A5 \ 10pp \ Free.

Usk Valley Walk 304

Gwent	80 km / 50 miles

Developed by Gwent County Council, the Walk follows the Usk valley upstream from the old Roman fortress of Caerleon, past the historic market town of Usk, via riverside, field and woodland paths and some minor roads to Abergavenny. Here it takes to the Monmouthshire and Brecon Canal towpath, which it follows to Brecon. Mainly an easy waterside walk, there are two climbs, to the Kemeys Ridge north of Caerleon, and to Glanusk Park west of Crickhowell; both of these offer fine views of the valley and hills beyond.

Start	Caerleon, Gwent	ST342902
Finish	Brecon, Powys	SO043286
On OS maps	160, 161, 171	
Waymark	Named yellow arrows	

Publication(s)
Booklet: *Usk Valley Walk* (Gwent County Council). 1989 \ A5 \ £1.50 (+ 50p).

Vanguard Way 305

E Sussex, Gtr London, Kent, Surrey	100 km / 63 miles

The Way, developed by Vanguards Rambling Club to lead from the suburbs of London to the sea, heads south-east from Croydon and crosses Selsdon Nature Reserve and the North Downs to Crockham Hill and Forest Row. From here it continues across the high Weald and through the woods and heaths of Ashdown Forest to Blackboys Youth Hostel and Alfriston. It then crosses the South Downs to Exceat and follows the coast to Seaford.

Start	East Croydon, Gtr London	TQ329657
Finish	Seaford, E Sussex	TV482991
On OS maps	176, 177, 187, 188, 198, 199	

Publication(s)
Paperback: *Vanguard Way* (Vanguards Rambling Club). 1986\
A5\40pp\£1.35 (+ 30p).
Paperback: *Wealdway and the Vanguard Way* by Kev Reynolds (Cicerone Press). ISBN: 0902363859. 1987\116 x 176\160pp\ £4.99.

Vectis Trail 306

IOW	120 km / 75 miles

A walk round the Isle of Wight following quiet country footpaths which lead to some of the most attractive places away from the tourist areas. The route has been conveniently planned in six sections, each one with accommodation near the start or finish so that shorter walks can be undertaken during a week's holiday on the island.

Start and Finish	Yarmouth, IOW	SZ355897
OS maps	196	

Publication(s)
Paperback: *Vectis Trail* by Iris Evans and Barbara Aze (RA Isle of Wight). 210 x 149\32pp\£2.00.

Ver-Colne Valley Walk 307

Herts	24 km / 15 miles

Named after the rivers Ver and Colne, this route links Watford, St Albans (the Roman name of which was Verulamium) and Redbourn. The latter boasts the oldest cricket club in the country (founded in 1666), St Albans has a large abbey church and Roman remains, and there are several former watermills along the route. The Ver provides a chalk stream habitat of significant wildlife value.

It is hoped to extend this route along the former railway line to Rickmansworth, thereby connecting to the Grand Union Canal and the Colne Valley Way (10 miles Staines to Cowley).

Start	Redbourn, Herts	TL103120
Finish	Watford, Herts	TQ116959
On OS maps	166	

Waymark	River symbol within standard waymarks

Publication(s)
Leaflet: *Ver-Colne Valley Walk* (Hertfordshire County Council).
1987 \ A4/3 \ Free.

Viking Way   308

Humberside, Leics, Lincs	225 km / 141 miles

The Way does not follow a Viking route but is so named because it crosses an area occupied by Norse invaders during the "Dark Ages". From the banks of the river Humber the Way heads south-east across the Lincolnshire Wolds to Caistor, and then goes along the Bain valley to Horncastle, from where the Spa Trail is followed along the trackbed of a former railway to Woodhall Spa. From here it heads west along the Witham valley, crossing flat fenland to Lincoln.

From the cathedral city it turns south along the limestone escarpment of Lincoln Cliff and over Lincoln Heath, before tracing the route of the prehistoric Sewstern Lane to reach Woolsthorpe Locks on the Grantham Canal. Another section of Sewstern Lane and other old tracks are followed to Thistleton from where the Way takes field paths and lanes past Greetham, Exton and Rutland Water to Oakham.

Start	Barton-upon-Humber, Humberside	TA028227
Finish	Oakham, Leics	SK861088
On OS maps	112, 113, 121, 122, 130, 141	
Waymark	Viking helmet/shield	

Publication(s)
Folder: *Glanford Explorer* (Humberside County Council).
A5 \ £2.00 (+ 30p).
Paperback: *Viking Way* by John Stead (Cicerone Press). ISBN:
1852840579. 1990 \ 116 x 176 \ 168pp \ £5.99.
Leaflet: *Viking Way* (Leicestershire County Council). A4/3 \ £0.15.
Booklet: *Viking Way* (Lincolnshire County Council). ISBN:
0861111109. 1992 \ A5 \ 28pp \ £1.50.
Badge available from RA Lincs and S Humberside Area.

Walkways: Bala/Snowdon   309

Gwynedd	44 km / 28 miles

Running west across grass moors to near Arenig Fawr, the route turns north over the valley of the Tryweryn and past Llyn Celyn. It climbs over the east side of the Migneint and drops into the Conwy valley at Ysbyty Ifan. Here it turns west on paths and tracks which were a prehistoric route. The hills and valleys grow wilder as the walk goes over low hills to Penmachno and a harsher moor to Dolwyddelan, then from a Roman bridge over the pass south of Moel Siabod to the head of Llyn Gwynant.

Start	Bala, Gwynedd	SH928364
Finish	Snowdon, Gwynedd	SH607546
OS maps	115, 116, 124, 125	

Publication(s)
Looseleaf: *Walkways Series 1: Bala to Snowdon* by J S Roberts (Walkways). 1984\235 x 175\£1.30 (+ 40p).

Walkways: Birmingham/Church Stretton   310

Salop, Staffs, W Midlands	82 km / 51 miles

From Birmingham New Street there is the choice of a walk along the canal or a journey by bus to the start at Kinver. This is a hilly route, mainly across grass pasture-land, to the Severn, which is crossed by ferry before a ridge is climbed which gives good views. The walk then goes over the many small, wooded hills of mid-Shropshire, which flatten as it reaches the foot of Brown Clee – at 1,500ft the highest point on the route. From this upland plateau the route descends across a valley, then climbs Wenlock Edge and goes on into the hills near Hope Bowdler (overlooking Church Stretton).

Start	Birmingham New St, W Midlands	SP064864
Finish	Church Stretton, Salop	SO451945
OS maps	138, 139	

Publication(s)
Looseleaf: *Birmingham to Church Stretton* by John Roberts (Walkways). ISBN: 0947708133. 1986\235 x 175\£1.30 (+ 40p).

Walkways: Birmingham/Ludlow   311

Heref & Worc, Salop, Staffs, W Midlands	77 km / 48 miles

From the centre of Birmingham there is a choice of following the canal towpath or taking a bus ride to the start. Starting with a ridge walk along Kinver Edge, the walk passes over two more ridges to the Severn. It then continues through the oaks and pines of Wyre Forest to Cleobury Mortimer. A long climb up to Titterstone Clee, at 1,750ft the highest point on the route, is followed by a walk south down its back. The route is then over grassland with one high point at Caynham Camp, and along the river Tame to Ludlow.

Start	Birmingham New St, W Midlands	SP064864
Finish	Ludlow, Salop	SO510745
OS maps	137, 138, 139	

Publication(s)
Looseleaf: *Walkways Series 2: Birmingham to Ludlow* by J S Roberts
(Walkways). ISBN: 0947708065. 1984\235 x 175\£1.30 (+ 40p).

Walkways: Llangollen/Bala 312

Clwyd, Gwynedd	54 km / 34 miles

This is a variable route of mountain and moorland with some
forest. It starts in the Welsh National Eisteddfod town of Llangollen on the river Dee and then goes up and around Horseshoe
valley. From Glyndyfrdwy there is a steep climb up to the moors
followed by some open moorland walking; at Llanarmon Dyffryn
Ceiriog the route turns to head west over Foel Wen in the Berwyn
Hills. This is the highest point on the route. The walk drops some
600ft into the Aberhirnant Forest to follow through undulating
woodland and finally reach the river Dee at Bala.

Start	Llangollen, Clwyd	SJ215420
Finish	Bala, Gwynedd	SH928364
OS maps	117, 125	

Publication(s)
Looseleaf: *Walkways Series 1: Llangollen to Bala* by J S Roberts
(Walkways). ISBN: 0947708146. 1987\235 x 175\£1.30 (+ 40p).

Walkways: Ludlow/Rhayader 313

Heref & Worc, Powys, Salop	67 km / 42 miles

The walk starts with a long climb over the Wigmore Dome, then a
drop straight into the gorge of the Teme, a secret place where birds
nest on the limestone cliffs. There is another steep climb, then a
sharp drop to the waterside village of Leintwardine and the reedy
water-meadows. There is more climbing before the descent to
Knighton and the Welsh border. The route now follows an undulating way across a remote, little-known pastoral landscape. A final
climb over Gwastedyn Hill gives views of the Wye and Elan valleys
before the descent to Rhayader.

Start	Ludlow, Salop	SO510745
Finish	Rhayader, Powys	SN968679
OS maps	136, 137	

Publication(s)
Looseleaf: *Walkways Series 2: Ludlow to Rhayader* by J S Roberts
(Walkways). ISBN: 0947708030. 1984\235 x 175\£1.30 (+ 40p).

Walkways: Rhayader/Aberystwyth 314

Dyfed, Powys	74 km / 46 miles

A strenuous route across the Cambrian Mountains and the "Green Desert" of the Elenith valley in central Wales. The route is a remote and hilly one from Wye Falls through an old oak wood and over the tops into the Elan valley. Then there is a scenic walk south by the reservoirs and a climb westwards into the wilder Claerwen valley. A little river leads through a harsh, wet upland and into the remote Tywy Forest. The route heads north to pass Strata Florida Abbey and the Teifi Pools; it then continues over barren moors, with the odd remains of old metal mines, to near Devil's Bridge. Finally there is a walk down the Rheidol valley to finish on the beach at Aberystwyth.

Start	Rhayader, Powys	SN968679
Finish	Aberystwyth, Dyfed	SN580813
OS maps	135, 136	

Publication(s)
Looseleaf: *Walkways Series 2: Rhayader to Aberystwyth* by J S Roberts (Walkways). ISBN: 0947708049. 1985 \ 235 x 175 \ £1.30 (+ 40p).

Wanderlust Way 315

Humberside	32 km / 20 miles

Originally called the Bradley 20, but renamed in memory of Nev Cole, a founder member of the Wanderlust Rambling Club, Grimsby, this Way is an elongated circuit passing through attractive small villages and across the woods and farmland of the undulating Lincolnshire Wolds, from where there are views across the mouth of the Humber Estuary.

Start and Finish	Bradley Woods, Humberside	TA242059
OS maps	113	
Waymark	Green and yellow "WW"	

Publication(s)
Folder: *Cleethorpes Explorer* (Humberside County Council). A5 \ £2.00 (+ 30p).
Badge and certificate (£1.25 / - / 6"x4" SAE) available from Alec Malkinson.

Wardens' Way 316

Glos	22 km / 14 miles

Developed by the Cotswold Wardens, the Way provides a link between the Oxfordshire Way at Bourton-on-the-Water with the

Cotswold Way at Winchcombe. Whereas its sister route, the Windrush Way, takes to the hills, the Wardens Way winds through the villages of Lower and Upper Slaughter, Naunton and Guiting Power.

Start	Bourton-on-the-Water, Glos	SP170209
Finish	Winchcombe, Glos	SP025283
On OS maps	163	
Waymark	Double "W"	

Publication(s)
Paperback: *Wardens' Way and Windrush Way* (Cotswold Warden Office). 1991\A5\32pp\£1.50 (+ 25p).

Waskerley Way 317

Durham	25 km / 16 miles

One of a series of railway-lines bought by local authorities, and developed for use by walkers and cyclists; horseriders may use them with a permit. The Waskerley Way connects the Derwent Walk from Tyneside and the Consett and Sunderland Railway Path at the southern edge of Consett with the Wear Valley at Stanhope.

Start	Hownes Gill, Durham	NZ099495
Finish	Crawley, Durham	NY997423
On OS maps	87, 88	

Publication(s)
Folder: *Railway Walks in County Durham* (Durham County Council). 1990\A5\10pp\£0.99 (+ 75p).
Folder: *Railway Walks in Derwentside* (Derwentside District Council). A4/3\4pp\£0.80.

Watersheds Walk 318

W Yorks	40 km / 25 miles

The Walk is a high-level traverse of the high moorlands surrounding the Worth Valley, taking in Hainworth, Nab Hill, Top Withens (where it crosses both the Pennine Way and Bronte Way), Ponden, the Earl Crag monuments and Goose Eye.

Start and Finish	Keighley Railway Station, W Yorks	SE065413
OS maps	104	

Publication(s)
Paperback: *Watersheds Walk* by Jim Jarratt (Smith Settle). ISBN: 1870071166. 1988\210 x 148\46pp\£2.95.

Waveney Way   319

Suffolk	27 km / 17 miles

Eventually the Waveney Way is planned to form a 70-mile circular route around the District boundary. It will use the Angles Way along the Waveney Valley and the Suffolk Coast Path, and will link Lowestoft, Oulton Broad, Beccles, Bungay, Halesworth and Southwold.

At present, all that is open is the 17-mile Lothingland Loop, opened in 1986, which runs to the north of Lowestoft and Oulton Broad, passing through the villages of Corton, Blundeston, Lound, Somerleyton and Oulton.

Start and Finish	Lowestoft, Suffolk	TM548926
OS maps	134	
Waymark	Green directional arrow in white circle	

Publication(s)
Leaflet: *Waveney Way: No 1 Lothingland Loop* (Waveney District Council). 1986\A4/3\Free.

Wayfarer's Walk   320

Berks, Hants	113 km / 71 miles

From Emsworth this first long distance path to be developed by Hampshire County Council heads west on a route now used by the Solent Way, before turning north to cross the chalk ridge of Portsdown, in the direction of Hambledon, with its cricketing associations. It crosses the Meon valley, and then goes north over the agricultural heartland of the county and through the attractive villages of Hinton Ampner and Cheriton to reach New Alresford. The Walk continues over undulating downland to the Candover valley and Dummer before climbing to the crest of the North Hants Ridgeway, the highest chalk ridge in southern England. The ridge track is followed westwards over Watership Down and Walbury Hill to reach Inkpen Beacon.

Start	Emsworth, Hants	SU753055
Finish	Inkpen Beacon, Berks	SU365622
On OS maps	174, 185, 196, 197	
Waymark	Black "WW" on white background	

Publication(s)
Paperback: *Along and Around the Wayfarer's Walk* by Linda Herbst and others (Hampshire County Council). ISBN: 0948176040. 1993\210 x 148\96pp\£4.95.

Wealdway 321

E Sussex, Kent	128 km / 80 miles

A varied route which was devised by a group of ramblers and developed with the support of local and district councils, linking the Thames to the English Channel and crossing the Kent and Sussex Weald. The Way crosses the North Downs and follows a meandering southerly route through attractive villages, over farm-and woodland and along the river Medway to Tonbridge. It skirts Tunbridge Wells and crosses the woods and open heaths of the sandy heights of the Ashdown Forest to Uckfield, where it crosses undulating farmland to Arlington, Wilmington and Jevington before climbing to the crest of the South Downs to meet the South Downs Way on Willingdon Hill, near Eastbourne.

Start	Gravesend, Kent	TQ647744
Finish	Eastbourne (YH), E Sussex	TV588981
On OS maps	177, 178, 188, 198, 199	
Waymark	"WW" on standard arrows	

Publication(s)
Hardback: *Guide to the Wealdway* by John H N Mason (Constable and Co Ltd). ISBN: 0094648204. 1984 \ 171 x 114 \ £6.95.
Booklet: *The Wealdway* by Geoffrey King (Dr Ben Perkins). A5 \ 36pp \ £3.50.
Leaflet: *Wealdway Accommodation Guide* (Dr Ben Perkins). £1.00 (+ SAE).
Paperback: *Wealdway and the Vanguard Way* by Kev Reynolds (Cicerone Press). ISBN: 0902363859. 1987 \ 116 x 176 \ 160pp \ £4.99.

Wear Valley Way 322

Durham	74 km / 46 miles

Originally invented as a challenge walk by Alan Earnshaw and now adopted by Wear Valley DC, the route crosses forest and farmland from the impressive Killhope Wheel and other remains of the lead mining era to Cowshill, and then climbs to the open fells high above the river Wear. It passes through old lead mining villages and past old works and quarries; it follows the trackbed of a high-level mineral line before crossing the valley at Frosterley to go over Pikeston Fell to the south of the river, and descend through the Hamsterley Forest to follow paths along or near the river to Willington.

Start	Killhope Wheel, Durham	NY827430
Finish	Willington, Durham	NZ218345
OS maps	87, 92, 93	
Waymark	Named discs with pithead logo	

Publication(s)
Leaflet: *Wear Valley Way* (Wear Valley District Council). 1993\
A4/3\£1.00.

Weardale Way 323

Durham, Tyne & Wear	125 km / 78 miles

The Way follows the river Wear upstream from the sea, with a few excursions to the surrounding hillsides, and goes through the urban areas around Monkswearmouth, Durham and Bishop Auckland, across farmland to the moors and old lead mining areas, and past Killhope Wheel to reach Cowshill.

Start	Monkwearmouth, Tyne & Wear	NZ408587
Finish	Cowshill, Durham	NY855405
On OS maps	86, 87, 88, 91, 92, 93	
Waymark	Named signposts	

Publication(s)
Paperback: *Weardale Way* by J K E Piggin (Dalesman Publishing Ltd). ISBN: 0852067895. 1984\205 x 135\48pp\£1.10.

Weaver Valley Way 324

Cheshire	32 km / 20 miles

The Weaver Valley Way follows the towpath of the Weaver Navigation, a navigable river still used by commercial ships serving the salt industry of Cheshire in the area around Northwich. Passing through an attractive wooded valley, the Way also passes the Anderton Boat Lift, built to lift vessels from the river to the Trent and Mersey Canal. It finishes at Winsford.

Start	Bottom Flash, Cheshire	SD657655
Finish	Frodsham (Bridge), Cheshire	SJ529784
OS maps	117, 118	

Publication(s)
Booklet: *Longer Trails in Vale Royal* by Carl Rogers (Vale Royal Borough Council). 1993\A5\76pp\£1.95.

Weavers Way 325

Norfolk	90 km / 56 miles

The Weavers Way uses public footpaths, three lengths of disused railway line and some minor roads in north-east Norfolk between Cromer and Great Yarmouth. The railway line and minor road sections are also available for use by horseriders and cyclists. The

Way has been developed by Norfolk County Council since 1980, and passes through very varied scenery, from the attractive mixed farmland and woodland of north Norfolk to the extensive, traditional grazing marshes of the Broadland river valleys. Notable landmarks to be seen along the Way include a number of fine flint churches, several big country houses, and a large number of windpumps. The name of the Way acknowledges the importance of the weaving industry in the area in the past.

Start	Cromer, Norfolk	TG215420
Finish	Great Yarmouth, Norfolk	TG522081
On OS maps	133, 134	
Waymark	Named boards	

Publication(s)
Booklet: *Peddars Way Guide and Accommodation List* (Peddars Way Association). 1994\A5\24pp\£1.80 (+ 25p).
Leaflet: *Weavers Way* (Norfolk County Council). 1990\A4/3\Free (+ SAE).

Wessex Ridgeway 326

Devon, Dorset, Wilts	219 km / 137 miles

One of the links in a prehistoric route which crossed England from the Wash to the south Devon coast, this route continues the Ridgeway south over an area rich in prehistoric remains.

From Marlborough, it runs west and south, passing on its way the great stone circle at Avebury. It crosses the Vale of Pewsey to skirt the northern edge of Salisbury Plain, and then continues south over the beautiful Wylye valley, climbing to Win Green Hill, Wiltshire's highest point.

Entering Cranborne Chase, the walk crosses into Dorset, then over the Stour, gaining height to give spectacular views over Blackmoor Vale. At Cerne Abbas the 180ft figure of the Cerne Giant can be seen. From Pilsden Pen, the highest point in Dorset, the views over the Marshwood Vale and the Somerset Levels in the north are outstanding. After a short foray into Devon and with tantalising glimpses of the sea, the walk finally descends to Lyme Regis.

Start	Marlborough, Wilts	SU187685
Finish	Lyme Regis, Dorset	SY347922
OS maps	173, 183, 184, 193, 194, 195	
Waymark	Wessex wyvern	

Publication(s)
Paperback: *Walk the Wessex Ridgeway in Dorset* by Priscilla Houstoun (Wincanton Press). ISBN: 094869937X. 1994\215 x 160\96pp\£5.95.

Paperback: *Wessex Ridgeway* by Alan Proctor (Ramblers' Association). 1988\210 x 149\50pp\£2.50.

West Gordon Way 327

Grampian	34 km / 21 miles

A joint development of the Forestry Commission and Gordon District Council, the first part of the Way was opened in 1989. It runs through Bennachie and Whitehaugh Forests, and will shortly be extended to Rhynie. Apart from the forests, there is farmland and heather moor, and the route runs over several hills (the highest point being around 500m), providing good views over the Don Valley and the Grampians beyond.

Start	Esson's Carpark, Grampian	NJ700217
Finish	Rhynie, Grampian	NJ500270
OS maps	37	
Waymark	Hexagonal "GW" logo	

Publication(s)
Leaflet: *Bennachie and the West Gordon Way* (Gordon District Council). 1993\A4/3\Free.

West Highland Way 328

Central, Highland, Strathclyde	152 km / 95 miles

Scotland's first national long distance path, this was opened in 1980. From Milngavie it heads in a north-westerly direction, crossing a variety of terrain which becomes more rugged as it moves northwards, and passing between the major mountain groups. The Way follows the eastern side of Loch Lomond, crossing the slopes of the Ben to Crianlarich and the Bridge of Orchy. It crosses the western edge of Rannoch Moor and passes the entrances to Glen Etive and Glen Coe to reach Kinlochleven. The final section follows General Caulfield's military road over the slopes of the Mamores, crossing wild country with extensive views of the Ben Nevis range, to reach Fort William.

The recently opened and not yet officially named Kelvin/Allander Walkway links the start of the route at Milngavie via the banks of the rivers Allander and Kelvin with the Clyde Walkway at Bell's Bridge in the centre of Glasgow. Details from Strathclyde Regional Council.

Start	Milngavie, Strathclyde	NS555745
Finish	Fort William, Highland	NN105742
On OS maps	41, 50, 56, 57, 64	
Waymark	Spannered thistle	

Publication(s)
Softback: *Guide to the West Highland Way* by Tom Hunter (Constable and Co Ltd). ISBN: 0094690901. 1988 \ 171 x 114 \ 192pp \ £8.95.
Stripmap: *The West Highland Way* (Footprint). £2.95.
Folder: *The West Highland Way* by Robert Aitken (HMSO Scotland). ISBN: 0114942080. 1990 \ 220 x 135 \ 192pp \ £9.95.
Leaflet: *West Highland Way* (Scottish Natural Heritage). 1994 \ A4/3 \ Free.

West Lakes Way 329

Cumbria · 112 km / 70 miles

Designed as a tour of western Lakeland, the route starts from the Georgian port of Whitehaven, climbs to St Bees Head, then follows a gentle lowland stretch to Ennerdale Bridge. From here it goes up Ennerdale Fell, along Pillar Ridge and down Black Sail Pass to Wasdale Head. Climbing over Scafell Pike, the highest point in England, it continues into Eskdale and Hardknott Pass, onto Harter Fell, the Duddon valley to Seathwaite and Ulpha, and over Thwaites Fell to the Sunkenkirk stone circles. It descends to the coast at Haverigg, and ends at Hodbarrow Point in the Duddon Estuary.

The book provides an alternative route for poor weather conditions.

Start	Whitehaven, Cumbria	NX973182
Finish	Millom, Cumbria	SD182781
OS maps	89, 96	

Publication(s)
Booklet: *The West Lakes Way* by Stuart Burgess (Copeland Borough Council). A5 \ 40pp \ £1.00.

West Mendip Way 330

Avon, Somerset · 48 km / 30 miles

The Way was created to commemorate the Queen's Silver Jubilee in 1977, and was a joint venture between local rotary clubs, with the assistance of county and local councils. As its name suggests, it follows the western edge of the limestone hills of the Mendips, passing through villages nestling in the shadow of the hills. From the cathedral city of Wells, the Way visits the tourist cave of Wookey Hole and crosses the Mendip plateau to Priddy, to pass close to Cheddar Gorge and Shipham. From here it crosses Crook Peak and Bleadon Hill to reach Uphill on the Bristol Channel.

Start	Wells, Somerset	ST549461
Finish	Uphill, Avon	ST315585
On OS maps	172, 182, 183	

Waymark	Named posts and named discs with Rotary International logo

Publication(s)
Booklet: *The West Mendip Way: A Walk across the Mendips* by Andrew Eddy (Weston-super-Mare Civic Society). ISBN: 0951036815. 1991\A5\44pp\£1.75 (+ 50p).

West Yorkshire Way 331

W Yorks	240 km / 150 miles

The Way is a circular route around the county boundary, designed to be easily accessible by public transport and covering a wide range of terrain: Pennine Moors in the west, limestone slopes in the north, the remnants of the South Yorks coalfield in the south.

It passes Ilkley, Wetherby, Micklefield, Knottingley, South Elmshall, Darton, Denby Dale, Holme, Marsden, Walsden and Oxenhope, and uses parts of the Ebor Way, Leeds Countryway, Pennine, Calderdale and Bronte Ways.

Start and Finish	Steeton & Silsden BR, W Yorks	SE037448
OS maps	104, 105, 110, 111	

Publication(s)
Softback: *The West Yorkshire Way* by Nicholas Parrott (Sigma Leisure). ISBN: 1850583277. 1993\A5\114pp\£6.95.

Westmorland Boundary Way 332

Cumbria	274 km / 171 miles

A meandering anti-clockwise circuit over the western Pennines, along river valleys, past lakes and over the open fells of the Lake District National Park, following a route very roughly approximating to the boundary of the historic county of Westmorland. From Kendal it crosses Farleton Fell to Kirkby Lonsdale and then heads north to Sedbergh, Wild Boar Fell, Dufton and Cross Fell, where it turns west and meanders across the Lake District via Shap, Patterdale and Helvellyn (at 3,118ft the highest point on the route), then on to Grasmere. It then turns south-east to Ambleside and Windermere, and returns to Kendal.

Start and Finish	Kendal, Cumbria	SD520931
OS maps	90, 91, 97, 98	

Publication(s)
Paperback: *In Search of Westmorland* by Charlie Emett (Cicerone Press). ISBN: 0902363662. 116 x 176\200pp\£5.50.

Westmorland Heritage Walk 333

Cumbria, N Yorks	320 km / 200 miles

An anti-clockwise near-circular route roughly based on the boundaries of the old county of Westmorland but making diversions to include the best walking country. The high-level route is 320km and the alternative low-level one is 290km.

Start and Finish	Arnside, Cumbria	SD461788
OS maps	90, 91, 96, 97, 98	

Publication(s)
Softback: *Westmorland Heritage Walk* by Mark Richards and Christopher John Wright (Cicerone Press). ISBN: 0902363948. 1988 \ 116 x 176 \ 256pp \ £7.99.

Westmorland Way 334

Cumbria	158 km / 99 miles

A scenic, relatively low-level, loop-shaped route across the historic county of Westmorland and the Lake District National Park. It follows footpaths, tracks and country lanes along river valleys and across farmland and the open fells, via Shap, Pooley Bridge, Patterdale, Grasmere, Troutbeck and Kendal to reach Arnside on Morecambe Bay.

Start	Appleby-in-Westmorland, Cumbria	NY683204
Finish	Arnside, Cumbria	SD461788
OS maps	90, 91, 97	

Publication(s)
Paperback: *Westmorland Way* by Paul Hannon (Hillside Publications). ISBN: 0950921254. 1983 \ 208 x 168 \ 88pp \ £4.95.

Wey-South Path 335

Surrey, W Sussex	58 km / 36 miles

From Guildford the Path follows the towpath of the Godalming Navigation (this is part of the canalised river Wey, a tributary of the Thames) to its junction with the Wey-Arun Canal. From here it follows the old towpath or farmland and woodland paths as near as possible to the line of the Wey-Arun Canal, to meet the river Arun near Amberley. Short sections of the Canal have been restored, but in places it has been almost completely obliterated – it was last used as a waterway link between the Thames and the south coast in 1871.

Start	Guildford, Surrey	SU994493

Finish	Amberley, W Sussex	TQ026118
On OS maps	186, 187, 197	

Publication(s)
Paperback: *Wey-South Path* by Aeneas Mackintosh (Wey and Arun Canal Trust Ltd). 120 x 225\24pp\£2.50 (+ 30p).

White Peak Way 336

Derby	128 km / 80 miles

A circular walk designed to be completed in seven easy stages, using youth hostels as staging posts. The book describes a meandering circuit which visits many of the limestone dales of the White Peak area of the Peak District National Park, including Dove Dale, Miller's Dale and Hay Dale. The route also passes Chatsworth House and Park, Hadden Hall and the Castleton Show Caves.

Start and Finish	Bakewell, Derby	SK217685
OS maps	110, 119	

Publication(s)
Paperback: *The White Peak Way* by Robert Haslam (Cicerone Press). ISBN: 1852840560. 116 x 176\96pp\£4.99.

Whithorn Pilgrim Way 337

Dum & Gall	40 km / 25 miles

Tradition has it that Ninian established the first organised centre of Christian life in northern Europe at Whithorn in AD398, and the Way follows ancient roadways through the Machars or Whithorn Peninsula. Stage 1 is from Glenluce via Mochrum to Whithorn, but eventually it is hoped to have a network of routes throughout the peninsula, to the Isle of Whithorn and Burrow Head, to Newton Stewart and on to the Southern Upland Way at Clatteringshaws Loch, and from Glenluce to New Luce, also on the Southern Upland Way. These extensions are described in the book, but not waymarked.

Start	Glenluce, Dum & Gall	NX198574
Finish	Whithorn, Dum & Gall	NX445404
OS maps	82, 83	
Waymark	Celtic cross logo	

Publication(s)
Paperback: *A Way to Whithorn* by Andrew Patterson (St Andrew Press). ISBN: 0715206907. 1993\110x210\162pp\£6.95.

Wimpole Way 338

Cambs	18 km / 11 miles

From Cambridge the Way loops south-westwards across farmland and through the villages of Caldecote and Kingston to the eighteenth-century Wimpole Hall and Park (NT), where it links with the Clopton Way.

Start	Cambridge, Cambs	TL435585
Finish	Wimpole Hall, Cambs	TL343511
On OS maps	154	
Waymark	Wimpole Way logo	

Publication(s)
Leaflet: *Wimpole Way* (Cambridgeshire County Council). 1993 \
A4/3 \ £0.40 (+ 50p).

Windrush Way 339

Glos	22 km / 14 miles

Developed by the Cotswold Wardens, the Way provides a link between the Oxfordshire Way at Bourton-on-the-Water with the Cotswold Way at Winchcombe. Whereas its sister route, the Wardens' Way, winds through villages, the Windrush Way takes to the hills with only remains of lost mediaeval villages en route.

Start	Bourton-on-the-Water, Glos	SP170209
Finish	Winchcombe, Glos	SP025283
On OS maps	163	
Waymark	Circle, top half white, bottom half black	

Publication(s)
Paperback: *Wardens' Way and Windrush Way* (Cotswold Warden Office). 1991 \ A5 \ 32pp \ £1.50 (+ 25p).

Witton Weavers Way 340

Lancs	51 km / 32 miles

The Witton Weavers is a complicated network of four circular routes (named the Beamers, Reelers, Tacklers and Warpers Trails), linked together to form a large loop to the west of Blackburn and Darwen. The route ranges from Witton Country Park to the west of Blackburn in the north via Abbey Village and Darwen Moor to Jumbles Reservoir on the northern outskirts of Bolton in the south. There is also a link into Darwen itself.

Start and Finish	Witton Park, Lancs	SD659273

OS maps	103, 109
Waymark	Mill logo on named standard markers

Publication(s)
Folder: *Witton Weavers Way: Blackburn & Darwen Borough-wide walk* (Blackburn Borough Council). 1993 \ A5 \ 4pp \ £2.00.

Wolds Way   341

Humberside, N Yorks	127 km / 79 miles

Proposed by the East Riding Area of the Ramblers' Association, the Wolds Way was officially opened in October 1982. It goes west along the river Humber, and then north around the western edge of the Wolds, across woods and arable land to Thixendale, where it turns east along the northern escarpment of the Wolds through dry valleys and sheep pasture before reaching the coast and the Cleveland Way at Filey.

Start	Hessle (Haven), Humberside	TA035256
Finish	Filey Brigg, N Yorks	TA126817
On OS maps	100, 101, 106, 107	
Waymark	National Trail Acorn	

Publication(s)
Softback: *Wolds Way* by Roger Ratcliffe (Aurum Press). ISBN: 1854101897. 1992 \ 210 x 130 \ £8.99.
Leaflet: *Wolds Way* (Countryside Commission Postal Sales). 1992 \ A4/3 \ Free.
Looseleaf: *Wolds Way Accommodation* (RA E Yorkshire & Derwent Area). A4 \ 1pp \ Free (+ SAE).
Badge (£0.75 / SAE) available from RA E Yorkshire & Derwent Area.

Worcestershire Way   342

Heref & Worc	77 km / 48 miles

Starting from Kingsford Country Park on Kinver Edge, where it meets the North Worcestershire Way and the Staffordshire Way, the route goes south-west through Eymore Wood to the river Severn; it then follows the river south, passing to the east of the Wyre Forest. At Bewdley, the Way leaves the river and continues south through Ribbesford Wood, over Abberley Hill, Penny Hill and then Ankerdine Hill before crossing the river Teme. The route then goes over Suckley Hills on the northern end of the Malvern Hills at Cowleigh. From here an extension over farmland to the west of the Malverns was opened in 1994, terminating at Hollybush.

Start	Kingsford, Heref & Worc	SO836821
Finish	Hollybush, Heref & Worc	SO763369

On OS maps	138, 149, 150
Waymark	Standard waymark with name in arrow

Publication(s)
Folder: *Worcestershire Way Guide & Map Pack* (Hereford and Worcester County Council). 1994\A5\£3.95.

Wychavon Way 343

Glos, Heref & Worc	66 km / 41 miles

Designed to link the Cotswold Way with the Severn near Ombersley and opened to commemorate the Silver Jubilee in 1977, the Way starts on the east bank of the river Severn, then turns east to Ombersley, continues east to Hampton Lovell, then on and around to the north of Droitwich where it turns south-east. The Way continues in this direction until it reaches Church Lench, where it turns south-west to Fladbury. Just after Netherton there is an optional detour up Bredon Hill, then on to Ashton under Hill, Gretton and the finish at Winchcombe on the Cotwsold Way.

Start	Holt Fleet, Heref & Worc	SO824633
Finish	Winchcombe, Glos	SP025283
On OS maps	138, 150, 163	
Waymark	Crown symbol "W"	

Publication(s)
Paperback: *The Wychavon Way* (Wychavon District Council). ISBN: 095080990X. 1993\A5\80pp\£2.95 (+ 50p).

Wye Valley Walk 344

Glos, Gwent, Heref & Worc, Powys	178 km / 111 miles

A beautiful walk that follows the banks of the river for most of its length. Formerly two routes from Chepstow to Hereford, and from Hay on Wye to Rhayader, and sometimes known by its Welsh name of Llwybr Bro Gwy, the missing stretch is now incorporated.

Climbing out of Chepstow to pass Lovers Leap, the Walk follows undulating, wooded tracks to descend to the Wye at Tintern Abbey. It then climbs to several good vantage points before crossing over the Wye at Redbrook to continue along the riverside to Monmouth. The route then meanders on to pass English Bicknor, Welsh Bicknor and Goodrich Castle; here it leaves the Wye to go across country to Ross-on-Wye before reaching the cathedral city of Hereford.

Passing cider orchards, parkland and farmland, the Way continues to Bredwardine, and the viewpoint of Merbach Hill before reaching Hay-on-Wye with its bookshops.

From here, it continues past Builth Wells and Newbridge to the finish at Rhayader, sometimes along the river valley and sometimes climbing hills giving extensive views over the valleys to the Black Mountains and Brecon Beacons.

Start	Chepstow, Gwent	ST529924
Finish	Rhayader, Powys	SN968679
On OS maps	136, 146, 147, 148, 149, 160, 161, 162, 172	
Waymark	Named arrows with yellow spot	

Publication(s)

Paperback: *Aerofilms Guide: Offa's Dyke (South) and River Wye Valley* by Des Hannigan (Ian Allan Publishing). ISBN: 0711021341. 1993 \ 286 x 140 \ 128pp \ £9.99.

Leaflet: *Llwybr Bro Gwy / Wye Valley Walk* (Powys County Council). 1984 \ A4/3 \ £0.50.

Paperback: *Walking Down the Wye* by David Hunter (Cicerone Press). ISBN: 1852841052. 1992 \ 116 x 176 \ £6.99.

Folder: *Wye Valley Walk* (Gwent County Council). 1991 \ 205 x 130 \ £3.50.

Yoredale Way   345

Cumbria, N Yorks	161 km / 101 miles

The Way follows the course of the river Ure from York to its source on Abbotside Common, 2,000ft above sea level near Kirkby Stephen. It passes through Boroughbridge, Ripon, Middleham and Wensleydale, where it passes Aysgarth and Hardraw Falls before climbing to Ure Head and descending to follow the river Eden to Kirkby Stephen.

Start	York, N Yorks	SE603522
Finish	Kirkby Stephen, Cumbria	NY775087
OS maps	91, 98, 99, 105	

Publication(s)

Paperback: *Yoredale Way* by J.K.E. Piggin (Dalesman Publishing Ltd). ISBN: 0852065922. 200 x 125 \ 72pp \ £1.25.

ANYTIME CHALLENGE WALKS – REGIONS

A Scotland & Cheviots
B Tyne & Wear
C North Pennines
D Lake District
E Yorkshire Dales
F North York Moors
G Yorkshire Wolds
H South Pennines
I Lancashire
J Canal Walks

K Peak District
L North Wales
M East Midlands
N Shropshire & Worcestershire
O East Anglia
P Mid & South Wales
Q Surrey
R Wiltshire
S Devon & Cornwall

ANYTIME CHALLENGE WALKS

A: Scotland and Cheviot Hills
Cheviot Hills 2,000ft Summits Walk

Northumb	40 km / 25 miles

This hard upland walk, originally devised by the Tyne Tees Group of the LDWA, links the six distinct summits in the Cheviot Hills that exceed the 2,000ft contour: Cheviot, Windy Gyle, Bloodybush Edge, Cushat Law, Comb Fell and Hedgehope. An alternative start from Wooler, adding 10 miles, is also described. This is a long walk over rough terrain, involving 5,000ft of ascent, and good navigation skills are essential.

Start and Finish	Hawsen Burn, Northumb	NT954225
OS maps	75, 80	

Publication(s)
Looseleaf: *Cheviot Hills 2,000ft Summits Walk* (LDWA Northumbria Group). Free (+ SAE). Certificate (£0.10 / C5 SAE) available from LDWA Northumbria Group.

Gallo Way Round

Dum & Gall, Strathclyde	80 km / 50 miles

A circular high-level route, with 12,500ft of ascent over 30 tops in the three main ranges of the Galloway Hills. Views are extensive from the route which dips into the skirts of forestry plantations three times. The bulk of the way is over the tops with only odd traces of paths, and will test navigation. The mixed terrain can be very tough through heather, bog and rocks, but is short turf above 2,000ft.

Start and Finish	Bruce's Stone, L Trool, Dum & Gall	NX415803
OS maps	77	

Publication(s)
Looseleaf: *Gallo Way Round* (Glyn Jones). Free (+ SAE). Certificate (£0.50 / A4 SAE) available from Glyn Jones.

Three Peaks of Cheviot Walk

Northumb	48 km / 30 miles

This hard upland walk, originally devised by Gwyn Rose, links three of the shapeliest peaks in the Cheviot Hills: The Schil, Windy Gyle and Hedgehope. An alternative start from Wooler, adding 10 miles, is also described. This is a long walk over rough terrain involving 5,700ft of ascent and good navigational skills are essential. The walk is only open between April and September, and no completions will be recorded outside this period.

Start and Finish	Hawsen Burn, Northumb	NT954225
OS maps	74, 75, 80	

Publication(s)
Looseleaf: *Three Peaks of Cheviot* (LDWA Northumbria Group). A4 \ Free (+ SAE). Certificate (£0.20 / C5 SAE) available from LDWA Northumbria Group.

B: Tyne and Wear

Shieldsman Walk

Tyne & Wear	53 km / 33 miles

The Shieldsman is a walk along the coast and countryside of Tyneside. The route passes many places of historic interest, including South Shields Roman Fort, Jarrow's Saxon church and North Tyneside Steam Railway, and crosses the river Tyne twice, by pedestrian tunnel and ferry. The limestone cliffs of South Shields are of outstanding geological and natural history interest while the picturesque valley of Hollywell Dene leading to Seaton Sluice is the highlight of the walk which is an exploration of a familiar yet neglected area. Donations for each completion to the RNLI would be appreciated.

Start and Finish	South Shields, Tyne & Wear	NZ370676
OS maps	88	

Publication(s)
Leaflet: *Shieldsman Walk* (David Kidd). 1990 \ A4 \ Free (+ SAE). Certificate (- / A4 SAE) available from David Kidd.

Tyne and Wear 20

Tyne & Wear	34 km / 21 miles

A circular route over undulating countryside which is quite steep in some areas, following tracks and riverside paths through or over Ryton Willows, Clara Vale, Bradley Hall, Greenside Hill, Penny

Hill, Bowser Hole, Milkwell Burn Woods, High Spen, Blackhall Mill, Liddells Fell and Blaydon Burn.

Start and Finish	Newburn Bridge, Tyne & Wear	NZ165652
OS maps	88	

Publication(s)
Looseleaf: *Tyne and Wear 20* (J Tinniswood). A4\Free (+ 9"x4" SAE). Badge and certificate (£1.00 / - / SAE) available from J Tinniswood.

C: North Pennines

Dog Walk

Cumbria	52 km / 33 miles

This route, named from Dufton – Orton – Grayrigg, includes some pleasant scenery on minor roads and paths, and can be linked at Tebay with the Cat Walk to create a 70 mile route. It includes Appleby and a look at the river Eden, and the river Lune in the Tebay area. The finish point is Kapellan, the Cumbria Animal Rescue centre, a favourite charity of the late A Wainwright. All donations welcome.

Start	Dufton, Cumbria	NY689250
Finish	Grayrigg, Cumbria	SD568968
OS maps	91, 97	

Publication(s)
Looseleaf: *Dog Walk* (Frank Hodson). Free (+ 9"x4" SAE). Badge and certificate (£1.00 / - / 9"x6" SAE) available from Frank Hodson.

Eden Trail

Cumbria	55 km / 34 miles

A delightful walk through the tranquil Eden Valley, with options in route length (min. 24 miles) including a high-level route which traverses Cross Fell (the highest English peak outside the Lake District). The walk is closely associated with the Settle to Carlisle Railway and the North Pennines.

Start and Finish	Appleby-in-Westmorland, Cumbria	NY683204
OS maps	91	

Publication(s)
Looseleaf: *Eden Trail* (North Pennine Walks). £0.50 (+ A5 SAE). Badge and certificate (£1.50 / £0.50 / A5 SAE) available from North Pennine Walks.

Greaver's Trail

Durham	42 km / 26 miles

Named after the old lead-miners' walking routes, the Trail is a pleasant walk running through central Weardale, based on the dale's new steam-operated railway. A family option enables half the walk to be undertaken at a time, with a steam-train journey back to the starting point if required. Half the route runs along the southern escarpment of the dale to Wolsingham Station; the return leg follows alongside the railway to Frosterley before climbing up the hillside to Rogerley and then descending back to Stanhope.

Start and Finish	Stanhope Station, Durham	NY998387
OS maps	87, 92	

Publication(s)
Looseleaf: *Greaver's Trail* (North Pennine Walks). £0.50 (+ A5 SAE). Badge and certificate (£1.50 / £0.50 / A5 SAE) available from North Pennine Walks.

Helm Wind Walk

Cumbria	32 km / 20 miles

The Walk takes its name from the notorious Helm Wind which often rages fiercely on the summit of Cross Fell, at 2,960ft the highest point on the route. Care should be taken when attempting the Walk, especially in poor weather conditions.

Start and Finish	Garrigill, Cumbria	NY744417
OS maps	87, 91	

Publication(s)
Looseleaf: *Helm Wind Walk* (LDWA East Lancs Group). Free (+ SAE). Badge and certificate (£0.85 / £0.15 / 9"x6" SAE) available from LDWA East Lancs Group.

Kirkby Lonsdale Parish Walk

Cumbria	40 km / 25 miles

Kirkby Lonsdale is the mother church of a very large parish involving seven churches altogether. The Rector, Canon Graham Betteridge, planned a route to include all these churches, and Frank Hodson of the LDWA made one or two variations. The route is a scenic one, which runs via Hutton Roof, Lupton, Mansergh, Middleton, Barbon and Casterton.

Start and Finish	Kirkby Lonsdale, Cumbria	SD611789
OS maps	97	

Publication(s)
Looseleaf: *Kirkby Lonsdale Parish Walk* (Frank Hodson). Free (+ 9"x4" SAE). Badge and certificate (£1.00 / - / 9"x6" SAE) available from Frank Hodson.

North Pennine Path

Cumbria, Durham, Northumb	176 km / 110 miles

Originally devised by Alan Earnshaw as a tough complement to the Wear Valley Way, this is a tough walk traversing the North Pennines. It can be started at a number of towns in the northern dales, and is designed as a tour of the Youth Hostels at Langdon Beck, Dufton, Ninebanks and Edmundbyers. It traverses unexplored highlands as well as taking in Weardale, Teesdale, the Eden Valley, South Tynedale, the Allendales and Derwentside.

Start and Finish	Stanhope Station, Durham	NY998387
OS maps	87, 91, 92	

Publication(s)
Looseleaf: *North Pennine Path* (North Pennine Walks). £0.50 (+ A5 SAE). Badge and certificate (£1.50 / £0.50 / A5 SAE) available from North Pennine Walks.

D: The Lake District
Back o' Skidda

Cumbria	45 km / 28 miles

A high-level circuit, with over 7,600ft of ascent, across the relatively unfrequented mountains of the northern Lake District, including the summits of High Pike, Great Calva, Skiddaw, Blencathra and Bannerdale Crags.

Start and Finish	Mosedale, Cumbria	NX357323
OS maps	90	

Publication(s)
Looseleaf: *Back o' Skidda* (Joyce Sidebottom). Free (+ 9"x4" SAE). Badge and certificate (- / SAE / - / SAE) available from Joyce Sidebottom.

Duddon Horseshoe

Cumbria	32 km / 20 miles

A hard mountain walk for experienced walkers that follows an undulating route around the Duddon valley to cross both Hardknott Pass and Wrynose Pass, two of the highest road passes in the Lakeland area.

Start and Finish	Seathwaite, Cumbria	NY235119
OS maps	96	

Publication(s)
Looseleaf: *Duddon Horseshoe* (Brian Richmond). Free (+ SAE). Badge and certificate (£1.00 / - / SAE) available from Brian Richmond.

Duddon Landscape Walk

Cumbria	37 km / 23 miles

A high-level circuit of one of the Lake District's finest valleys, pioneered by the West Lancashire Group of the LDWA to raise money for the National Trust Lake District Appeal. Starting in the attractive market town of Broughton-in-Furness, it traverses the fells of the Duddon/Esk watershed, including the majestic Harter Fell and the rugged Dunnerdale Fells.

Start and Finish	Broughton, Cumbria	SD212875
OS maps	96	

Publication(s)
Looseleaf: *The Duddon Landscape Walk* (John Tootle). A4\3pp\Free (+ SAE). Badge and certificate (£1.50/-/10"x8" SAE) available from John Tootle.

Grasmere Skyline Classic Walk

Cumbria	32 km / 20 miles

A superb high mountain walk over some of the highest mountains in the eastern and central fells.

Start and Finish	White Moss Common, Cumbria	NY348065
OS maps	90	

Publication(s)
Looseleaf: *Grasmere Skyline Classic Walk* (Brian Richmond). Free (+ SAE). Badge and certificate (£0.85 / £0.15 / SAE) available from Brian Richmond.

High Street Stroll

Cumbria	48 km / 30 miles

A scenic high-level route over the mountains of the central and eastern Lake District, avoiding tourist spots and visiting Harter

Fell, Nabs Moor, Swindale, Mardale and High Street. No time limit.

Start and Finish	Ambleside, Cumbria	NY376045
OS maps	90	

Publication(s)
Looseleaf: *High Street Stroll* (Joyce Sidebottom). Free (+ 9"x4" SAE). Badge and certificate (- / SAE / - / SAE) available from Joyce Sidebottom.

Lakeland Challenge Walk

Cumbria	29 km / 18 miles

Tough 6,000ft ascent of ten lakeland peaks in a circular walk from Langdale, firstly via Stickle Tarn and the Langdale Pikes to Esk Hause, followed by the ascent of Scafell Pike, returning via Bowfell, Crinkle Crags and Pike of Blisco.

Start and Finish	Dungeon Ghyll, Cumbria	NY295066
OS maps	89, 90	

Publication(s)
Paperback: *John Merrill's Lakeland Challenge Walk* by John Merrill (Trail Crest Publications Ltd). ISBN: 0907496504. 1987 \ 140 x 210 \ 32pp \ £2.75. Badge and certificate (£2.75 / post free) available from Trail Crest Publications Ltd.

Lost Lancs Way

Cumbria	80 km / 50 miles

When Cumbria was formed in 1971, it included part of Lancashire, north of the sands. This route follows on footpaths and minor roads the old boundary with Cumberland and Westmorland. The rail line links the start and finish points, but there is no Sunday service.

After a scenic look at the Duddon Valley, the route goes over Wrynose Pass to Elterwater, the midway point and a good place for an overnight stop. It then takes the Windermere shore path and goes over the lake by ferry, followed by the lovely Winster valley to finish in Grange-over-Sands.

Start	Green Road Station, Cumbria	SD190840
Finish	Grange-over-Sands, Cumbria	SD412781
OS maps	89, 90, 96, 97	

Publication(s)
Looseleaf: *Lost Lancs Way* (Frank Hodson). Free (+ SAE). Badge and certificate (£1.00 / £0.50 / SAE) available from Frank Hodson.

North Western Fells

Cumbria	80 km / 50 miles

A route visiting all the peaks in Wainwright's "North Western Fells", which involves 18,000ft of ascent.

Start and Finish	Rannerdale Knotts, Cumbria	NY162182
OS maps	89	

Publication(s)
Looseleaf: *North Western Fells* (A G Foot). Free (+ 9"x4" SAE). Certificate (£1.50 post free) available from A G Foot.

Pennington Round

Cumbria	40 km / 25 miles

A walk over moorland countryside visiting the John Barrow monument overlooking the delightful market town of Ulverston. It includes a few miles of the Cumbria Way.

Start and Finish	Beckside, Cumbria	SD235822
OS maps	96	

Publication(s)
Looseleaf: *The Pennington Round* (Brian Richmond). 1pp\£0.20 (+ SAE). Badge and certificate (£0.85 / £0.15 / SAE) available from Brian Richmond.

Rydal Round

Cumbria	45 km / 28 miles

9,000ft of ascent on well-used mountain paths. Highlights are fine weather views from Fairfield, Kidsty Pike, Thornthwaite Beacon and Red Screes with pub stops at Patterdale and Kirkstone Pass. A compass will be needed in mist.

Start and Finish	Pelter Bridge, Cumbria	NY365059
OS maps	90	

Publication(s)
Looseleaf: *Rydal Round* (Jim Strother). Free (+ 9"x4" SAE). Certificate (£1.00 post free) available from Jim Strother.

That's Lyth

Cumbria	40 km / 25 miles

The route encircles the Lyth Valley, and includes Cunswick Scar, Scout Scar and Whitbarrow Scar. It also includes Witherslack, and crosses the Lyth valley from Gilpin Bridge to Levens. The unusual totem pole stile at Gilpin Bridge is a feature of the walk, as is the limestone scenery and striking views.

Start and Finish	Scout Scar, Cumbria	SD489923
OS maps	97	

Publication(s)
Looseleaf: *That's Lyth* (Frank Hodson). Free (+ 9"x4" SAE). Badge and certificate (£1.00 / - / 9"x6" SAE) available from Frank Hodson.

Thirlmere Round

Cumbria	35 km / 22 miles

A high-level walk touching 15 of the highest eastern central fell tops. A high mountain walk for experienced walkers only.

Start and Finish	Grasmere, Cumbria	NY339072
OS maps	96, 97	

Publication(s)
Looseleaf: *The Thirlmere Round* (Brian Richmond). 2pp \ £0.30 (+ SAE). Certificate (£0.30 / SAE) available from Brian Richmond.

Ullswater Circuit

Cumbria	74 km / 46 miles

A strenuous fell walk in the eastern and central fells with 8,000ft of ascent.

Start and Finish	Pooley Bridge, Cumbria	NY470247
OS maps	90	

Publication(s)
Looseleaf: *Ullswater Circuit* (Paul Miller). Free (+ 1st class). Certificate (- / 1st class) available from Paul Miller.

Whicham Valley Five Trigs Walk

Cumbria	31 km / 19 miles

A rough mountain walk with very few footpaths in the first half. Knowledge of map and compass use is essential.

Start and Finish	Duddon Bridge, Cumbria	SD199882
OS maps	96, 97	

Publication(s)
Looseleaf: *The Whicham Valley Five Trigs Walk* (Brian Richmond).
Free (+ SAE). Badge (£0.85 / SAE) available from Brian Richmond.

E: Yorkshire Dales
Apostles Walk

Lancs, W Yorks	128 km / 80 miles

The route was first described in 1974 for a walk to raise funds for the united benefice of Harden and Wilsden. It is an almost circular walk from the outskirts of Bradford to the southern part of the Yorkshire Dales, along roads, towpaths and the Dales Way, and visiting twelve churches.

Start and Finish	Wilsden, W Yorks	SE094362
OS maps	98, 103, 104	

Publication(s)
Looseleaf: *Apostles Walk* (A T Ashworth). 1pp \ Free (+ 9"x4"SAE).
Badge (£1.00 / SAE) available from A T Ashworth.

Cavendish 27 Circuit

N Yorks	43 km / 27 miles

A route encircling the Barden Fell, an area of outstanding beauty and varied scenery, full of history. From Bolton Abbey the route follows the river Wharfe to Bolton Bridge, and then takes in the villages of Draughton, Eastby, Embsay, Hasby, Rylstone, Cracoe, Thorpe, Burnsall and Howgill before climbing up to Simon's Seat, an outstanding viewpoint.

Start and Finish	Bolton Abbey Hall, N Yorks	SE071540
OS maps	98, 103, 104	

Publication(s)
Looseleaf: *Cavendish 27 Circuit* (L Turner). 1pp \ Free (+ 9"x4" SAE). Badge and certificate (£1.50 / - / 9"x4" SAE) available from L Turner.

Crag and Cove Walk

N Yorks	32 km / 20 miles

A circular walk in the Pennine limestone Dales, which may be started from Arncliffe, Malham or Conistone, as there are parking limitations in these villages. The walk features dramatic limestone cliffs of the Mid-Craven geological fault at Malham and Gordale. The area formed an important part of the Cistercian monastic estates of Fountains Abbey in the Middle Ages.

Start and Finish	Arncliffe, N Yorks	SD932718
OS maps	98	

Publication(s)
Looseleaf: *Crag and Cove Walk* (Mike Barnham). Free (+ SAE).

Dales Traverse

N Yorks	40 km / 25 miles

A circuit of Upper Wharfedale, the route climbs to Wassa Hill beneath the imposing Kilnsey Crag, then goes on to the top of Hill Castles Scar, following the Scar northwards to Kettlewell. It continues up Cam Head to Buckden Pike, at 2,302ft the highest point on the route, and descends to Litton. It returns via Yew Cogar Scar and Great West Scar and follows Mastiles Lane, a former drovers' road, before climbing over Kilnsey Moor to the finish. Proceeds from sales of badges go to the Wheatfields Hospice.

Start and Finish	Kilnsey, N Yorks	SD974679
OS maps	98	

Publication(s)
Looseleaf: *Dales Traverse* (Simon Townson). Free (+ 9"x4" SAE). Badge and certificate (£1.50 / - / 9"x6" SAE) available from Simon Townson.

Nidd Vale Circuit

N Yorks	42 km / 26 miles

A circular route in the Nidd valley and Masham area of North Yorkshire. There is a time limit of 12 hours.

Start and Finish	Lofthouse, N Yorks	SE101737
OS maps	99	

Publication(s)
Looseleaf: *Nidd Vale Circuit* (Simon Townson). Free (+ SAE). Badge and certificate (£1.00 / £0.50 / 9"x6" SAE) available from Simon Townson.

Otley Nine Leagues

N Yorks, W Yorks	43 km / 27 miles

A circular walk taking in woodland, moorland, riverside and field walking in the Wharfe and Washburn valleys. The official start is the White House Visitor Centre on the north-facing slope of Otley Chevin. The terrain covered by the walk is not difficult for the practised walker but a knowledge of map and compass use may be found useful at dusk or in bad weather.

Start and Finish	Otley Chevin, W Yorks	SE203445
OS maps	104	

Publication(s)
Looseleaf: *Otley Nine Leagues* (D W Haller). Free (+ 9"x4" SAE). Badge (£1.00 / Banker SAE) available from D W Haller.

Three Crags Walk

N Yorks, W Yorks	25 km / 16 miles

A walk passing Alms Cliff, Caley and Cow and Calf crags, and offering good views of lower Wharfedale. A good introduction to longer walks. The use of Pathfinder maps 671 and 672 is recommended.

Start and Finish	Weeton Station, N Yorks	SE276476
OS maps	104	

Publication(s)
Looseleaf: *Three Crags Walk* (Peter Bayer). £0.50 (+ A5 SAE). Badge (£1.50 / 4"x2" SAE) available from Peter Bayer.

Three Feathers Walk (Kettlewell)

N Yorks	55 km / 34 miles

The Three Feathers Walks are a series of three walks each set in a different national park. To qualify for a badge, all the routes must be completed within a calendar year. Each is a circular walk, and they may be completed in any order. The three routes are set in the Yorkshire Dales (Kettlewell), the N York Moors (Kilburn) and the Peak District (Yorkshire Bridge). All routes are arduous and must be planned accordingly.

Start and Finish	Kettlewell, N Yorks	SD971724
OS maps	98	

Publication(s)
Looseleaf: *Three Feathers Walks* (Keith Bown). A4\Free (+ SAE).
Badge (£1.50) available from Keith Bown.

Three Moors Walk

N Yorks, W Yorks	48 km / 30 miles

A circular walk taking in the Chevin, Rombalds Moor and Round
Hill (Langbar/Middleton Moor). It includes some of the more obscure paths hence offering a navigational challenge as well as
needing stamina. The use of Pathfinder maps 662, 671 and 672 is
recommended.

Start and Finish	Otley, W Yorks	SE204455
OS maps	104	

Publication(s)
Looseleaf: *Three Moors Walk* (Peter Bayer). £0.50 (+ A5 SAE).
Badge (£1.50 / 4"x2" SAE) available from Peter Bayer.

Three Peaks Walk

N Yorks	39 km / 24 miles

A classic challenge walk linking the trig points on Pen-y-ghent
(2,278ft), Whernside (2,416ft) and Ingleborough (2,376ft), and involving over 5,000ft of ascent. In recent years, the route has become
so badly eroded that costly remedial work has had to be carried out
on the footpaths. For this reason, many walkers have decided not
to walk it. Details of the Three Peaks of Yorkshire Club can be
obtained from the Pen-y-ghent Cafe in Horton (0729 860333).

Start and Finish	Horton in Ribblesdale, N Yorks	SD809725
OS maps	98	

Publication(s)
Hardback: *Walks in Limestone Country* by A Wainwright (Michael
Joseph). ISBN: 0718140117. 1992\178 x 120\£8.99.

Three Rivers Walk

N Yorks, W Yorks	40 km / 25 miles

A walk via the rivers Aire, Wharfe and Washburn, offering fields,
rivers, moors and woods. The use of Pathfinder maps 662, 671, 672,
682 is recommended.

Start	Shipley, W Yorks	SE149376
Finish	Otley, W Yorks	SE204455
OS maps	104	

Publication(s)
Looseleaf: *Three Rivers Walk* (Peter Bayer). £0.50 (+ A5 SAE).
Badge (£1.50 / 4"x2" SAE) available from Peter Bayer.

Trollers Trot

N Yorks	43 km / 27 miles

A varied route in the Yorkshire Dales using footpaths over moorland, alongside riverbanks, through forests and fields. Part of the route passes over access land which on certain days (except Sundays) is closed to the public for grouse-shooting.

Start and Finish	Bolton Abbey, N Yorks	SE072539
OS maps	98	

Publication(s)
Leaflet: *Trollers Trot* (John Sparshatt). A4 \ Free (+ SAE). Badge and certificate (£1.50 / - / A4 SAE) available from John Sparshatt.

Yorkshire Dales Challenge Walk

N Yorks	40 km / 25 miles

A circular challenge walk through the Yorkshire Dales National Park. It includes much high moorland.

Start and Finish	Kettlewell, N Yorks	SD971724
OS maps	98	

Publication(s)
Paperback: *John Merrill's Yorkshire Dales Challenge Walk* by John Merrill (Trail Crest Publications Ltd). ISBN: 0907496865. 32pp \ £2.75. Badge and certificate (£2.75 / post free) available from Trail Crest Publications Ltd.

Yorkshire Ridings 200 Furlongs

N Yorks, W Yorks	40 km / 25 miles

A circular walk taking in woodland and open moorland. Some parts of the route are not at all well marked and the route instructions should be used in close conjunction with the OS maps. Ability to use map and compass will be found useful.

Start and Finish	Otley, W Yorks	SE204455
OS maps	104	

Publication(s)
Looseleaf: *Yorkshire Ridings 200 Furlongs* (D W Haller). Free (+ 9"x4" SAE). Badge (£1.00 / Banker SAE) available from D W Haller.

F: North Yorkshire Moors
Bilsdale Circuit

N Yorks	48 km / 30 miles

A strenuous circuit with over 4,000ft of ascent, mainly along tracks over the high moors to the north of Helmsley. It takes its name from the Bilsdale TV mast, visible for most of the walk, and from the dale which it circuits. From Newgate Bank viewpoint the route heads north-east through plantations on Roppa Edge and Helmsley Moor before joining the Bilsdale bridleway over Slape Wath Moor and into Tripdale, from where ancient earthworks are followed to join the Lyke Wake Walk and Cleveland Way routes on Urra Moor. These are followed west over the Cleveland Ridge to Carlton Bank Top where the Circuit turns south past the TV mast, 1,200ft up on West Moor, and swings east to the finish.

Start and Finish	Newgate Bank Top, N Yorks	SE564890
OS maps	93, 100	

Publication(s)
Paperback: *Bilsdale Circuit* by Michael Teanby (Dalesman Publishing Ltd). ISBN: 0852066368. 1981\120 x 180\32pp\£0.90.
Looseleaf: *Bilsdale Circuit* (Michael Guest). Free (+ 9x4 SAE). Badge and certificate (£0.80 / £0.20 / SAE) available from Michael Guest.

Hambleton Hobble

N Yorks	50 km / 31 miles

A circular route with 2,500ft of ascent centred around Black Hambleton, one of the Tabular Hills, on the western edge of the North York Moors National Park; it includes moorland, arable land, forests and villages.

Start and Finish	Osmotherley, N Yorks	SE461985
OS maps	100	

Publication(s)
Leaflet: *Hambleton Hobble* (Lyke Wake Club). £0.20 (+ SAE). Badge (£1.25 / SAE) available from Lyke Wake Club.

Lyke Wake Walk

N Yorks	67 km / 42 miles

The route was pioneered by local farmer Bill Cowley in 1955, and has since become one of the best-known and most popular walks. When the first crossing was made, much of the route over deep heather moor was undefined, but there is now a well-worn and, in places, wet and eroded path. For this reason, many walkers no longer walk the route, and both the Shepherds Round and the Lyke Wake Way have been devised as alternatives to reduce the pressure on it.

From Scarth Wood the Walk follows the northern escarpment of the high moors over Carlton Bank, Cringle Moor, the Wainstones and Hasty Bank to Botton Head. From here it heads east, crossing Farndale, Rosedale, Wheeldale and Goathland Moors, and passing the "golf balls" of the early warning station on Fylingdale Moor to reach the sea.

Start	Osmotherley, N Yorks	SE461985
Finish	Ravenscar, N Yorks	NZ970012
OS maps	93, 94, 99	

Publication(s)
Paperback: *Lyke Wake Walk* by Bill Cowley (Dalesman Publishing Ltd). ISBN: 0852069421. 1993 \ 205 x 135 \ 72pp \ £4.75. Badge and certificate (£1.25 / £0.25 / SAE) available from Lyke Wake Club.

Lyke Wake Way

N Yorks	80 km / 50 miles

This is a longer alternative to the classic Lyke Wake Walk, avoiding badly eroded moorland sections and linking Chop Gate, Church Houses, Rosedale Abbey, Egton Grange and Beck Hole.

Start	Osmotherley, N Yorks	SE461985
Finish	Ravenscar, N Yorks	NZ970012
OS maps	93, 94, 99	

Publication(s)
Paperback: *Lyke Wake Walk* by Bill Cowley (Dalesman Publishing Ltd). ISBN: 0852069421. 1993 \ 205 x 135 \ 72pp \ £4.75.

Monks Trod

N Yorks	32 km / 20 miles

From Byland Abbey, the route follows the old monk's footpath to Rievaulx, then continues by Caydale Mill and Murton Grange to join the Drove Road for Scarth Nick, a route used by Rievaulx monks to visit their granges at Welbury and elsewhere.

Start	Byland Abbey, N Yorks	SE549789
Finish	Scarth Nick, N Yorks	SE471994
OS maps	100	

Publication(s)
Paperback: *Lyke Wake Walk* by Bill Cowley (Dalesman Publishing Ltd). ISBN: 0852069421. 1993\205 x 135\72pp\£4.75.

Newtondale Trail

N Yorks	32 km / 20 miles

This relatively easy-going walk links together the terminal stations of the North Yorkshire Moors Railway, which follows Newton Dale northwards from Pickering across the moors to Grosmont. The Trail follows the Dale, some sections going close to the Railway and others following forest tracks and crossing the open moors high above the valley.

Start	Pickering, N Yorks	SE797842
Finish	Grosmont, N Yorks	NZ828053
OS maps	94, 100	

Publication(s)
Leaflet: *Newtondale Trail* (Mike Teanby). A4/3\Free (+ SAE). Badge (£1.20 / SAE) available from Mike Teanby.

North York Moors Challenge Walk

N Yorks	40 km / 25 miles

A strenuous circular challenge walk in the North York Moors National Park. The route includes high moorland.

Start and Finish	Goathland, N Yorks	NZ838014
OS maps	94	

Publication(s)
Paperback: *John Merrill's North Yorkshire Moors Challenge Walk* by John Merrill (Trail Crest Publications Ltd). ISBN: 0907496369. 32pp\£2.25. Badge and certificate (£2.75 / post free) available from Trail Crest Publications Ltd.

North York Moors Wobble

N Yorks	51 km / 32 miles

The circular route takes in Farndale, Rosedale and the valley of the river Swen; it uses some 5 miles of the old Rosedale Railway track, and crosses part of Rosedale Moor and Hamer Moor. It links 10 moorland pubs, and visits the beautiful villages of Cropton, Lastingham, Hutton-le-Hole, Rosedale, High and Low Mills and Gillamoor. Although a good day's walk, the Wobble can also provide a weekend walk if one of the pubs is used for an overnight stay.

Start and Finish	Gillamoor, N Yorks	SE684801
OS maps	100	

Publication(s)
Booklet: *North York Moors Wobble* (George Davies). 12pp\£3.00 (+ A4 SAE). Certificate (- / 9"x6" SAE) available from George Davies.

Rosedale Circuit

N Yorks	59 km / 37 miles

A tour of Rosedale, Farndale, Bransdale, Westerdale, Danby Dale, Great Fryup Dale and Glaisdale, the route includes many points of natural and historical interest, with moorland tracks and grassy dales. This is a strenuous route with 4,000ft of ascent.

Start and Finish	Rosedale Abbey, N Yorks	SE723959
OS maps	94, 100	
Waymark	"RC" for most of the way	

Publication(s)
Leaflet: *Rosedale Circuit* (G Kilvington). A4\Free (+ SAE). Badge and certificate (£1.10 / - / 9"x4" SAE) available from G Kilvington.

Samaritan Way

Cleveland, N Yorks	64 km / 40 miles

A strenuous high-level route across the North York Moors National Park, devised as a fund-raising venture by the Teesdale Samaritans. From Guisborough it heads in a southerly direction, crossing Commondale, Great Fryup Dale and Glaisdale and Farndale Moors to return via Westerdale, Baysdale and the Cleveland Way between the Captain Cook monument and High Cliff Nab.

Start and Finish	Guisborough, Cleveland	NZ615160
OS maps	93, 94, 100	

Publication(s)
Looseleaf: *Samaritan Way* (R T Pinkney). Free (+ SAE). Badge and
certificate (£1.25 / £0.25 / A4 SAE) available from R T Pinkney.

Seahorse Saunter

N Yorks	69 km / 43 miles

The route crosses the North York Moors to the old Nordic settle-
ment of Whitby on the east coast. Following a mixture of field
paths, bridleways and paved packhorse ways, the Saunter passes
through farmland, open moors and wooded valleys, in an ever-
changing facet of this popular national park. Most of the route is
easy to follow, but in poor weather conditions skill with map and
compass is required.

Start	Kilburn White Horse, N Yorks	SE514813
Finish	Whitby, N Yorks	NZ900117
OS maps	94, 100	

Publication(s)
Leaflet: *Seahorse Saunter* (Steve Watkins). A4 \ £0.20 (+ SAE).

Shepherd's Round

N Yorks	64 km / 40 miles

A tough circuit of the North York Moors with 5,000ft of climbing,
designed as an alternative to the complete Lyke Wake Walk. The
walking is firmer and more suited to large groups. From Scarth
Nick it follows the Cleveland Way and Lyke Wake Walk route for
12 miles over Clay Bank and Urra Moor, and then crosses the
moors via Fangdale Beck and Hawnby to return to the start.

Start and Finish	Scarth Nick, N Yorks	SE471994
OS maps	93, 94, 100	

Publication(s)
Paperback: *Lyke Wake Walk* by Bill Cowley (Dalesman Publishing
Ltd). ISBN: 0852069421. 1993 \ 205 x 135 \ 72pp \ £4.75.
Leaflet: *Shepherd's Round* (Lyke Wake Club). A4/3 \ £0.25 (+ SAE).
Badge (£1.25 / SAE) available from Lyke Wake Club.

Three Feathers Walk (Kilburn)

N Yorks	48 km / 30 miles

The Three Feathers Walks are a series of three walks each set in
a different national park. To qualify for a badge, all the routes must
be completed within a calendar year. Each is a circular walk, and
they may be completed in any order. The three routes are set in the

Yorkshire Dales (Kettlewell), the N York Moors (Kilburn) and the Peak District (Yorkshire Bridge). All routes are arduous and must be planned accordingly.

Start and Finish	Kilburn White Horse, N Yorks	SE514813
OS maps	100	

Publication(s)
Looseleaf: *Three Feathers Walks* (Keith Bown). A4 \ Free (+ SAE). Badge (£1.50) available from Keith Bown.

G: Yorkshire Wolds

East Thriding Treble Ten

Humberside	48 km / 30 miles

A figure-of-eight route over the southern chalk wolds of the historic East Riding of Yorkshire. It crosses farmland and mixed woodland, going through attractive dales and visiting Brantingham, South Cave and North Cave.

Start and Finish	Welton, Humberside	SE959272
OS maps	106	

Publication(s)
Looseleaf: *East Thriding Treble Ten* (Kim Peacock). SAE \ Free. Badge (£1.00) available from Kim Peacock.

High Hunsley Circuit

Humberside	39 km / 24 miles

A circuit over the wooded valleys and farmland of the southern Yorkshire Wolds, devised by Dennis Parker of the Beverley Group of the RA for challenge and sponsored walks. It is coincident with sections of the Wolds Way, and Beverley 20 link routes enable the basic mileage to be extended. Because of parking problems in Walkington, the walk may be started at any point on the route.

Start and Finish	Walkington, Humberside	SE999368
On OS maps	106, 107	

Publication(s)
Folder: *Beverley Explorer* (Humberside County Council). A5 \ £2.00 (+ 30p).
Leaflet: *High Hunsley Circular* (RA Beverley Group). A4 \ Free (+ 9"x4" SAE). Badge (£1.00 / 6"x4" SAE) available from RA Beverley Group.

Howden 20

Humberside	32 km / 20 miles

From Howden the walk heads west along the bank of the river Ouse, and north across flat farmland and along the Derwent valley via Asselby and Wressle to Bubwith, from where it meanders southwards over farmland back to Howden.

Start and Finish	Howden, Humberside	SE748283
On OS maps	105, 106	
Waymark	Standard arrows with "H20"	

Publication(s)
Folder: *Boothferry Explorer* (Humberside County Council). 1992\A5\£2.00 (+ 30p).
Looseleaf: *Howden Twenty* (Goole Rambling Club). Free (+ 9"x4" SAE). Badge and certificate (£0.50 / - / 6"x4" SAE) available from Goole Rambling Club.

North Wolds Walk

Humberside, N Yorks	32 km / 20 miles

This is a scenic, undulating route across the chalk hills and valleys of the Yorkshire Wolds; it passes through the picturesque villages of Millington, Great Givendale, Bishop Wilton, Kirby Underdale and Thixendale. There is a youth hostel at Thixendale, which is on the Wolds Way. The route was developed by Reckitts Rambling Club as a challenge walk; it is now an established recreational route.

Start and Finish	Millington Road End, N Yorks	SE836567
On OS maps	100, 105, 106	

Publication(s)
Looseleaf: *North Wolds Walk* (Reckitt & Colman Pharmaceuticals). A4\Free (+ 9"x4" SAE). Badge and certificate (£1.20 / £0.20 / 9"x4" SAE) available from Reckitt & Colman Pharmaceuticals.

H: South Pennines

Bronte Round

W Yorks	37 km / 23 miles

The circuit crosses open moorland to Haworth, passing Top Withins before returning to Hebden Bridge via riverside and farm paths. It links places associated with the Bronte family.

Start and Finish	Hebden Bridge, W Yorks	SD992272

OS maps	103, 104

Publication(s)
Booklet: *Bronte Round / Pendle and Ribble Round* by Derek Magnall (Derek Magnall). 1994\A5\36pp\£1.50 (+ 35p). Badge and certificate (£1.50 / - / SAE) available from Derek Magnall.

Crowthorn Crawl

Lancs	43 km / 27 miles

This circular walk in the West Pennine Moors was pioneered by the pupils at Crowthorn School (a branch of the National Childrens Home). It skirts the reservoir country north of Bolton before crossing Turton Moor to Darwen Tower, then across Darwen to the Haslingden Grane Valley. After passing through Snig Hole and Irwell Vale it follows a scenic section high above the river Irwell and then to the National Trust woods at Stubbins. The final part is across the MoD land at Wet Moss before descending to Crowthorn School and Entwistle Station.

Start and Finish	Entwistle, Lancs	SD728178
OS maps	103, 109	

Publication(s)
Looseleaf: *Crowthorn Crawl* (Peter Sleightholm). Free (+ 9"x4" SAE). Badge (£1.25 / 6"x4" SAE) available from Peter Sleightholm.

Cuckoo Walk

Gtr Man, W Yorks	29 km / 18 miles

A strenuous and at times boggy upland circuit developed by Marsden Scout Group. It goes via Wessenden Reservoir, Black Hill and White Moss and is partly coincident with the Pennine Way and several of the walks in this area.

Start and Finish	Marsden, W Yorks	SE049116
OS maps	110	

Publication(s)
Looseleaf: *The Cuckoo Walk* (D E Wilkins). Free (+ 6"x4" SAE). Badge and certificate (£0.90 / £0.10 / 6"x4" SAE) available from D E Wilkins.

Holme Valley Circular Challenge Walk

W Yorks	38 km / 24 miles

A varied route in the South Pennines in "Summer Wine" country. The Walk, mainly on footpaths and tracks, involves 4,000ft of ascent and is not as easy as it may look on the map. It is not the same as the Holme Valley Circular Walk.

Start and Finish	Meltham Infants School, W Yorks	SE093111
OS maps	110	

Publication(s)
Looseleaf: *Holme Valley Circular Challenge* (N F Scholes). Free (+ 9"x4" SAE). Badge and certificate (£2.00 / - / 9"x4" SAE) available from N F Scholes.

New Five Trig Points Walk

Gtr Man, W Yorks	29 km / 18 miles

The circuit along lanes, tracks and footpaths over the Pennine moors, and in parts coincident with the Pennine Way, was designed as a companion walk to the Saddleworth Five Trig Points Walk. It visits the trig points on Bishop Park, Tame Scout, Blackstone Edge, White Hill and Standedge.

Start and Finish	Delph, Gtr Man	SD985079
OS maps	109, 110	

Publication(s)
Looseleaf: *The New Five Trig Points Walk* (Bob Tait). A4 \ Free (+ SAE). Badge and certificate (£1.00 / £0.10 / 9"x5" SAE) available from Bob Tait.

Saddleworth Five Trig Points Walk

Gtr Man	32 km / 20 miles

A tough high-level circuit over open moorland and across peat groughs, with parts of the Walk being coincident with the Pennine Way and other routes in this area. As its name suggests, the route links five trig points on the Saddleworth Moors, namely Alphin Pike, Featherbed Moss, Black Hill, West Nab and Broadstone Hill.

Start and Finish	Greenfield, Gtr Man	SE002040
OS maps	109, 110	

Publication(s)
Looseleaf: *Saddleworth Five Trig Points Walk* (Bob Tait). A4 \ Free (+ SAE). Badge and certificate (£1.00 / £0.10 / 9"x5" SAE) available from Bob Tait.

Summer Wine Walk

W Yorks	32 km / 20 miles

A gentle stroll around countryside made famous by the "Last of the Summer Wine" TV series. Low moorland, open farmlands, woods and reservoirs are the main features of this highly scenic route – an ideal family walk.

Start and Finish	Holmfirth, W Yorks	SE143082
OS maps	110	

Publication(s)
Looseleaf: *Summer Wine Walk* (M P Berry). £0.50 (+ A5 SAE). Badge and certificate (£1.50 / £0.50 post free) available from M P Berry.

Ten Reservoirs Walk

Derby, Gtr Man	35 km / 22 miles

A tough circuit over the Saddleworth Moors, linking with the Pennine Way and several walks in this area. It visits Yeoman Hey, Greenfield, Black Moss, Swellands, Blakeley, Wessenden, Wessenden Head, Torside and Chew Reservoirs.

Start and Finish	Dovestone Reservoir, Gtr Man	SE014034
OS maps	110	

Publication(s)
Looseleaf: *The Ten Reservoirs Walk* (Bob Tait). A4 \ Free (+ SAE). Badge and certificate (£1.00 / £0.10 / 9"x5" SAE) available from Bob Tait.

I: Lancashire

Anglezarke Amble

Lancs	34 km / 21 miles

Pioneered by the W Lancs group of the LDWA in the Spring of 1982, the route over the western edge of the Pennines climbs Rivington Pike and Winter Hill (at 1,489ft the highest point on the route) before passing Belmont, Turton and Entwistle Reservoirs. Moor- and farmland paths are followed to Anglezarke, Chorley and Yarrow Reservoirs before returning to Rivington.

Start and Finish	Rivington Hall Barn, Lancs	SD633144
OS maps	109	

Publication(s)
Looseleaf: *Anglezarke Amble* (Robert Waller). Free (+ SAE). Badge and certificate (£1.50 / - / A4 SAE) available from Robert Waller.

Anglezarke Anguish

Lancs	32 km / 20 miles

The walk is in the West Pennine Moors Country Park taking in Leverhulme Park and going over the seven-arched romanesque-style bridge. It passes Pidgeon Tower and Rivington Pike, walking alongside three reservoirs, over rough moorland to the village of White Coppice. It returns along the side of the reservoirs. There is an alternative 10-mile route.

Start and Finish	Rivington Hall Barn, Lancs	SD633144
OS maps	109	

Publication(s)
Looseleaf: *Anglezarke Anguish Walk* (Norman Thomas). Free (+ SAE). Badge and certificate (£1.50 / - / SAE) available from Norman Thomas.

Bowland-Pendle Challenge Trail

Lancs	85 km / 53 miles

The Trail circumnavigates the Ribble Valley AONB, and was devised as a 24-hour challenge walk, though it can also be walked in two days using one of three camping barns. It can also be linked with the Pendle Way to make a figure-of-eight 100-mile walk. From Whalley it passes anti-clockwise via Pendle Hill, Downham, Sawley, Slaidburn, Whitendale, Langden Castle and Chipping.

Start and Finish	Whalley, Lancs	SD732362
OS maps	102, 103	

Publication(s)
Booklet: *The Bowland-Pendle Challenge Trail* by John Dixon (Aussteiger Publications). ISBN: 1872764061. 1993 \ A5 \ 32pp \ £3.75. Badge and certificate (£1.50 / post free) available from Aussteiger Publications.

Cat Walk

Cumbria, Lancs	64 km / 40 miles

The Cat Walk, named after the three villages of Carnforth, Arnside and Tebay, was first planned in 1986 to mark the opening of youth hostels in Kendal and Tebay. Along with Arnside, these can make good overnight stops. There is nice scenery around the coastal areas of Silverdale and Arnside, and the route continues via Heversham Head, Scout Scar and Kendal, northwards to Meal Bank and the lovely Borrowdale Valley, before descending to the Lune Valley at Tebay.

Start	Carnforth Station, Lancs	SD497707
Finish	Tebay, Cumbria	SD617044
OS maps	90, 91, 97	

Publication(s)
Looseleaf: *Cat Walk* (Frank Hodson). Free (+ 9"x4" SAE). Badge and certificate (£1.00 / 9"x4" SAE / £0.50 / 9"x6" SAE) available from Frank Hodson.

Four Pikes Hike

Gtr Man, Lancs, W Yorks	72 km / 45 miles

The name comes from the four Pikes of Rivington, Hoglow, Thievely and Stoodley. The route heads in a north-east direction, first climbing Rivington Pike, and then crossing the moors and farmland of the west Pennines via the other three pikes before descending to Hebden Bridge.

Start	Great House Barn, Lancs	SD628139
Finish	Hebden Bridge, W Yorks	SD992272
OS maps	103, 109	

Publication(s)
Looseleaf: *The Four Pikes Hike* (Derek Magnall). Free (+ SAE). Badge and certificate (£1.50 / - / SAE) available from Derek Magnall.

Giraffe Walk

Cumbria	45 km / 28 miles

The route includes the famous Giraffe tree on Arnside Knott, and takes in Gatebeck Bridge, Icehouse Wood, Red Bridge, Arnside Tower, Far Arnside, Fairy Steps and Endmoor. A scenic route on footpaths and minor roads including woodland, parklands and some good viewpoints in a limestone area.

Start and Finish	Endmoor, Cumbria	SD543853
OS maps	97	

Publication(s)
Looseleaf: *Giraffe Walk* (Frank Hodson). Free (+ SAE). Badge and certificate (£1.00 / SAE / £0.50 / 9"x6" SAE) available from Frank Hodson.

Heart of Bowland Walk

Lancs, N Yorks	29 km / 18 miles

A varied circuit of moorland, steep-sided valleys, rivers and forests in the picturesque Forest of Bowland.

Start and Finish	Slaidburn, Lancs	SD712524
OS maps	103	

Publication(s)
Looseleaf: *Heart of Bowland Challenge Walk* (David Connelly). Free (+ SAE). Badge and certificate (£1.50 / - / 10"x8" SAE) available from David Connelly.

Hyndburn Clog

Lancs	50 km / 31 miles

Devised to commemorate the RA's 50th anniversary in 1985, the Clog describes a circular route around Accrington, loosely following the boundary of the borough of Hyndburn. It passes through various types of countryside from pastures to open moorland with extensive views. It runs over the moors to the south of the town to Haslingden, and then north to Hapton and Altham, before turning west to Dean Clough and Parsonage Reservoirs, and then south back to Oswaldtwistle.

Start and Finish	Oswaldtwistle, Lancs	SD723277
OS maps	103	

Publication(s)
Leaflet: *Hyndburn Clog* (JJ Allen). 1985 \ 148 x 210 \ £0.20 (+ 9"x6" SAE). Badge and certificate (£0.50 / £0.60 / 6"x4" SAE) available from JJ Allen.

Peel Trail

Gtr Man, Lancs	56 km / 35 miles

The Trail is basically two loops, one on each side of the Irwell Valley. The oblong route follows farmland and urban paths to the south and crosses moorland to the north. The Trail is named after Sir Robert Peel, one-time Prime Minister and founder of the Metropolitan Police, and in whose honour a tower was erected in 1852 on Holcombe Moor to the north of the valley. The route passes the tower, which is visible for much of the walk.

Start and Finish	Bury, Gtr Man	SD809123
OS maps	109	

Publication(s)
Leaflet: *The Peel Trail* (Michael Burton). Free (+ 9"x4" SAE). Badge
and certificate (£0.75 / - / C5 SAE) available from Michael Burton.

Pendle and Ribble Round

Lancs	32 km / 20 miles

A circuit crossing Pendle Hill and dropping down to Downham,
Lancashire's prettiest village, before returning by riverside and
farm paths to Whalley.

Start and Finish	Whalley, Lancs	SD732362
OS maps	103	

Publication(s)
Booklet: *Bronte Round / Pendle and Ribble Round* by Derek Magnall (Derek Magnall). 1994\A5\36pp\£1.50 (+ 35p). Badge and
certificate (£1.50 / - / SAE) available from Derek Magnall.

Pendle Marathon

Lancs	43 km / 27 miles

The Pendle Marathon was set up by YHA members in 1982 as a
route using hostels. There is a choice between a circular route, or
a linear route to Slaidburn. These are the same to Pendle Hill
summit, but the circular route returns by a different route to Earby.
There is plenty of good scenery and scenic paths on the route which
includes Foulridge and Barley. The area was made famous by the
association with witches.

Start and Finish	Earby YH, Lancs	SD915469
OS maps	103	

Publication(s)
Looseleaf: *Pendle Marathon* (Frank Hodson). Free (+ SAE). Badge
and certificate (£1.00 / £0.50 / SAE) available from Frank Hodson.

Pioneers Round

Gtr Man, Lancs	32 km / 20 miles

Devised in 1994 to mark the 150th anniversary of the founding of
the Co-operative Movement, this very easy walk starts from Toad
Lane, the birthplace of the movement. It runs through the urban
area, and then visits Healey Dell, leads over open moorland to
Watergrove Reservoir and Hollingworth Lake, and returns to
Rochdale via Milnrow and the Rochdale Canal.

Start and Finish	Rochdale, Gtr Man	SD896136

OS maps   109

Publication(s)
Booklet: *The Pioneers Round* by Derek Magnall (Rochdale Pioneers Museum). 1994\A5\34pp\£1.50 (+ 35p). Badge and certificate (£1.50 / - / SAE) available from Rochdale Pioneers Museum.

Promised Land

Lancs	32 km / 20 miles

This is a mainly flat walk taking in the local viewpoints of Billinge Hill and Ashurst Beacon which offer views over Liverpool, the Welsh Hills, and the Lancashire Plain to Southport and Blackpool. It continues through the farming area of the Promised Land.

Start and Finish	Orrell, Lancs	SD534056
OS maps	108	

Publication(s)
Looseleaf: *The Promised Land* (C Roby). Free (+ 9"x4" SAE). Badge and certificate (£1.50 / - / 9"x12" SAE) available from C Roby.

Ramsbottom Round

Lancs	32 km / 20 miles

A circuit around Ramsbottom. It runs across open moorland to the west and east of the town, crossing the Irwell Valley by riverside and farm paths via the villages of Irwell Vale and Summerseat.

Start and Finish	Ramsbottom, Lancs	SD792168
OS maps	103, 109	

Publication(s)
Booklet: *Ramsbottom Round / Spanners Round* (Derek Magnall). 1992\A5\36pp\£1.50 (+ 35p). Badge and certificate (£1.50 / - / SAE) available from Derek Magnall.

Silvarn Round

Cumbria, Lancs	40 km / 25 miles

A varied route following the boundary of the Arnside and Silverdale AONB, including coastal paths, woodland trails and limestone hills.

Start and Finish	Carnforth Station, Lancs	SD497707
OS maps	97	

Publication(s)
Looseleaf: *Silvarn Round* (Derek Esmond). Free (+ SAE). Badge
and certificate (£1.50 / - / SAE) available from Derek Esmond.

Spanners Round

Gtr Man, Lancs	32 km / 20 miles

A circuit across open moorland and along riverside and farmland
paths, linking three reservoirs of the old Bolton Water Authority
with three reservoirs of the former Irwell Valley Water Board (now
all controlled by North West Water).

Start and Finish	Jumbles Reservoir, Gtr Man	SD736139
OS maps	103, 109	

Publication(s)
Booklet: *Ramsbottom Round / Spanners Round* (Derek Magnall).
1992\A5\36pp\£1.50 (+ 35p). Badge and certificate (£1.50 / - /
SAE) available from Derek Magnall.

Three Towers Circuit

Gtr Man, Lancs	56 km / 35 miles

The name comes from the three towers of Peel, Rivington and
Darwen. The last was built in 1896 to commemorate the granting
of the freedom of the moor to the public, and the Peel Tower was
erected in 1851 in memory of Sir Robert Peel. This route provides
some good walking through the West Pennine Moors Country Park.
Although it is a fairly easy route, about half of it goes over moorland
and does need some map-reading skills.

Start and Finish	Tottington, Gtr Man	SD776129
OS maps	103, 109	

Publication(s)
Looseleaf: *Three Towers Circuit* (LDWA East Lancs Group). Free
(+ SAE). Badge and certificate (£0.90 / £0.10 / 9"x6" SAE) available
from LDWA East Lancs Group.

Two Crosses Circuit

Gtr Man, Lancs	40 km / 25 miles

The name comes from the Roman Cross and the medieval Pilgrims
Cross. From the start the route follows the same path as the Three
Towers Circuit, to the Roman Cross at Affetside, which is on the
Manchester to Ribchester Roman road. The path climbs to reach
Turton Tower, then on to pass the Turton and Entwistle Reservoir
before an easy climb up and around Bull Hill to the site of the

Pilgrims Cross. From here there is an easy descent through a golf course to the finish. This is a good walk through the West Pennine Moors Country Park. Although it is a fairly easy route, about half of it goes over moorland and does need some map-reading skills.

Start and Finish	Tottington, Gtr Man	SD776129
OS maps	109	

Publication(s)
Looseleaf: *Two Crosses Circuit* (LDWA East Lancs Group). Free (+ SAE). Badge and certificate (£0.90 / £0.10 / 9"x6" SAE) available from LDWA East Lancs Group.

Weavers Shuttle

Lancs	64 km / 40 miles

Aiming to take in the best paths and views in E Lancashire, the walk extends over open moorland and pastures in the Rossendale, Burnley and Pendle Districts and takes in many historical buildings and areas connected with the Industrial Revolution, Pendle witches and the Bronte Sisters. Items of interest range from an Iron Age clapper bridge to drovers' roads and canal towpaths. The walk was originally devised and established in 1983 by the Burnley Mountaineering Club.

Start and Finish	Worsthorne, Lancs	SD876324
OS maps	103	

Publication(s)
Looseleaf: *Weavers Shuttle* (Max Tattersall). Free (+ 9"x6" SAE). Badge and certificate (£1.00 / - / SAE) available from Max Tattersall.

Wide Awake Walk

Lancs	35 km / 22 miles

The route covers mixed terrain including tracks, roads and open moorland. It is set in the Forest of Bowland which is designated as an Area of Outstanding Natural Beauty. During the grouse-shooting season, the moorland part of the walk is closed to the public on various dates. These can be checked with Lancashire County Council (0772 254868) who have responsibility for the Bowland Access Areas. The walk can be done on any Sunday. There is an alternative route giving less road walking.

Start and Finish	Dolphinholme, Lancs	SD516534
OS maps	102	

Publication(s)
Looseleaf: *Wide Awake Walk* (Maxine Hogbin). Free (+ 9"x4" SAE).
Badge and certificate (£1.00 / - / SAE) available from Maxine
Hogbin.

Wigan Pier Walk

Gtr Man, Lancs	43 km / 27 miles

A relatively easy-going route around the south-west plains of
Lancashire giving an insight into the industrial heritage of the
area (mining and the cotton industry). It takes in woods and
farmland, Harrock Hill with superb views to the coast, and parts
of the Leeds and Liverpool canal. There are three variations in
length: 15, 27 and 32 miles.

Start and Finish	Wigan Pier, Gtr Man	SD577053
OS maps	108	

Publication(s)
Looseleaf: *Wigan Pier Walk* (R Dean). Free (+ 9"x4" SAE). Badge
and certificate (£1.50 / - / 12"x9" SAE) available from R Dean.

J: Canal Walks

Waterwitch "100"

Cumbria, Gtr Man, Lancs	160 km / 100 miles

100 miles of exploring canals. Set up in 1992 to commemorate the
bicentenary of the Lancaster Canal, and the centenary of Eccles as
a borough, the route starts in Eccles (with an Eccles cake), and
ends in Kendal (with Kendal mint cake). It joins the canal at
Barton Aqueduct, and runs through Worsley and Wigan to near
Chorley where it leaves the waterways (Walton Summit Branch is
no longer a canal) to Preston. Then it follows the Lancaster Canal
to Glasson Dock and Tewitfield, and the final very scenic 15 miles
to Kendal. The final stretch is closed to boats, but there are hopes
to restore it in the future. See also Lancaster Canal.

Start	Eccles, Gtr Man	SJ777983
Finish	Kendal, Canal Head, Cumbria	SD519917
OS maps	97, 102, 108, 109	

Publication(s)
Paperback: *Walking the Lancaster Canal* by Gay Quilter (Gay
Quilter). £5.90.
Looseleaf: *Waterwitch "100"* (Frank Hodson). Free (+ 9"x4" SAE).
Badge and certificate (£1.00 / 9"x4" SAE / £0.50 / 9"x6" SAE)
available from Frank Hodson.

K: The Peak District

Bell Walk Major

Derby, S Yorks	58 km / 36 miles

The Bell Walk links the churches of Dronfield, Old Whittington, Norton, Dore, Hathersage, Totley and Holmesfield, all of which have bells and a close association with Dronfield. It is full of interest and variety, and takes the walker through woodland, past a little industry, across fields, by historical sites, in parkland, over moorland, through villages, by riverside, into valleys and within easy reach of 50 pubs. It was devised and first walked by the Dronfield Parish Church Bellringers, hence the name.

Start and Finish	Dronfield, Derby	SK353784
OS maps	110, 119	

Publication(s)
Looseleaf: *Bell Walk Major* (Vic Cox). Free (+ A5 SAE). Badge and certificate (£2.00 / - / A5 SAE) available from Vic Cox.

Churnet Valley Challenge Walk

Staffs	39 km / 24 miles

This circular walk is set just outside the Peak District National Park, in and around the unspoilt Churnet Valley. The route includes the old Staffordshire villages of Ipstones, Kingsley, Alton, Farley and Oakamoor; a small section of the restored Caldon Canal and part of the popular Staffordshire Way are two of the highlights of the walk. With 2,600ft of ascent, the walk can be completed within 12 hours without difficulty.

Start and Finish	Froghall, Staffs	SK027476
OS maps	119	

Publication(s)
Looseleaf: *Churnet Valley Challenge Walk* (Alan S Edwards). Free (+ SAE). Certificate (£0.30 / Large SAE) available from Alan S Edwards.

Cloud 7 Circuit

Cheshire, Staffs	53 km / 33 miles

Cloud 7 is so termed because there are seven hills called Cloud: Hen Cloud, five Clouds on The Roaches, and The Cloud by Congleton. The circuit covers an area between Leek, Buxton, Macclesfield and Congleton. The route is fairly tough with ascents of Hen Cloud, The Roaches, Shutlingsloe, Shining Tor, Teggs Nose, Croker Hill,

The Cloud , and Gun Hill, 5,400ft in total. There are two distances, 28 and 33 miles, and the walk can be started from any point.

Start and Finish	Roaches lay-by, Staffs	SK004621
OS maps	118, 119	

Publication(s)
Leaflet: *Cloud 7 Circuit* (Derek Nash). 1989\A4\Free (+ SAE). Badge and certificate (£1.30 / £0.50 / SAE) available from Derek Nash.

Dane Valley Circular

Cheshire, Derby, Staffs	38 km / 24 miles

The circular route on the Staffs/Cheshire border on the western edge of the Peak District is of a "Three Peaks" format taking in the summits of The Roaches (1,656ft), Shutlingsloe (1,659ft) and the excellent viewpoint of Gun Hill at 1,263ft. Other points of interest are Lud's church, a fantastic geological fault and place of worship of the 14th century Lollards, the packhorse bridge and panniers pool at Three Shire Heads, and the quaintly situated Macclesfield Forest Chapel. The route passes five pubs of which the "Cat and Fiddle" is the second highest in England.

Start and Finish	Meerbrook, Staffs	SJ990608
OS maps	118, 119	

Publication(s)
Looseleaf: *Dane Valley Circular* (J F Eardley). Free. Badge and certificate (£1.50 / £0.50 / SAE) available from J F Eardley.

Dark Peak Challenge Walk

Derby	38 km / 24 miles

This is a demanding high-level circular walk taking in Stanage Edge, Derwent Edge, Back Tor, Derwent Reservoir, Win Hill and Bamford. There is a total of 3,300ft of ascent.

Start and Finish	Hathersage, Derby	SK232815
OS maps	119	

Publication(s)
Paperback: *John Merrill's Dark Peak Challenge Walk* by John Merrill (Trail Crest Publications Ltd). ISBN: 0907496660. 1988\134 x 210\32pp\£2.95. Badge and certificate (£2.75 / post free) available from Trail Crest Publications Ltd.

Dunford Round

S Yorks	36 km / 23 miles

One of a series of five walks devised by Dunford Parish Council as part of their Parish Paths Partnership scheme. The route passes anti-clockwise via Crowedge and Dunford Bridge.

Start and Finish	Flouch Inn, S Yorks	SE197016
OS maps	110	

Publication(s)
Folder: *Dunford Parish Footpaths* (Allen Pestell). 1993\A4/3\5pp\£1.00.

Gritstone Edge Walk

Derby, S Yorks	43 km / 27 miles

Linear walk running generally downhill along the eastern edge system of the Peak District, taking in Derwent, Stanage, Burbage, Froggatt, Baslow and Chatsworth Edges.

Start	Flouch Inn, S Yorks	SE197016
Finish	Baslow, Derby	SK256725
OS maps	110, 119	

Publication(s)
Paperback: *Peak District End to End Walks* by John Merrill (Trail Crest Publications Ltd). ISBN: 0907496393. 1988\140 x 210\52pp\£2.75. Badge and certificate (£2.75 / post free) available from Trail Crest Publications Ltd.

High Peak Way

Derby, S Yorks	45 km / 28 miles

A tough walk including 6,500ft of ascent, set in the High Peak, which should not be attempted during the winter months. Transport is easy, as the start and finish points are both on the main Manchester/Sheffield rail route. The paths are easy to follow, but the moorland should be treated with respect in adverse conditions. Two villages are visited: Hope and Hathersage, where inns provide refreshment. The route also includes the Great Ridge between Mam Tor and Lose Hill – possibly the best 2 miles of "views" in the Peak District.

Start	Chinley, Derby	SK038826
Finish	Padley, Derby	SK251788
OS maps	109, 110, 119	

Publication(s)
Booklet: *The High Peak Way* (Alan S Edwards). 20pp\Free (+ A5 SAE). Badge and certificate (£2.25 / post free) available from Alan S Edwards.

Highlow Historic Hike

Derby	40 km / 25 miles

A tough walk in the north-eastern corner of the Peak District National Park. Terrain varies from the wild windswept moorland of White Edge and Offerton Moor to delightful stretches of the river Derwent, finishing at the stately splendour of Chatsworth Park. Nine pubs, tearooms, and many places of historical interest are passed en route.

Start and Finish	Baslow, Derby	SK256725
OS maps	110, 119	

Publication(s)
Looseleaf: *Highlow Historic Hike* (J F Eardley). Free (+ SAE). Badge and certificate (£1.50 / £0.50 / SAE) available from J F Eardley.

Limestone Dale Walk

Derby, S Yorks	39 km / 24 miles

Linear walk running north-south through the limestones dales of the White Peak, via Cunning, Woo, Deep and Horseshoe Dales to Earl Sterndale, and then Dovedale to Hartington, Milldale and Mapleton.

Start	Buxton, Derby	SK060735
Finish	Ashbourne, Derby	SK178469
OS maps	119, 128	

Publication(s)
Paperback: *Peak District End to End Walks* by John Merrill (Trail Crest Publications Ltd). ISBN: 0907496393. 1988\140 x 210\52pp\£2.75. Badge and certificate (£2.75 / post free) available from Trail Crest Publications Ltd.

Pride of the Peak Walk

Derby	48 km / 30 miles

This walk was produced in 1991, to commemorate the 40th anniversary of the Peak District National Park. The circular route provides a look at the wide variety of scenery to be found within the Peak District – limestone dales, gritstone edges, woodland, and several Derbyshire villages: Sheldon, Wardlow, Rowland, Hassop, Calver, Froggatt, Baslow and Edensor. Some of the area's finest historical features are also visited, including the Monsal Viaduct, Cressbrook Mill, and Chatsworth House, home of the Duke of Devonshire. It is quite a tough day out, with 3,700ft of ascent.

Start and Finish	Bakewell, Derby	SK217685
OS maps	119	

Publication(s)
Booklet: *Pride of the Peak Walk* by Alan S Edwards (Alan S Edwards). 1991\A5\30pp\£2.55. Badge and certificate (£2.25 / post free) available from Alan S Edwards.

Staffordshire Moorlands Challenge Walk

Staffs	38 km / 24 miles

A circular walk from the Churnet Valley, involving 2,000ft of ascent, the route takes in Froghall Wharf, the Weaver Hills, Ordley Dale, Alton and Ousal Dale.

Start and Finish	Oakamoor, Staffs	SK053448
OS maps	128	

Publication(s)
Paperback: *John Merrill's Staffordshire Moorlands Challenge Walk* by John Merrill (Trail Crest Publications Ltd). ISBN: 0907496679. 1988\137 x 210\32pp\£2.45. Badge and certificate (£2.75 / post free) available from Trail Crest Publications Ltd.

Three Counties Challenge Walk

Cheshire, Derby, Staffs	45 km / 28 miles

Tough moorland route straggling the borders of Cheshire, Staffordshire and Derbyshire in the Peak District. It runs via The Roaches, Shutlingsloe, Tegg's Nose, Shining Edge and Three Shires Head.

Start and Finish	Tittesworth Reservoir, Staffs	SJ994605
OS maps	118, 119	

Publication(s)
Paperback: *Three Counties Challenge Walk* by John Merrill (Trail Crest Publications Ltd). ISBN: 1874754152. 1993\210 x 130\32pp\£2.95. Badge and certificate (£2.75 / post free) available from Trail Crest Publications Ltd.

Three Feathers Walk (Yorkshire Bridge)

Derby, S Yorks	45 km / 28 miles

The Three Feathers Walks are a series of three walks each set in a different national park. To qualify for a badge, all the routes must be completed within a calendar year. Each is a circular walk, and they may be completed in any order. The three routes are set in the Yorkshire Dales (Kettlewell), the N York Moors (Kilburn) and the Peak District (Yorkshire Bridge). All routes are arduous and must be planned accordingly.

Start and Finish	Yorkshire Bridge, Derby	SK201850
OS maps	110	

Publication(s)
Looseleaf: *Three Feathers Walks* (Keith Bown). A4\Free (+ SAE). Badge (£1.50) available from Keith Bown.

Three Reservoirs Challenge

Derby, S Yorks	40 km / 25 miles

A strenuous and varied day's walking around the reservoirs of the upper Derwent. Situated in the north Derbyshire Peak District, the Upper Derwent Valley is an Area of Outstanding Natural Beauty flanked by high Gritstone Edges; the steep-sided valley contains one of the most spectacular reservoir systems in central England.

Start and Finish	Ladybower, Derby	SK205865
OS maps	110	

Publication(s)
Paperback: *The Three Reservoirs Challenge* (Mountain Peaks Climbing Club). A5\20pp\£2.40 (+ 30p). Certificate (£0.20 / A4 SAE) available from Mountain Peaks Climbing Club.

White Peak Challenge Walk

Derby	40 km / 25 miles

A strenuous circular challenge walk in the Peak National Park. The route follows the most rugged parts of the Peak, passing via Rowsley, Birchover, Youlgreave, Monyash, Flagg, Taddington and Great Longstone.

Start and Finish	Bakewell, Derby	SK217685
OS maps	119	

Publication(s)
Paperback: *John Merrill's White Peak Challenge Walk* by John Merrill (Trail Crest Publications Ltd). ISBN: 0907496776. 1988\134 x 210\32pp\£2.45. Badge and certificate (£2.75 / post free) available from Trail Crest Publications Ltd.

White Peak Rollercoaster

Derby, Staffs	38 km / 24 miles

This circular walk is set in the southern part of the Peak District National Park, and based around the Dove, Hamps and Manifold valleys. Many "picture postcard" scenes are visited, including Dovedale, Thors Cave, and Wetton Mill; the route starts in Alstonefield, and includes the villages of Milldale, Ilam, Grindon, Wetton, Butterton and Warslow. A fairly tough day out with numerous ascents and descents (a total of 4,500ft of climbing).

Start and Finish	Alstonefield, Staffs	SK131556
OS maps	119	

Publication(s)
Looseleaf: *White Peak Rollercoaster* (Alan S Edwards). A4\4pp\ Free (+ SAE). Badge and certificate (£2.00 / post free) available from Alan S Edwards.

L: North Wales

Open to Offa's

Clwyd	45 km / 28 miles

Based in the Moel Fammau AONB, this circuit with 5,900ft of ascent takes in a wide variety of terrain from fields and woodlands to limestone escarpments and hilltop forts.

Start and Finish	Cilcain, Clwyd	SJ176652
OS maps	116	

Publication(s)
Looseleaf: *Open to Offa's* (Paul Miller). Free (+ 9"x4" SAE). Badge and certificate (£1.50 / - / 1st class) available from Paul Miller.

Snowdon Challenge Walk

Gwynedd	48 km / 30 miles

5,000ft of ascent to the top of Snowdon and back, this is a tough day's walk. From Caernarvon Bay, it climbs via Penygroes and the Ranger Path, and then descends again via the Rhyd-ddu path.

Start and Finish	Pontllyfni, Gwynedd	SH435526
OS maps	115	

Publication(s)
Paperback: *John Merrill's Snowdon Challenge Walk* by John Merrill (Trail Crest Publications Ltd). ISBN: 0907496792. 1992\210 x 130\40pp\£2.95. Badge and certificate (£2.75 / post free) available from Trail Crest Publications Ltd.

Snowdonia 24hr Circuit

Gwynedd	72 km / 45 miles

A tough rollercoaster-type circuit of approx 16,500ft of ascent, which includes the Snowdon Horseshoe, Glyders, Carneddau and Moel Siabod massifs. Can be started at Capel Curig, Pen-y-Pass, Nant Peris or Ogwen, and can be walked in either direction.

Start and Finish	Capel Curig, Gwynedd	SH721583
OS maps	115	

Publication(s)
Looseleaf: *Snowdonia 24hr Circuit* (E Dalton). Free (+ 9"x4" SAE). Certificate (- / 9"x6" SAE) available from E Dalton.

Snowdonia Panoramic Walk

Gwynedd	48 km / 30 miles

A high-level strenuous walk with approx 12,500ft of ascent, running over ridge paths of Snowdonia, including the summits of Carnedd Llewelyn (Carneddau, 1,062m) and Snowdon (1,085m), and finishing over the seven peaks of the beautiful Nantlle ridge.

Start	Aber, Gwynedd	SH662720
Finish	Nebo, Gwynedd	SH479505
OS maps	115	

Publication(s)
Leaflet: *Snowdonia Panoramic Walk* (E Dalton). 1987\A4\£1.50 (+ 9"x6" SAE). Certificate (- / 9"x6" SAE) available from E Dalton.

Welsh 3000s Double Crossing

Gwynedd	87 km / 54 miles

First promoted in 1981 as an open challenge walk, operating between May and the end of September and demanding a very high level of physical fitness and navigational ability, this is a double crossing of the classic Welsh 3000s route with 28 summits, including Snowdon, Crib Goch, the Glyders, Tryfan and the Carneddau and over 25,000ft of ascent. Certificates are available for completion within 32 hours. In the interests of safety, no solo attempts are acceptable and walkers must notify the organiser of intended crossings at least two weeks in advance.

Ed Dalton's version includes 15 peaks, rather than the 14 included in Peter Travis's original.

Start and Finish	Llyn Anafon, Gwynedd	SH699699
OS maps	115	

Publication(s)
Looseleaf: *Welsh 3000s Double Crossing* (E Dalton). Free (+ 9"x4" SAE).
Looseleaf: *Welsh 3000s Double Crossing* (P Travis). Free (+ 9"x4" SAE). Certificate (£1.00 post free) available from P Travis.

M: East Midlands
Belmont 30

Lincs	48 km / 30 miles

A good testing walk taking in some of Lincolnshire's finest Wolds views, and passing through many small hamlets and villages. It also gives an insight into the Lincolnshire farming industry. At the time of going to press, an alternative 25-mile route is being written.

Start and Finish	Tetford, Lincs	TF334746
OS maps	122	

Publication(s)
Looseleaf: *Belmont 30* (Mike Surr). Free (+ SAE). Badge (£1.50 / SAE) available from Mike Surr.

Caistor Challenge

Lincs	40 km / 25 miles

This walk through rural Lincolnshire gives an insight into the history of the county through the eight churches on which the route is based, together with farming and forestry. There are some very scenic views of the Lincolnshire Wolds.

Start and Finish	Caistor, Lincs	TA117013
OS maps	113	

Publication(s)
Looseleaf: *Caistor Challenge* (Mike Surr). Free (+ SAE). Badge and certificate (£1.40 / £0.10 / SAE) available from Mike Surr.

Charnwood Forest Challenge Walk

Leics	40 km / 25 miles

A circular walk around the hill country to the north-east of Leicester. It passes Newtown Lifford, Ulverscroft Priory, Bardon Hill, Mount St Bernard Abbey, Beacon Hill and Woodhouse Eaves.

Start and Finish	Bradgate Park, Leics	SK543114
OS maps	129	

Publication(s)
Paperback: *Charnwood Forest Challenge Walk* by John Merrill (Trail Crest Publications Ltd). ISBN: 0907496644. 1992\132 x 210\32pp\£2.50. Badge and certificate (£2.75 / post free) available from Trail Crest Publications Ltd.

Hardwick Hobble

Derby, Notts	45 km / 28 miles

The route follows both well-used and unused footpaths. The views into the Derbyshire Peak District are very good on clear days, and Hardwick Park is full of history with many interesting features.

Start and Finish	Mansfield, Notts	SK527619
OS maps	120	

Publication(s)
Looseleaf: *Hardwick Hobble* (South Normanton Walking Club). £1.00 (+ 9"x4" SAE). Certificate (- / 9"x6" SAE) available from South Normanton Walking Club.

Little John Challenge Walk

Notts	45 km / 28 miles

A circular walk through Sherwood Forest, the heart of Robin Hood country, which includes forests, gorges, meandering rivers and historic houses, and passes Church Warsop, Cuckney, Cresswell Crags, Clumber Park, Bothamsall and Ollerton.

Start and Finish	Edwinstowe, Notts	SK626669
OS maps	120	

Publication(s)
Paperback: *The Little John Challenge Walk* by John Merrill (Trail Crest Publications Ltd). ISBN: 0907496466. 1986\132 x 210\32pp\£2.25. Badge and certificate (£2.75 / post free) available from Trail Crest Publications Ltd.

Rutland Water Challenge Walk

Leics	38 km / 24 miles

Clockwise circular route around the largest man-made reservoir in Europe.

Start and Finish	Rutland Water, Leics	SK935083
OS maps	141	

Publication(s)
Paperback: *The Rutland Water Challenge Walk* by John Merrill (Trail Crest Publications Ltd). ISBN: 0907496881. 36pp \ £2.95. Badge and certificate (£2.75 / post free) available from Trail Crest Publications Ltd.

Six Shires Circuit

Beds, Bucks, Cambs, Leics, Lincs, Northants	330 km / 206 miles

This large circuit links the Nene, Torpel, Ermine Street, Roman, Spaldwick, Three Shires, Grafton and Knightley Ways into 15 sections to form one circular route. The price for the publication includes 15 certificates.

Start and Finish	Wellingborough, Northants	SP888683
OS maps	141, 142, 152, 153	

Publication(s)
Booklet: *Six Shires Circuit* (Waendel Walkers Club). £10.00. Badge (£2.50 / A5 SAE) available from Waendel Walkers Club.

Tennyson Twenty

Lincs	32 km / 20 miles

The route circles the village of Somersby, birthplace of Alfred, Lord Tennyson, Victorian Poet Laureate. It passes through some of the finest scenery in the Lincolnshire Wolds – an Area of Outstanding Natural Beauty. The walk passes many small isolated villages and deserted hamlets as well as a nature reserve, a pottery and four pubs. There are no really long or steep climbs, but enough ups and downs to test the walker and give marvellous views over to the coast.

Start and Finish	Hagworthingham, Lincs	TF344696
OS maps	122	

Publication(s)
Looseleaf: *Tennyson Twenty* (Martyn Bishop). Free (+ SAE). Badge and certificate (£1.50 / post free) available from Martyn Bishop.

Vermuyden Way

Humberside	32 km / 20 miles

The Vermuyden Way, created by the county council, is now run by the Vermuyden group of the LDWA, and follows an elongated circuit over the rich arable land and along many of the artificial water courses, or drains, of the Isle of Axholme. The first half of the walk is over what was, until the 17th century, marshland and fen. Dutch drainage engineer Cornelius Vermuyden was commissioned by King Charles I to drain it in 1626 and did so in spite of much local opposition. The second half is across the low hills of the Isle which stood proud of the wetlands flooded by the rivers Trent, Idle, Torn and Don. It passes Epworth Rectory, birthplace of John Wesley.

Start and Finish	Belton, Humberside	SE782054
OS maps	112	
Waymark	Stickers with "VW"	

Publication(s)
Folder: *Boothferry Explorer* (Humberside County Council). 1992 \ A5 \ £2.00 (+ 30p).
Looseleaf: *Vermuyden Way* (Frank Lawson). Free (+ 9"x4" SAE).
Badge and certificate (£1.00 / - / 10"x7" SAE) available from Frank Lawson.

N: Shropshire and Worcestershire

Abberley Amble

Heref & Worc	32 km / 20 miles

The Amble goes in the opposite direction to the Alpine Walk that also starts from Bewdley, so by linking the two you have a very tough 40-miler. It runs over mixed terrain, with ascents, descents, woods, valleys, brooks and rivers. It passes Tickenhill, Snuffmill, Golden Valley, Deasland, Joans Hills, Glasshamton Monastery, The Burf (a cider house), the river Severn, Ribbesford Woods and returns to Bewdley via Grubbers Alley.

Start and Finish	Bewdley, Heref & Worc	SO788754
OS maps	138	

Publication(s)
Leaflet: *Abberley Amble* (Eric Perks). 1989 \ A4 \ £0.75 (+ 9"x6" SAE). Badge and certificate (£1.75 / - / 9"x6" SAE) available from Eric Perks.

Carpet Baggers 50

Heref & Worc, Salop, Staffs	80 km / 50 miles

From the Brintons Sports Centre in Oldington, the route passes first through the riverside town of Bewdley, then along the Severn valley before climbing into Seckley Wood. Descending, the route goes past the Severn Valley station at Arley, then crossing the old miners bridge at Highley, it reaches the village of Arveley. Following lanes and footpaths, it then goes through the villages of Claverley, Seisdon and Trysull before ascending Abbot's Hill. Turning south on the Staffs Way, it reaches the picturesque village of Enville before climbing over Kinver Edge and descending via the wooded areas of Arley and Eymore Wood back to the river Severn.

Start and Finish	Brintons, Oldington, Heref & Worc	SO815736
OS maps	138	

Publication(s)
Looseleaf: *Carpet Baggers 50* (Eric Perks). £0.75 (+ 9"x6" SAE). Badge and certificate (£1.00 / - / 9"x6" SAE) available from Eric Perks.

Chaddesley Chase

Heref & Worc	35 km / 22 miles

From the picturesque village of Chaddesley Corbett the walk heads east across open fields to Chaddesley, Santery Hill, Nutnells and High Woods, giving outstanding views. Entering the Dartford area, the route follows streams and country lanes across farmland to Pepper Wood and Fairfield, Belbroughton, Drayton and Hillpool Mill (formerly the Brintons Carpet Mill). It returns to the start via Blakedown and the moated Harvington Hall.

Start and Finish	Chaddesley Corbett, Heref & Worc	SO892736
OS maps	138, 139	

Publication(s)
Looseleaf: *Chaddesley Chase* (Eric Perks). £0.75 (+ 9"x6" SAE). Badge and certificate (£1.00 / - / 9"x6" SAE) available from Eric Perks.

Kinver Clamber

Heref & Worc, Staffs	32 km / 20 miles

From the edge of the Black Country, this circular walk uses forestry tracks, canal paths, open fieldpaths and ridge paths. It passes Enville with its Hall, Kinver Edge with its rock dwellings, Caunsall and Whittingham. It picks up the Roman Road to return to Stourbridge.

Start and Finish	Stourbridge, Heref & Worc	SO882840
OS maps	138, 139	

Publication(s)
Looseleaf: *Kinver Clamber* (Eric Perks). £0.75 (+ 9"x6" SAE). Badge and certificate (£1.00 / - / 9"x6" SAE) available from Eric Perks.

Malvern Hills Challenge Walk

Heref & Worc	32 km / 20 miles

Involving 3,000ft of ascent, this walk around the Malvern Hills heads south via Little Malvern on the lower slopes and returns north along the ridge.

Start and Finish	Old Wyche, Malvern, Heref & Worc	SO773442
OS maps	150	

Publication(s)
Paperback: *The Malvern Hills Challenge Walk* by John Merrill (Trail Crest Publications Ltd). ISBN: 0907496954. 32pp\£2.95. Badge and certificate (£2.75 / post free) available from Trail Crest Publications Ltd.

Mini-Alps

Heref & Worc	32 km / 20 miles

From the Old Wyche, the route goes north over Worcestershire Beacon and North Hill, descends to Old Hollow, and then turns west to Six Acre Wood. It then turns north to Whithams Hill, south to Limbridge Wood, Weobley Cross and Colwall. Continuing southeast on fieldpaths, it heads for Hatfield Coppice and climbs up to Herefordshire Beacon, where it follows the ridge path north to the Malvern Hills Hotel and the start.

Start and Finish	Old Wyche, Malvern, Heref & Worc	SO773442
OS maps	149, 150	

Publication(s)
Looseleaf: *Mini-Alps* (Eric Perks). £0.75 (+ 9"x6" SAE). Badge and certificate (£1.00 / - / 9"x6" SAE) available from Eric Perks.

Severn Valley Way

Heref & Worc, Salop	50 km / 31 miles

In 1980, to celebrate its 50th anniversary and the opening of Ironbridge Youth Hostel, the Wolverhampton Rambling Club held an organised challenge walk along the Severn valley, and this has been an annual event ever since. It follows rights of way from Stourport through Bewdley, Upper Arley, Hampton Loade and Bridgnorth to the finish at Coalbrookdale. At Ironbridge there is the famous Abraham Darby ironbridge and the Ironbridge Gorge museum, with relics of the birth of the Industrial Revolution.

Start	Stourport-on-Severn, Heref & Worc	SO808709
Finish	Ironbridge, Salop	SJ671043
OS maps	127, 138	

Publication(s)
Looseleaf: *The Severn Valley Way* (Wolverhampton Rambling Club). A4 \ 1pp \ Free (+ SAE).

Shropshire Challenge Walk

Salop	122 km / 76 miles

The Walk links five youth hostels at Ludlow, Wheathill, Wilderhope Manor, Bridges and Clun, all in the lovely South Shropshire Hills. It climbs the Long Mynd, the Clees, Caer Caradoc and Wenlock Edge, and is partly coincident with the Shropshire Way. The terrain is a mixture of moorland, field paths, tracks and roads.

Start and Finish	Ludlow, Salop	SO510745
OS maps	137, 138	

Publication(s)
Paperback: *Shropshire Challenge Walk* (Youth Hostels Association). 147 x 210 \ £0.50.

Six Shropshire Summits

Powys, Salop	56 km / 35 miles

This extremely scenic route over the six hills in Shropshire that are over 1,500ft high was pioneered in 1962 by Vivian Bird OBE, a feature writer on the Sunday Mercury. The walk can be done in either direction using any chosen route, but each of the trig points on Corndon, Brown Clee, Long Mynd, Stiperstones, Titterstone Clee, and the cairn on Caer Caradoc must be touched. A badge and certificate are available if the walk is completed in more than eight hours.

Start	Corndon Hill, Salop	SO301971
Finish	Clee Hill, Salop	SO594771
OS maps	137	

Publication(s)
Looseleaf: *Six Shropshire Summits* (Vivian Bird OBE). A4 \ 1pp \
Free (+ SAE). Badge and certificate (£0.60 / - / SAE) available from
Vivian Bird OBE.

Wyre Forest Alpine Walk

Heref & Worc		32 km / 20 miles

A circular walk in the Wyre Forest district of Worcestershire, the
route encircles the Severn Valley and is always within sound of the
Severn Valley Railway. The walk is quite demanding, as it seeks
out all the climbs and viewpoints. It therefore requires a good
standard of fitness.

Start and Finish	Bewdley, Heref & Worc	SO788754
OS maps	138	

Publication(s)
Looseleaf: *Wyre Forest Alpine Walk* (Eric Perks). £0.75 (+ 9"x6"
SAE). Badge and certificate (£1.00 / - / 9"x6" SAE) available from
Eric Perks.

O: East Anglia

Daffodil Dawdle

Cambs		42 km / 26 miles

A circular route linking villages to the south-west of Cambridge.

Start and Finish	Cambridge, Mill Lane, Cambs	TL447581
OS maps	154	

Publication(s)
Looseleaf: *Daffodil Dawdle* (John Searle). Free (+ SAE). Badge and
certificate (£1.25 / - / A4 SAE) available from John Searle.

Flower of Suffolk

Suffolk		42 km / 26 miles

A circular route using coastal and heathland paths. There is also
a choice of shorter 10- and 17-mile circuits.

Start and Finish	Walberswick, Suffolk	TM498746

OS maps   156

Publication(s)
Looseleaf: *Flower of Suffolk* (John Searle). Free (+ 9"x4" SAE).
Badge and certificate (£1.25 / - / A4 SAE) available from John
Searle.

Poppyline Marathon

Norfolk	42 km / 26 miles

An undulating route in North Norfolk, which includes inland paths
and parts of the North Norfolk Coast Path.

Start and Finish	Sheringham, Norfolk	TG159430
OS maps	133	

Publication(s)
Looseleaf: *Poppyline Marathon* (John Searle). A4\1pp\Free (+
SAE). Badge and certificate (£1.25 / - / A4 SAE) available from John
Searle.

P: Mid and South Wales
Gower Gallop

W Glam	39 km / 24 miles

Arranged by Swansea Outdoor Group, there are two routes to the
Gower Gallop. The 24-mile "A" route crosses Cefn Bryn to Hardings
Down, descends to Port Eynon Bay and then returns back along
the coast to Pennard. The 19-mile "B" walk cuts down from Cefn
Bryn to Port Eynon, otherwise the route is the same as "A".

Start and Finish	Pennard, W Glam	SS553882
OS maps	159	

Publication(s)
Looseleaf: *The Gower Gallop* (Rob Lewis). Free (+ C6 SAE). Certificate (- / A4 SAE) available from Rob Lewis.

Red Kite Trail

Dyfed, Powys	119 km / 74 miles

The southern Cambrian Mountains are one of the largest areas of
magnificent wilderness left in England and Wales. These routes
between four towns (Llanwrtyd Wells, Tregaron, Rhayader and
Pumsaint) have been devised to traverse the best of this area and
enable the walker to see the scenery of lakes and mountains which
conceals the home of the red kite and other rare birds of prey. The

route is composed of four legs between (hotel) checkpoints of approximately 16-22 miles (you devise your own route). Good navigational skills are required.

Start and Finish	Llanwrtyd Wells, Powys	SN879467
OS maps	146, 147	

Publication(s)
Looseleaf: *Red Kite Trail* (Neuadd Arms Hotel). A4/3 \ Free (+ SAE). Badge and certificate (£2.00 / SAE / - / A4 SAE) available from Neuadd Arms Hotel.

Q: Surrey
North to South Surrey Walk

Berks, Surrey	64 km / 40 miles

This Walk, from Surrey's most northerly point to its most southerly, was pioneered by the Surrey Group of the LDWA in 1976. It shows the variety of Surrey's countryside, starting by the flooded gravel pits in earshot of Heathrow, and passing via Runnymede Memorial, Windsor Park, Chobham Common, through woods and fields to the west of Guildford, and by more wooded commons, over Gibbet Hill to finish by the edge of Blackdown.

Start	Colnbrook, Berks	TQ030771
Finish	Haslemere edge, Surrey	SU914312
OS maps	176, 186	

Publication(s)
Looseleaf: *North-South Surrey* (Keith Chesterton). A4 \ Free (+ SAE).

R: Wiltshire
Old Sarum Challenge

Wilts	40 km / 25 miles

A circular route from Amesbury over chalk downland linking Old Sarum and intervening villages.

Start and Finish	Amesbury, Wilts	SU161417
OS maps	184	

Publication(s)
Looseleaf: *Old Sarum Challenge* (Richard Archard). Free (+ 9"x6" SAE). Badge and certificate (£1.00 / £0.50 / 9"x6" SAE) available from Richard Archard.

S: Devon and Cornwall

Land's End Round

Cornwall	80 km / 50 miles

A walk combining coastal scenery with an attractive rural link to create a challenging circuit. Starting from Mousehole on the south Cornish coast, the route crosses the county to the north coast at St Ives. The SW Coast Path is then followed around Land's End back to Mousehole.

Start and Finish	Mousehole, Cornwall	SW470264
OS maps	203	

Publication(s)
Looseleaf: *The Land's End Round* (Dave and Anne Carrivick). A4 \ Free (+ 9"x4" SAE). Certificate (£1.00 post free) available from Dave and Anne Carrivick.

Sidmouth Saunter

Devon	40 km / 25 miles

A circuit combining coastal footpath and picturesque E Devon scenery. There is also a shorter 13-mile route.

Start and Finish	Sidmouth, Army Cadet Hut, Devon	ST128872
OS maps	192	

Publication(s)
Looseleaf: *Sidmouth Saunter* (Terry Bound). Free (+ SAE). Badge and certificate (£1.00 / - / A4 SAE) available from Terry Bound.

ROUTES BY DISTANCE

Path	Miles	Km	Page
South West Coast Path	600	960	126-127
Ulster Way	570	912	148
Pennine Bridleway	313	500	107
Southern Coast to Coast Walk	283	453	128
Cambrian Way	274	438	19
Alternative Pennine Way	268	429	8
Pennine Way	251	402	108-109
Macmillan Way	227	363	86
Midshires Way	225	360	91
Snowdonia to the Gower	222	355	123
Thames Path	213	341	140
Southern Upland Way	213	340	128-129
London Countryway	206	330	84-85
Six Shires Circuit	206	330	212
Marches Way	204	326	87
Trans Pennine Trail	200	320	144
Westmorland Heritage Walk	200	320	163
Fife Interbus Walks	191	306	48
Coast to Coast Walk	190	304	27
Pembrokeshire Coast Path	183	292	106-107
Tarka Trail	181	290	137
Offa's Dyke Path	178	285	100-101
Westmorland Boundary Way	171	274	162
Sarn Helen	160	256	118-119
Hospice Coast to Coast	154	246	65
Sussex Border Path	152	243	134-135
Reivers Way	150	240	111
Settle to Carlisle Walk	150	240	120-121
West Yorkshire Way	150	240	162
Lakeland Fringe	147	235	74
Around the Lakes	145	232	10
Teesdale Way	144	230	138
North Downs Way	142	227	97
Grand Union Canal Walk	141	225	53
Harcamlow Way	141	225	59
Saxon Shore Way	141	225	119
Viking Way	141	225	151
Shropshire Way	140	224	122-123
Wessex Ridgeway	137	219	159
Greater Manchester Boundary Walk	130	208	54
Thirlmere Way	130	208	140-141
Leeds and Liverpool Canal	127	203	79
Cumbria Coastal Way	125	200	32
Round Northmavine Trek	125	200	115

List of Routes by Distance

Path	Miles	Km	Page
Trent Valley Way	84	135	145
Centenary Way (North Yorkshire)	83	133	20
Cotswolds	83	133	30-31
Eskdale Way	83	132	46
Fife Coast Path	82	131	48
Dales Way	81	130	33
Essex Way	81	130	46
Apostles Walk	80	128	179
Cumberland Way	80	128	32
Wealdway	80	128	157
White Peak Way	80	128	164
Wolds Way	79	127	166
Dark Peak Boundary Walk	78	125	35
Weardale Way	78	125	158
Angles Way	78	124	9
Eden Way	78	124	44
Shropshire Challenge Walk	76	122	216
Hadrian's Wall Walk	75	120	58
Vectis Trail	75	120	150
Red Kite Trail	74	119	218
Barnsley Boundary Walk	74	118	13
Kirklees Way	73	116	71
North Wales Coastal Footpath	73	116	98
Ribble Way	73	116	112
Jack Mytton Way	72	115	69
Lancashire Trail	71	113	75
Wayfarer's Walk	71	113	156
Cumbria Way	70	112	32-33
Ebor Way	70	112	42-43
West Lakes Way	70	112	161
Swan's Way	68	108	135
Severn Way	66	105	121
d'Arcy Dalton Way	65	104	33
Isle of Wight Coastal Footpath	65	104	68
Oxfordshire Way	65	104	103
Oxfordshire Trek	64	103	103
Great Glen Way	63	100	54
Round Unst Trek	63	100	116-117
Vanguard Way	63	100	149
Black and White Village Trail	62	99	14-15
Best of Lakeland	60	96	14
Furness Trail	60	96	50
Landsker Borderlands Trail	60	96	77
Leeds Country Way	60	96	79
Milton Keynes Boundary Walk	60	96	92
Northumbrian Coastline	60	96	99
Solent Way	60	96	124
Stour Valley Path	60	96	132
Three Castles Path	60	96	141
Three Forests Way	60	96	142
Nev Cole Way	58	92	95

Path	Miles	Km	Page
Lancaster Canal	57	91	76
Weavers Way	56	90	158-159
Taff Trail	55	88	136
Allerdale Ramble	54	87	7
Trans Pennine Walk	54	87	144-145
Welsh 3000s Double Crossing	54	87	209
Bowland-Pendle Challenge Trail	53	85	194
Nidderdale Way	53	85	95
Walkways: Birmingham/Church Stretton	51	82	152
Calderdale Way	50	80	18
Carpet Baggers 50	50	80	214
Chesterfield Round	50	80	22
Cleveland Way (Missing Link)	50	80	25
Clyde Walkway	50	80	26
Dartmoor Perambulation	50	80	35
Daugleddau Trail	50	80	36
Gallo Way Round	50	80	170
Land's End Round	50	80	220
Lea Valley Walk	50	80	78-79
Lost Lancs Way	50	80	176
Lyke Wake Way	50	80	185
Minster Way	50	80	92-93
Morecambe Bay Shoreline	50	80	93
North Western Fells	50	80	177
Recedham Way	50	80	111
Suffolk Coast Path	50	80	133
Usk Valley Walk	50	80	149
Speyside Way	48	77	129
Walkways: Birmingham/Ludlow	48	77	152-153
Worcestershire Way	48	77	166-167
Tabular Hills Link Walk	48	76	135
Avon Community Forest Path	47	75	10-11
Test Way	46	74	139
Ullswater Circuit	46	74	178
Walkways: Rhayader/Aberystwyth	46	74	154
Wear Valley Way	46	74	157
Four Pikes Hike	45	72	195
Pendle Way	45	72	107
Plogsland Round	45	72	109
Rossendale Way	45	72	114-115
Snowdonia 24hr Circuit	45	72	209
St Peter's Way	45	72	130-131
Ainsty Bounds Walk	44	70	7
Middlesex Greenway	43	69	90
Seahorse Saunter	43	69	188
Lyke Wake Walk	42	67	185
Walkways: Ludlow/Rhayader	42	67	153
Wychavon Way	41	66	167
Around the Carneddau	40	64	10
Bronte Way	40	64	17
Burnley Way	40	64	18

List of Routes by Distance

Path	Miles	Km	Page
Gritstone Edge Walk	27	43	204
Itchen Way	27	43	68-69
Otley Nine Leagues	27	43	181
Pendle Marathon	27	43	197
Trollers Trot	27	43	183
Wigan Pier Walk	27	43	201
Flower of Suffolk	26	42	217
Greaver's Trail	26	42	173
Lipchis Way	26	42	84
North Worcestershire Hills Marathon	26	42	98
North Worcestershire Path	26	42	98-99
Poppyline Marathon	26	42	218
Ramblers Route	26	42	110
Saints Way/Forth an Syns	26	42	117
Sirhowy Valley Walk	26	42	123
Nidd Vale Circuit	26	42	180
Daffodil Dawdle	26	42	217
Ouse Valley Way	26	41	102
Bollin Valley Way	25	40	16
Caistor Challenge	25	40	210
Charnwood Forest Challenge Walk	25	40	211
Cheviot Hills 2,000ft Summits Walk	25	40	170
Dales Traverse	25	40	180
Forest Way	25	40	48-49
Highlow Historic Hike	25	40	205
Kirkby Lonsdale Parish Walk	25	40	173
North York Moors Challenge Walk	25	40	186
Old Sarum Challenge	25	40	219
Ox Drove Way	25	40	103
Pennington Round	25	40	177
Rotherham Round Walk	25	40	115
Sidmouth Saunter	25	40	220
Silvarn Round	25	40	198
Tame Valley Way	25	40	137
That's Lyth	25	40	178
Three Reservoirs Challenge	25	40	207
Three Rivers Walk	25	40	182
Two Crosses Circuit	25	40	199
Watersheds Walk	25	40	155
White Peak Challenge Walk	25	40	207
Whithorn Pilgrim Way	25	40	164
Yorkshire Dales Challenge Walk	25	40	183
Yorkshire Ridings 200 Furlongs	25	40	183
Churnet Valley Challenge Walk	24	39	202
Clarendon Way	24	39	24
Gower Gallop	24	39	218
High Hunsley Circuit	24	39	189
Holme Valley Circular Walk	24	39	65
Limestone Dale Walk	24	39	205
Three Peaks Walk	24	39	182
Cross Bucks Way	24	38	31

List of Routes by Distance

Path	Miles	Km	Page
Dane Valley Circular	24	38	203
Dark Peak Challenge Walk	24	38	203
Holme Valley Circular Challenge Walk	24	38	191
Maelor Way	24	38	86
Rutland Water Challenge Walk	24	38	212
Salter's Way	24	38	118
Staffordshire Moorlands Challenge Walk	24	38	206
White Peak Rollercoaster	24	38	208
Bronte Round	23	37	190
Elham Valley Way	23	37	44
Round Preston Walk	23	37	116
South Bucks Way	23	37	125
Duddon Landscape Walk	23	37	175
Centenary Circle	23	36	20
Dunford Round	23	36	204
Haslemere Circular Walk	23	36	61
Chaddesley Chase	22	35	214
Delamere Way	22	35	37
Hidden Valley Walk	22	35	63
Lambourn Valley Way	22	35	74-75
Maldon Millennium	22	35	86-87
Sefton Coastal Footpath	22	35	120
Ten Reservoirs Walk	22	35	193
Thirlmere Round	22	35	178
Wide Awake Walk	22	35	200
Anglezarke Amble	21	34	193
Exe Valley Way	21	34	47
Hangers Way	21	34	59
Harrogate Ringway	21	34	60
Holderness Way	21	34	64-65
Marriott's Way	21	34	88
Spen Way Heritage Trail	21	34	129
Tyne and Wear 20	21	34	171
West Gordon Way	21	34	160
Abberley Amble	20	32	213
Anglezarke Anguish	20	32	194
Consett and Sunderland Railway Path	20	32	29
Crag and Cove Walk	20	32	179
Duddon Horseshoe	20	32	174
Epperstone Park to Southwell Minster	20	32	44-45
Grasmere Skyline Classic Walk	20	32	175
Hanslope Circular Ride	20	32	59
Harrogate-Dales Way	20	32	60-61
Helm Wind Walk	20	32	173
Hillingdon Trail	20	32	64
Howden 20	20	32	190
Kinver Clamber	20	32	214
Knaresborough Round	20	32	72
Leeds-Dales Way	20	32	80
Malvern Hills Challenge Walk	20	32	215
Mid Suffolk Footpath	20	32	89

List of Routes by Distance

Path	Miles	Km	Page
Darent Valley Path	15	24	34
Eden Valley Walk	15	24	43
Epping Forest Centenary Walk	15	24	45
Templer Way	15	24	138-139
Ver-Colne Valley Walk	15	24	150-151
Frome Valley Walkway	14	22	49
Wardens' Way	14	22	154-155
Windrush Way	14	22	165
Grafton Way	13	21	52-53
Limestone Link	13	21	82
Ogwr Ridgeway Walk	13	21	101
Tissington Trail	13	21	143
Lark Valley Path	13	20	78
Medlock Valley Way	13	20	88
Staunton Way	13	20	131
Derwent Walk	12	19	37
Etherow/Goyt Valley Way	12	19	46-47
Knightley Way	12	19	72
Lanchester Valley Walk	12	19	77
Longster Trail	11	18	85
Wimpole Way	11	18	165
Clopton Way	11	17	26
Brandon/Bishop Auckland Walk	10	16	17
Goyt Way	10	16	52
Knights' Way	9	14	72-73
Baker Way	8	13	12
Two Ridges Link	8	13	146
Deerness Valley Walk	8	12	36-37
Shipley-Dales Way	7	11	122

LIST OF ADDRESSES

A G Publications, Attorney Garth, Motherby, Penrith, Cumbria, CA11 0RJ

Peter Abbott, 5 Hillstone Close, Greenmount, Bury, Lancashire, BL8 4EZ

Alan Sutton Publishing Ltd, Phoenix Mill, Far Thrupp, Stroud, Gloucestershire, BL5 2BU

JJ Allen, 5 Moorgate Cottages, Astley Bank, Darwen, Lancashire, BB3 2QB

Allerdale District Council, Holmewood, Cockermouth, Cumbria, CA13 0DW

The Appletree Press Ltd, 7 James Street South, Belfast, BT2 8DL

Richard Archard, 57 Countess Road, Amesbury, Wiltshire, SP4 7AS

A T Ashworth, 22 Laneside, Haworth Road, Wilsden, Bradford, BD15 0LH

Aurum Press, 25 Bedford Avenue, London, WC1B 3AT

Aussteiger Publications, 8 Back Skipton Road, Barnoldswick, Colne, Lancashire, BB8 5NE

Avon County Council, Avon House, Haymarket, Bristol, Avon, BS99 7DE

Aylesbury Vale District Council, Countryside Management Project, Haydon Mill, Rabans Lane, Aylesbury, Buckinghamshire, HP19 3ST

Mike Barnham, 10 Netheredge Drive, Knaresborough, North Yorkshire, HG5 9DA

Barnsley Metropolitan Borough Council, Leisure and Amenities Department, County Way, Barnsley, S70 2TL

Barrow Borough Council, Development Division, Town Hall, Duke Street, Barrow in Furness, Cumbria, LA14 2LD

Bartholomew & Times Books, 12 Duncan Street, Edinburgh, EH9 1TA

Basildon District Council, Countryside Section, Wat Tyler Country Park, Wat Tyler Way, Pitsea, Essex, SS16 4UW

Peter Bayer, 12 Brooklands Lane, Menston, Ilkley, West Yorkshire, LS29 6PJ

Beacon Regional Park, Liz Stuffins, Beacon Lodge, 551 Beacon Road, Walsall, WS9 0QW

Bedfordshire County Council, Countryside Access Officer, Leisure Services Dept, County Hall, Cauldwell Street, Bedford, MK42 9AP

Berkshire County Council, Babtie Public Services Division, Shire Hall, Shinfield Park, Reading, RG2 9XG

M P Berry, 99 Scar Lane, Milnsbridge, Huddersfield, HD3 4PW

Vivian Bird OBE, 486 Shirley Road, Hall Green, Birmingham 28

Martyn Bishop, 79 Sydney Street, Boston, Lincolnshire, PE21 8NZ

Blackburn Borough Council, Tourist Information, King George's Hall, Northgate, Blackburn, Lancashire, BB2 1AA

Blackwater Valley Team, Ash Lock Cottage, Government Road, Aldershot, Hampshire, GU11 2PS, Steve Bailey

Bollin Valley Project, County Offices, Chapel Lane, Wilmslow, Cheshire, SK9 1PU

Terry Bound, 3 Alpha Street, Heavitree, Exeter, Devon, EX1 2SP

Keith Bown, Dale House, 35 Bawtry Road, Listerdale, Rotherham, South Yorkshire, S66 0AR

Bracknell Forest District Council, Recreational Paths Officer, The Look-Out, Nine Mile Ride, Bracknell, Berks, RG12 3QW

British Waterways Board, Customer Services, Willow Grange, Church Road, Watford, Hertfordshire, WD1 3QA

Buckinghamshire County Council, Recreational Paths Officer, County Engineer's Department, County Hall, Aylesbury, Buckinghamshire, HP20 1UY

Burnley Borough Council, Tourist Information, Burnley Mechanics, Manchester Road, Burnley, Lancashire, BB11 1JA

Michael Burton, 6 Carrwood Hey, Ramsbottom, Bury, Lancashire, BL0 9QT

Caerphilly Mountain Countryside Servce, Taff Gorge Countryisde Centre, Heol-y-Fforest, Tongwynlais, Cardiff, CF4 7JR

Metropolitan Borough of Calderdale, Leisure Services Department, Wellesley Park, Halifax, W Yorkshire, HX2 0AY

Cambridgeshire County Council, Department of Property, Shire Hall, Castle Hill, Cambridge, CB3 0AP

Carnegie Press, 18 Maynard Street, Preston, Lancashire, PR2 2AL

Dave and Anne Carrivick, Elm View, Trispen, Truro, Cornwall, TR4 9AZ

Castlemead Publications, 12 Little Mundells, Welwyn Garden City, Hertfordshire, AL7 1EW

Chelmsford Borough Council, Technical Services Department, Civic Centre, Chelmsford, Essex, CM1 1JE

Cheshire County Council, Information and Leisure Services, Goldsmith House, Hamilton Place, Chester, CH1 1SE

Keith Chesterton, "Firle", Chestnut Avenue, Guildford, Surrey, GU2 5HD

Chiltern Society, c/o Mrs Penny Perriss, East Lodge, Essex Lane, Kings Langley, Hertfordshire, WD4 8PN

Cicerone Press, 2 Police Square, Milnthorpe, Cumbria, LA7 7PY

Cleveland County Council, Dept of Environment, Gurney House, Gurney Street, Middlesbrough, Cleveland, TS1 1JJ

Stephen J Collins, 51 Russell Gardens, Sipson, Middlesex, UB7 0LR

David Connelly, 35 Maypark, Bamber Bridge, Preston, PR5 8JB

Constable and Co Ltd, 3 The Lanchesters, 162 Fulham Palace Road, London, W6 9ER

Copeland Borough Council, Tourist Information Office, The Market Hall, Market Place, Whitehaven, Cumbria, CA28 7JG

Cordee Ltd, 3a De Montfort Street, Leicester, LE1 7HD

Cornwall County Council, Countryside Access Section, Radnor Road, Scorrier, Redruth, Cornwall, TR16 5EH

Cotswold Warden Office, Gloucestershire County Council, Shire Hall, Gloucester, GL1 2TN

Countryside Books, 2 Highfield Avenue, Newbury, Berkshire, RG14 5DS

Countryside Commission Postal Sales, PO Box 124, Walgrave, Northampton, NN6 9TL

Countryside Council for Wales, Plas Penrhos, Ffordd Penrhos, Powys, Bangor, Gwynedd, LL57 2LQ

Vic Cox, 36 Elwood Road, Bradway, Sheffield, S17 4RH

Cumbria County Council, Planning Dept, County Offices, Kendal, Cumbria, LA9 4RQ

Dalby Forest Visitor Centre, Low Dalby, Pickering, North Yorkshire, YO18 7LT

Dales Way Association, c/o David Smith, Dalegarth, Moorfield Road, Ilkley, W Yorkshire, LS29 8BL

Dalesman Publishing Ltd, Stable Courtyard, Broughton Hall, Skipton, N Yorks, BD23 3AE

E Dalton, Mountain View, Fachell, Hermon, Bodorgan, Gwynedd, LL62 5LL

George Davies, 33 Fir Tree Road, Fernhill Heath, Worcester, WR3 8RE

R Dean, 33 Brookfield Road, Upholland, Skelmersdale, Lancashire, WN8 0NZ

Derbyshire County Council, Chief Planning and Highways Officer, County Offices, Matlock, Derbyshire, DE4 3AG

Derbyshire Dales District Council, Town Hall, Matlock, Derbyshire, DE4 3NN, Planning Officer

Derwentside District Council, Leisure Development, The Louisa Centre, Front Street, Stanley, Co Durham, DH8 0TE

Devon Books, Chinon Court, Lower Moor Way, Tiverton Business Park, Tiverton, Devon, EX16 6SS

Devon County Council, County Engineer and Planning Officer, County Hall, Exeter, EX2 4QW

Diadem Books, 3a De Montfort Street, Leicester, LE1 7HD

Paddy Dillon, 82 Arthur Street, Barrow-in-Furness, Cumbria, LA14 1BH

Doncaster Metropolitan Borough Council, Amenities and Leisure Department, Countryside Unit, Cooke Street, Bentley, Doncaster

Dumfries and Galloway Regional Council, Dept of Physical Planning, English Street, Dumfries, DG1 2DD

Durham County Council, County Hall, Durham, DH1 5UQ, Environment Department

Dyfed County Council, Planning Department, 40 Spilman Street, Carmarthen, Dyfed, SA31 1LQ

East Devon District Council, Rural Affairs Officer, Knowle, Sidmouth, Devon, EX10 8HL

J F Eardley, 2 Steele Close, Cheddleton, Leek, Staffs, ST13 7EN

Alan S Edwards, 6 Brittain Road, Cheddleton, Leek, Staffordshire, ST13 7EH

C Dexter Ellis, 4 Prospect Place, Holmfirth, W Yorks, HD7 1RH

Gordon Emery, 27 Gladstone Road, Chester, CH1 4BZ

Epping Forest Superintendent, The Warren, Loughton, Essex, IG10 4RW

Derek Esmond, 75 Grosvenor Place, Carnforth, Lancashire, LA5 9DL

Essex County Council, Planning Dept, County Hall, Chelmsford, Essex, CM1 1LF

Etherow/Goyt Valley Wardens, Etherow Country Park, George St, Compstall, Stockport, SK6 5JD

A G Foot, Coombe House, Brithem Bottom, Cullompton, Devon, EX15 1NQ

Footpath Guides, Old Hall, East Bergholt, Colchester, CO7 6TG

Footpath Touring, Sea Chimneys, Southdown, Beer, Devon, EX12 3AE

Footprint, Stirling Surveys, Unit 54, Stirling Enterprise Park, Stirling, FK7 7RP

Forest Enterprise N Scotland, 21 Church Street, Inverness, IV1 1EL

Richard French, Expedition North, Sedbergh, Cumbria, LA10 5LS

Friends of The Ridgeway, c/o Nigel Forward, 90 South Hill Park, London, NW3 2SN

Gloucestershire County Council, Public Rights of Way Office, County Surveyors Dept, Shire Hall, Gloucester, GL1 2TH

Gomer Press, Wind Street, Llandysul, Dyfed, SA44 4BQ

Goole Rambling Club, c/o Wendy Wales, 29 Mount Pleasant Road, Goole, Yorkshire, DN14 6LH

Gordon District Council, Planning Dept, Gordon House, Blackhall Road, Inverurie, AB51 9WA

Grand Union Canal Walk Project Officer, British Waterways, The Stop House, The Wharf, Braunston, Northamptonshire, NN11 7JQ

Green Chain Working Party, John Humphries House, Stockwell St, Greenwich, London, SE10 9JN

Grey Stone Books, 83 Glenshiels Avenue, Hoddlesden, Darwen, Lancashire, BB3 3LS

Michael Guest, 7 Barton Close, Thornaby on Tees, Cleveland, TS17 0HH

Gwent County Council, County Planning Officer, County Hall, Cwmbran, Gwent, NP44 2XF

D W Haller, 11 Cambridge Terrace, Otley, W Yorkshire, LS21 1JS

Hampshire County Council, Countryside & Community Dept, Mottisfont Court, High Street, Winchester, Hants, SO23 8ZF

Les Hardman, 80 Bolton Road, Marland, Rochdale, Lancashire, OL11 4QX

Harrogate Borough Council, Tourist Information, Royal Baths Assembly Rooms, Crescent Road, Harrogate, North Yorkshire, HG1 2RR

Heart of England Way Association, 20 Throckmorton Road, Alcester, Warwickshire, B49 6QA

Hendon Publishing Co, Hendon Mill, Nelson, Lancashire

Hereford and Worcester County Council, Countryside Service, County Hall, Spetchley Road, Worcester, WR5 2NP

Hertfordshire County Council, Countryside and Community, Dept of Planning & Environment, County Hall, Hertford, SG13 8DN

London Borough of Hillingdon, Recreation Unit, 2 East 05, Civic Centre, High Street, Uxbridge, UB8 1UW

Hillside Publications, 11 Nessfield Grove, Keighley, West Yorkshire, BD22 6NU

HMSO Scotland, 71 Lothian Road, Edinburgh, EH3 9AZ

Frank Hodson, Toll Bar Cottage, Underbarrow, Kendal, Cumbria, LA8 8HB

Maxine Hogbin, 32 Barleyfield, Bamber Bridge, Preston, Lancashire, PR5 8JH

Holme Valley Civic Society, c/o Tourist Information Centre, 49-51 Huddersfield Road, Holmfirth, West Yorkshire, HD7 1JP

Glen Hood, 329 Kingston Road, Willerby, Hull, HU10 6PY

Humberside County Council, Technical Services Dept, County Hall, Beverley, North Humberside, HU17 9XA

Huntingdon District Council, Planning Dept, Pathfinder House, St Mary's Street, Huntingdon, Cambridgeshire, PE18 6TN

Hyndburn Borough Council, Development Services, Leisure Division, Town Hall, Blackburn Road, Accrington, BB5 1LA

Ian Allan Publishing, Coombelands House, Coombelands Lane, Addlestone, Surrey, KT15 1HY

Icknield Way Association, c/o Roy Wheeler, 19 Boundary Road, Bishop's Stortford, Herts, CM23 5LE

Dave Irons, 57 Reservoir Road, Selly Oak, Birmingham, B29 6ST

Isle of Man Government, Rights of Way Officer, Dept of Highways, Ports and Properties, Sea Terminal Building, Douglas, Isle of Man

Isle of Man Dept of Tourism & Transp't, 13 Victoria Street, Douglas, Isle of Man

Isle of Wight County Council, County Surveyor, County Hall, Newport, Isle of Wight, PO30 1UD

David Johnson, The Hollies, Stainforth, Settle, North Yorkshire, BD24 9PQ

Glyn Jones, Bing, Kirkinner, Wigtownshire, DG8 9BZ

Richard Kenchington, 15 Mitre Copse, Bishopstoke, Nr Eastleigh, Hampshire, SO5 6QE

Kent County Council, Planning Department, Springfield, Maidstone, Kent, ME14 2LX

David Kidd, 14 Froude Avenue, South Shields, Tyne and Wear, NE34 9TB

G Kilvington, Rambling Club Section, Blackburn Leisure Association, British Aerospace, Brough, North Humberside, HU15 1EQ

Kirklees Metropolitan Council, Countryside Unit, The Stables, Ravensknowle Park, Wakefield Road, Huddersfield, HD5 8DJ

Kirklees Metropolitan Council, Oakwell Hall Country Park, Nutter Lane, Birstall, Nr Batley, WF17 9LG

Ian & Caroline Kirkpatrick, 6 Tor View, Horrabridge, Yelverton, Devon, PL20 7RE

Kittiwake Press, c/o Laurence Main, 9 Mawddwy Cottages, Minllyn, Dinas Mawddwy, Machynlleth, SY20 9LW

Lancaster City Council, Tourist Information Centre, 29 Castle Hill, Lancaster, LA1 1YN

Lancashire County Council, P O Box 160, East Cliff County Offices, Preston, Lancashire, PR1 3EX

Langbaurgh Loop, "Bywood", Victoria Terrace, Saltburn-by-the-Sea, Cleveland, TS12 1JE

Lawrence and Wishart Ltd, 144a Old South Lambeth Road, London, SW8 1XX

Frank Lawson, 74 Tatenhill Gardens, Cantley, Doncaster, South Yorkshire, DN4 6TL

LDWA East Lancs Group, c/o J S Abbott, 18 Hillstone Close, Greenmount, Bury, BL8 4EZ

LDWA Northumbria Group, c/o Mike Rayner, 1 Corriedale Close, Pity Me, Durham, DH1 5GY

Leading Edge Press and Publishing, The Old Chapel, Burtersett, Hawes, North Yorkshire, DL8 3PB

Lee Valley Regional Park Authority, Countryside Service, Holyfield Hall Farmhouse, Stubbins Hall Lane, Crooked Mile, Waltham Abbey, Essex EN9 2EG

Leeds Metropolitan Borough Council, Leisure Services Countryside Service, Rights of Way Section, Home Farm, Temple Newsam Estate, Leeds, LS15 0BJ

Leicestershire County Council, County Hall, Glenfield, Leicester, LE3 8RJ, Planning & Transportation Dept

Leicestershire Libraries & Information, 99 Burleys Way, Leicester, LE1 3TZ

Rob Lewis, 89 Gelli Fawr, Treboeth, Swansea, West Glamorgan, SA6 7PW

Lincolnshire County Council, County Offices, Newland, Lincoln, LN1 1YL, Recreational Services Dept

Lincolnshire Fieldpath Association, c/o Major (retd) Brett Collier, Chloris House, 208 Nettleham Road, Lincoln, LN2 4DH

Liphook Rambling Club, c/o David & Margaret Clark, 21 Chestnut Close, Liphook, Hants, GU30 7JA

Lyke Wake Club, PO Box 24, Northallerton, N Yorkshire, DL6 3HZ

Derek Magnall, Spanners Retreat, 5 Caldy Drive, Holcombe Brook, Ramsbottom, BL0 9TY

Mainstream Publishing Co Ltd, 7 Albany Street, Edinburgh, EH1 3UG

Alec Malkinson, 2 Southern Walk, Scartho, Grimsby, DN33 2PG

Management Update Ltd, c/o Powney's Bookshop, 4-5 St Alkmund's Place, Shrewsbury, Shropshire, SY1 1UJ

Matthews/Bitten Publications, Glen View, London Road, Abridge, Essex, RM4 1UX

Medlock Valley Warden Service, The Stables, Park Bridge, Ashton under Lyne, OL6 8AQ

Men-an-Tol Studio, School House, Newbridge, Penzance, Cornwall

Meridian Books, 40 Hadzor Road, Oldbury, Warley, West Midlands, B68 9LA

Mersey Valley Partnership, Camden House, York Place, Runcorn, Cheshire, WA7 5BD

Merthyr and Cynon Valley Groundwork, Fedw Hir, Llwydcoed, Aberdare, CF44 0DX

Michael Joseph, 27 Wright's Lane, London, W8 5TZ

Mid-Cheshire Footpath Society, c/o Mrs Sheila Greenwood, Wynscot, Gazebank, Norley, Warrington, WA6 8LJ

Mid Suffolk District Council, Planning & Leisure, 131 High Street, Needham Market, Suffolk, IP6 8DL

Paul Miller, 72 St Ives Way, Halewood, Liverpool, L26 7YW

Peter Miller, 107 Hamelin Road, Darlands, Gillingham, Kent, ME7 3ER

Milton Keynes Borough Council, Recreation Footpaths Officer, PO Box 113, Civic Offices, 1 Saxon Gate East, Central Milton Keynes, Bucks MK9 3HN

Missing Link Recorder, 80 Howe Road, Norton, Malton, North Yorkshire, YO17 9BL

Montgomery Waterway Restoration Trust, c/o Mrs M. Awcock, "Oakhaven", Longden-on-Tern, Shropshire, TF6 6LJ

Moray District Council, Dept of Leisure & Libraries, High Street, Elgin, IV30 1BX

Mountain Peaks Climbing Club, 2 Chapel Cottages, Main Road, Hathersage, Derbyshire, S30 1BB

Derek Nash, White Lodge, Birmingham Road, Shenstone, Lichfield, Staffordshire, WS14 0LB

Neuadd Arms Hotel, Gordon Green, Llanwrtyd Wells, Powys

Norfolk County Council, Dept of Planning & Property, County Hall, Martineau Lane, Norwich, NR1 2DH, Dept of Planning & Property

North Pennine Walks, Stanhope Station, Bondisle Way, Stanhope, Weardale, Co Durham, DL13 0YS

North York Moors National Park, Information Service, The Old Vicarage, Bondgate, Helmsley, Yorks, YO6 5BP

North York Moors Adventure Centre, Park House, Ingleby Cross, Northallerton, North Yorkshire, DL6 3PE

North Yorkshire County Council, Highways & Transportation Dept, County Hall, Northallerton, North Yorkshire, DL7 8AH

Northamptonshire County Council, Countryside Services, 9 Guildhall Road, Northampton, NN1 1DP

Northavon District Council, Planning Department, Council Offices, Castle Street, Thornbury, Bristol, BS12 1HF

Northern Ireland Tourist Board, 59 North Street, Belfast, BT1 1NB

Nottinghamshire County Council, Planning & Economic Development Dept, Trent Bridge House, Fox Road, West Bridgford, Nottingham, NG2 6BJ

Offa's Dyke Association, Old Primary School, West Street, Knighton, Powys, LD7 1EW

Ogwr Borough Council, Borough Planning Officer, Civic Offices, Angel Street, Bridgend, Mid Glamorgan

Oldham Metropolitan District Council, 84 Union St, Oldham, Lancashire, OL1 1DN

Ordnance Survey, Romsey Road, Maybush, Southampton, SO9 4DH

Oxford Fieldpaths Society, c/o Alison Kemp, Lockey House, Langford, Lechlade, Gloucestershire, GL7 3LF

Elizabeth Pamplin, Little Critchmere, Manor Crescent, Haslemere, Surrey

Patrick Stephens Ltd, Thorson Publishing Group, Wellingborough, Northamptonshire, NN8 2RQ

Kim Peacock, 26 Fulford Crescent, Ganton Way, Kingston Road, Willerby, Hull, HU10 6NR

Peak District National Park, Baslow Road, Bakewell, Derbyshire, DE4 1AE

Peddar Publications, Croft End, Bures, Suffolk, CO8 5JN

Peddars Way Association, 150 Armes Street, Norwich, Norfolk, NR2 4EG

Pembrokeshire Coast National Park, County Offices, Haverfordwest, Dyfed, SA61 1QZ

Pendle Borough Council, Bank House, Albert Road, Colne, Lancashire

Penguin Books Ltd, Bath Road, Harmondsworth, Middlesex, UB7 0DA

Pennine Way Association, c/o Chris Sainty, 29 Springfield Park Avenue, Chelmsford, Essex, CM2 6EL

Dr Ben Perkins, 11 Old London Road, Brighton, Sussex, BN1 8XR

Eric Perks, "Selbhome", 10 Cordle Marsh Road, Bewdley, Worcestershire, DY12 1EW

Allen Pestell, 8 Sledbrook Crescent, Crowedge, Sheffield, S30 5HD

Peterborough City Council, Planning Dept, Town Bridge, Bridge St, Peterborough, PE1 1HB

R T Pinkney, 11 Pine Road, Ormesby, Middlesbrough, Cleveland, TS7 9DH

Power Publications, c/o Countryside Books, 6 Pound St, Newbury, Berkshire, RG14 6AB

Powys County Council, County Planning Office, Shire Hall, Llandrindod Wells, Powys, LD1 5LG

Gay Quilter, 12 Shaw Hall Close, Greenfield, Oldham, OL3 7PG

Ramblers' Association, 1-5 Wandsworth Road, London, SW8 2XX

RA Beverley Group, per Dennis Parker, 11 Elmsall Drive, Beverley, North Humberside, HU17 7HL

RA Bolton Group, c/o Lawrence Hubbard, 2 Coniston Road, Blackrod, Bolton, BL6 5DN

RA Buckinghamshire, 12 Wykeham Way, Haddenham, Aylesbury, Buckinghamshire, HP17 8BL

RA Chelmer & Blackwater Group, c/o Ways Through Essex, Essex County Council

RA Chesterfield & NE Derbyshire, c/o Mr A W Hunt, 108 Peveril Road, Newbold, Chesterfield, Derbyshire, S41 8SH

RA Devon Area, c/o JR Turner, Coppins, The Poplars, Pinhoe, Exeter, EX4 9HH

RA E Berkshire Group, c/o Pat Hayers, 16 Lanterns Walk, Farthingales, Maidenhead, Berkshire, SL6 1TG

RA E Yorkshire & Derwent Area, c/o Sheila M Smith, 65 Ormonde Avenue, Beresford Avenue, Beverley High Road, Hull, HU6 7LT

RA Gloucestershire Area, 12 Shepherds Way, Northleach, Cheltenham, GL54 3ED

RA Harrogate Group, c/o Peter Goldsmith, 20 Pannal Ash Grove, Harrogate, HG2 0HZ

RA Isle of Wight, per Mr C R Johns, 19 Manor Road, Lake, Sandown, Isle of Wight, PO36 9JA

RA Lincs and S Humberside Area, c/o Chloris House, 208 Nettleham Road, Lincoln, LN2 4DH

RA Manchester Area, c/o Terry Perkins, 34 Grangethorpe Drive, Burnage, Manchester, M19 2LG

RA Norfolk Area, 150 Armes St, Norwich, Norfolk, NR2 4EG

RA Peterborough Group, c/o Trevor Noyes, 8 Welmore Rd, Glinton, Peterborough, PE6 7LU

RA Preston Group, c/o Fred Coulthurst, 17 St Andrews Avenue, Ashton, Preston, PR2 1JL

Reckitt & Colman Pharmaceuticals, Laboratory Services, R H Watson, Kingston-upon-Hull, North Humberside, HU8 7DS

A Richmond, 40 St Mary's Avenue, Birchley, Billinge, Wigan, WN5 7QL

Brian Richmond, 31 Dartmouth Street, Barrow-in-Furness, Cumbria, LA14 3AS

Richmondshire District Council, Tourism Officer, Swale House, Frenchgate, Richmond, N Yorkshire, DL10 4JE

Ridgeway Officer, Countryside Section, Library Headquarters, Holton, Oxford, OX9 1QQ

River Foss Amenity Society, 147 York Road, Haxby, York, YO3 8EU

C Roby, 2 Wilkesley Avenue, Standish, Nr Wigan, Lancashire, WN6 0UZ

Rochdale Pioneers Museum, Toad Lane, Rochdale, OL12 0NU

Rossendale Borough Council, Planning Officer, 6 St James Square, Bacup, Lancashire

Rossendale Groundwork Trust Ltd, New Hall Hey Road, Rawtenstall, Lancashire, BB4 6HR

Rotherham Metropolitan Borough Council, Director of Amenities and Recreation, Recreation Offices, Grove Road, Rotherham, S60 2ER

Sandhill Press Ltd, 17 Castle Street, Warkworth, Morpeth, Northumberland, NE65 0UW

Scarborough Borough Council, Tourism & Amenities Department, Londesborough Lodge, The Crescent, Scarborough

Scarthin Books, The Promenade, Cromford, Derbyshire, DE4 3QF

N F Scholes, Pendowner, Britannia Road, Morley, Leeds, LS27 0DW

Scottish Rights of Way Society, Unit 2, John Cotton Business Centre, 10/2 Sunnyside, Edinburgh, EH7 5RA

Scottish Natural Heritage, Battleby, Redgorton, Perth, PH1 3EW

John Searle, 52 The Broad Walk, Eynesbury, Huntingdon, Cambridgeshire, PE19 2SG

Metropolitan Borough of Sefton, Planning & Environment, Vermont House, 375 Stanley Road, Bootle, L20 3RY

The Shetland Times Ltd, 71/79 Commercial Street, Lerwick, Shetland, ZE1 0AJ

Shire Publications, Cromwell House, Church Street, Princes Risborough, Aylesbury, Buckinghamshire, HP17 9AJ

Shropshire County Council, Leisure Services Department, Winston Churchill Building, Radbrook Centre, Radbrook Road, Shrewsbury, SY3 9BJ

List of Addresses

Joyce Sidebottom, 15 Grosvenor Way, Horwich, Bolton, Greater Manchester, BL6 6DJ

Sigma Leisure, 1 South Oak Lane, Wilmslow, Cheshire, SK9 6AR

Owen Silver, 6 Shorehead, St Andrews, Fife, KY16 9RG

Peter Sleightholm, 31 Oaks Lane, Bradshaw, Bolton, BL2 3BR

Smith Settle, Ilkley Road, Otley, W Yorks, LS21 3JP

South Downs Way Officer, Sussex Downs Conservation Board, Chanctonbury House, Church Road, Storrington, West Sussex, RH20 4LT

South Lakeland District Council, Leisure Services Dept, South Lakeland House, Lowther Street, Kendal, Cumbria, LA9 4UF

South Norfolk District Council, South Norfolk House, Swan Lane, Long Stratton, Norfolk, NR15 2XE

South Normanton Walking Club, c/o Peter and Lorraine Matkin, Westfield Lane SPO, Westfield Lane, Mansfield, Notts, NG19 6AQ

South Somerset District Council, Brympton Way, Yeovil, Somerset, BA20 1PU

South West Way Association, 'Windlestraw', Penquit, Ermington, Nr Ivybridge, Devon, PL21 0LU

SPARC, The Old School, Station Road, Narberth, Dyfed, SA67 8DU

John Sparshatt, 30A Sandholme Drive, Burley in Wharfedale, Ilkley, W Yorkshire, LS29 7RQ

Sports Council for Northern Ireland, House of Sport, Upper Malone Road, Belfast, BT9 5LA

St Andrew Press, 121 George Street, Edinburgh, EH2

St Mary's Hospice Appeal Centre, PO Box 6, Ulverston, Cumbria, LA12 9SJ

Staffordshire County Council, Planning & Economic Development, Martin Street, Stafford, ST16 2LE

D & S Stewart, 99 Woodside, Gillingham, Kent, ME8 0PW

Stile Publications, 24 Lisker Drive, Otley, W Yorks, LS21 1DQ

Strathclyde Regional Council, Dept of Physical Planning, Strathclyde House, 20 India Street, Glasgow, G2 4PF

Jim Strother, Galava Shiel, Borrans Road, Ambleside, LA22 0EN

Suffolk County Council, Planning Department, St Edmund House, Ropewalk, Ipswich, Suffolk, IP4 1LZ

Mike Surr, 10 Albany Place, Louth, Lincs, LN11 8EY

Surrey County Council, Highways & Transportation Department, County Hall, Penrhyn Road, Kingston-upon-Thames, Surrey, KT1 2DY

Society of Sussex Downsmen, Publications Editor, 254 Victoria Drive, Eastbourne, East Sussex, BN20 8QT

Sustrans Ltd, Rockwood House, Barn Hill, Stanley, Co Durham, DH9 8AW

Sustrans Scotland, 53 Cochrane Street, Glasgow, G1 1HL

Don Sweeting, The Levels, Portington Road, Eastrington, Goole, DN14 7QE

Taff Ely Borough Council, Planning Department, Mill Street, Pontypridd, Mid Glamorgan, CF3 2TU

Bob Tait, 3 Ridings Court, Dobcross, Nr Oldham, OL3 5DB

Tameside Leisure Services, Tame Valley Warden Service, Council Offices, Wellington Road, Ashton under Lyne, OL6 6DL

Tarka Project Officer, Bideford Station, Railway Terrace, Bideford, Devon, EX39 4BB

Max Tattersall, 79 Ormerod Road, Burnley, Lancashire, BB11 2RU

Mike Teanby, The Old School House, Village Street, Adwick le Street, Doncaster, DN6 7AA

Teesside Hospice Care Foundation, 10a Cambridge Road, Middlesborough, TS5 5NQ

Norman Thomas, The Parsonage, off Ainsworth Avenue, Horwich, Bolton, Lancashire, BL6 6LS

Thornhill Press, Unit 3, Fountain Way, Parkend, nr Lydney, Glos, GL15 4HH

J Tinniswood, 12 Beaconsfield Terrace, Chopwell, Newcastle-upon-Tyne, NE17 7JG

John Tootle, 10 Haredon Close, Bamber Bridge, Preston, PR5 6WL

Simon Townson, 22 St John's Crescent, Harrogate, North Yorkshire, HG1 3AB

Trail Crest Publications Ltd, Milne House, Speedwell Mill, Miller's Green, Wirksworth, Derbyshire, DE4 4BL

Trans Pennine Trail Officer, c/o Department of Planning, Barnsley Metropolitan Borough Council, Central Offices, Kendray Street, Barnsley, S70 2TN

P Travis, 23 Kingsway East, Newcastle-under-Lyme, Staffordshire, ST5 3PY

L Turner, 3 Ringwood Crescent, Leeds, West Yorkshire, LS14 1AL

Vale Royal Borough Council, Tourism Officer, Wyvern House, The Drumber, Winsford, Cheshire, CW7 1AH

Vanguards Rambling Club, c/o 109 Selsdon Park Road, South Croydon, CR2 8JJ

Waendel Walkers Club, c/o Michael Dunnett, 68 Wellingborough Road, Irthlingborough, Northamptonshire, NN9 5RF

Walker's Guides, 103 Minster Court, Liverpool, L7 3QD

Walking Routes, 16 Ash Court, Rhyl, Clwyd, LL18 4NZ

Walking World Ireland, 109 Old County Road, Crumlin, Dublin 12, Ireland

Walkways, 8 Hillside Close, Bartley Green, Birmingham, B32 4LT

Robert Waller, 45 Shire Bank Crescent, Fulwood, Preston, Lancashire, PR2 4QE

Ray Wallis, 75 Ancaster Avenue, Kingston-upon-Hull, HU5 4QR

Walsall Metropolitan Borough Council, Leisure Services, Darwall Street, Walsall, West Midlands

Wanderlust Rambling Club, c/o Mr Don Shaw, 5 Pelham Crescent, Keelby, Nr Grimsby, South Humberside, DN37 8EW

Warwickshire County Council, Planning & Transport Dept, PO Box 43, Shire Hall, Warwick, CV34 4SX

Steve Watkins, 3 Farriers Croft, Copmanthorpe, York, YO2 3XE

Waveney District Council, Chief Executive's Department, Town Hall, High Street, Lowestoft, Suffolk, NR32 1HS

Wear Valley District Council, Economic Development & Tourism Dept, Civic Centre, Crook, County Durham, DL15 9ES

West Glamorgan County Council, Countryside Section, Environment & Highways Dept, County Hall, Swansea, West Glamorgan, SA1 3SN

West Sussex County Council, Planning Dept, County Hall, Tower Street, Chichester, W Sussex, PO19 1RL

Westmorland Gazette, 22 Stricklandgate, Kendal, Cumbria, LA9 4NE

Weston-super-Mare Civic Society, 3-6 Wadham Street, Weston-super-Mare, Avon, BS23 1JY

Wey and Arun Canal Trust Ltd, 24 Griffiths Avenue, Lancing, W Sussex, BN15 0HW

Wharncliffe Publishing Ltd, 47 Church Street, Barnsley, S Yorkshire, S70 2AS

Mrs Doreen Whitehead, East Stonesdale Farm, Keld, Richmond, North Yorkshire, DL11 6LJ

D E Wilkins, 22 Lane Ings, Marsden, Huddersfield, HD7 6JP

Willow Publishing, Willow Cottage, 36 Moss Lane, Timperley, Altrincham, Cheshire, WA15 6SZ

Wiltshire County Council, Dept of Planning and Highways, County Hall, Trowbridge, Wiltshire, BA14 8JD

Wimpole Books, Pip's Peace, Kenton, Stowmarket, Suffolk, IP14 6JS

Wincanton Press, National School, North Street, Wincanton, Somerset, BA9 9AT

Wolverhampton Rambling Club, c/o Derek Newman, 68 Farrington Road, Ettingshall Park, Wolverhampton, WV4 6QH

Wrexham Maelor Borough Council, Guildhall, Wrexham, Clwyd, LL11 1AY

David Wright, 94 Wyville Road, Frome, Somerset, BA11 2BT

Wychavon District Council, Directorate of Technical Services, Civic Centre, Queen Elizabeth Drive, Pershore, Worcestershire, WR10 1PT

Wye Valley AONB Joint Advisory Cttee, Hadnock Road, Monmouth, Gwent

Yatton Ramblers, c/o Marian Barraclough, 92 Claverham Road, Yatton, Bristol, BS19 4LE

Youth Hostels Association, Trevelyan House, 8 St Stephen's Hill, St Albans, Hertfordshire, AL1 2DY

YHA Northern Region, PO Box 11, Matlock, Derbyshire, DE4 2XA

INDEX

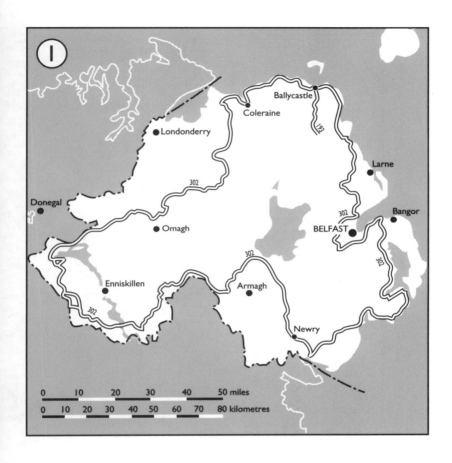

Key to maps

═══════	National Trails
▬ ▬ ▬ ▬ ▬	National Trails planned
─────────	Canal Routes
┅┅┅┅┅┅	Waymarked Routes
▬▬▬▬▬▬	Waymarked Routes planned
───────	Other Routes
┈┈┈┈┈┈	Other Routes planned

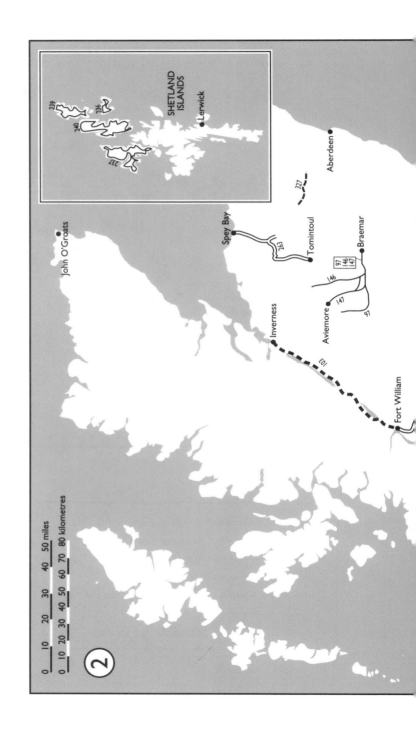

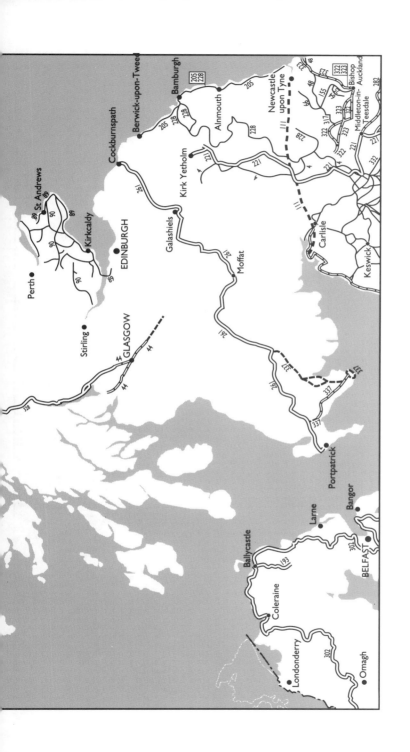

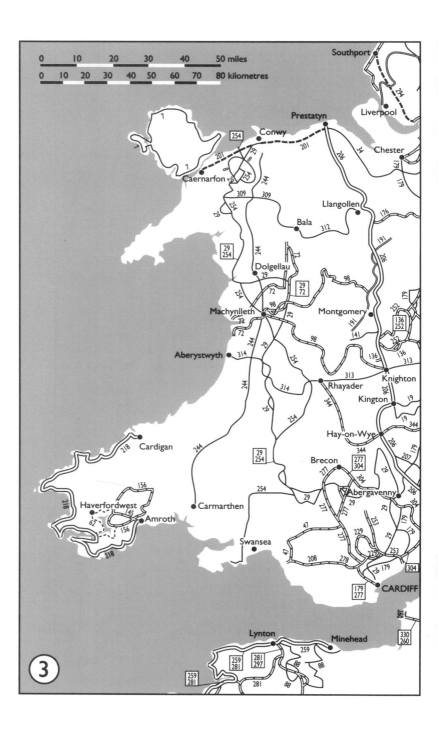

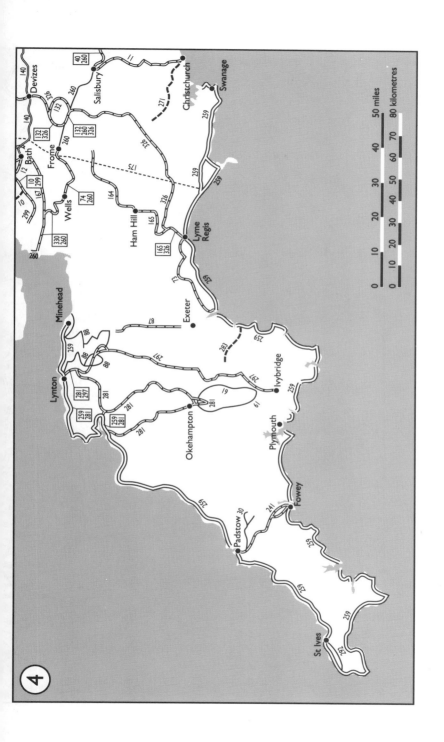

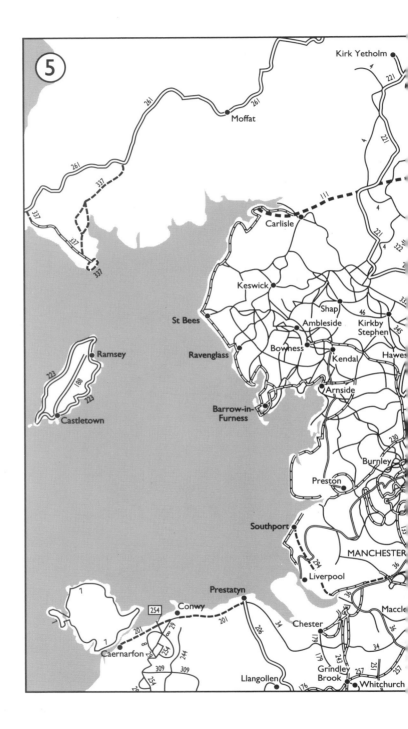

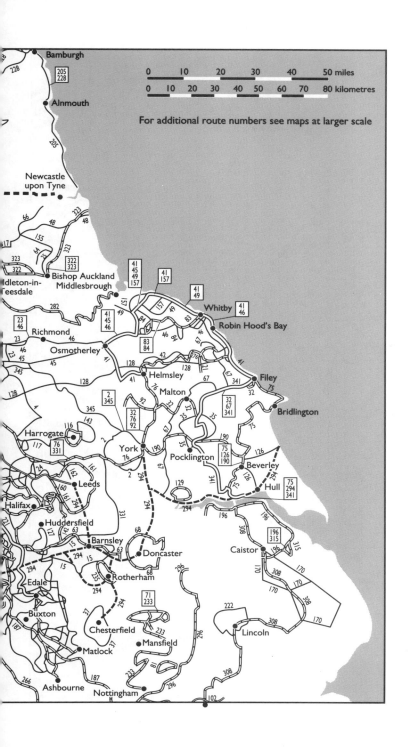

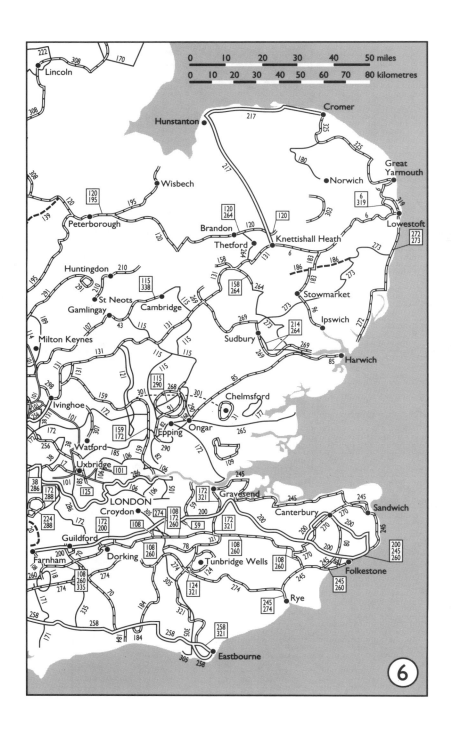

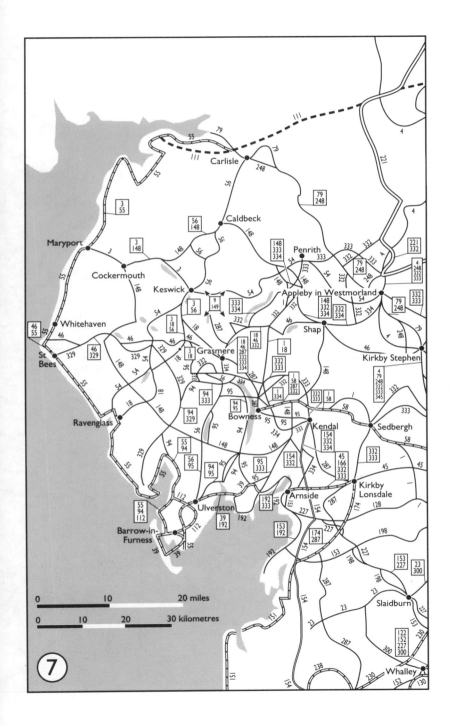

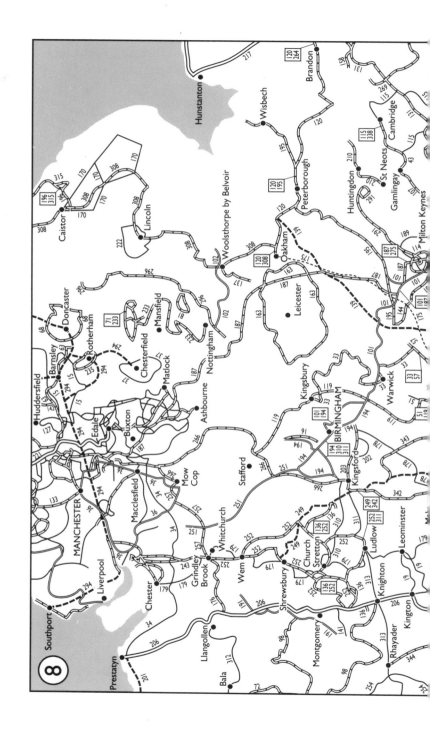

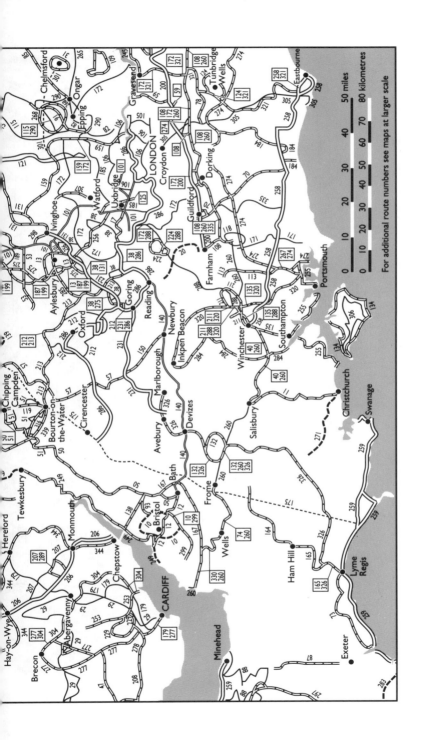

For additional route numbers see maps at larger scale

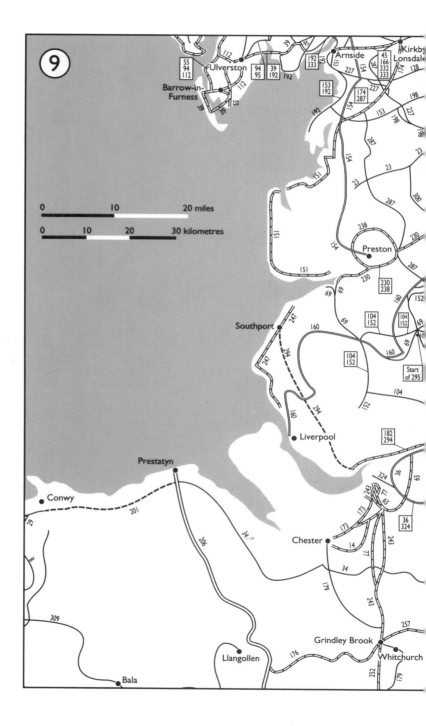

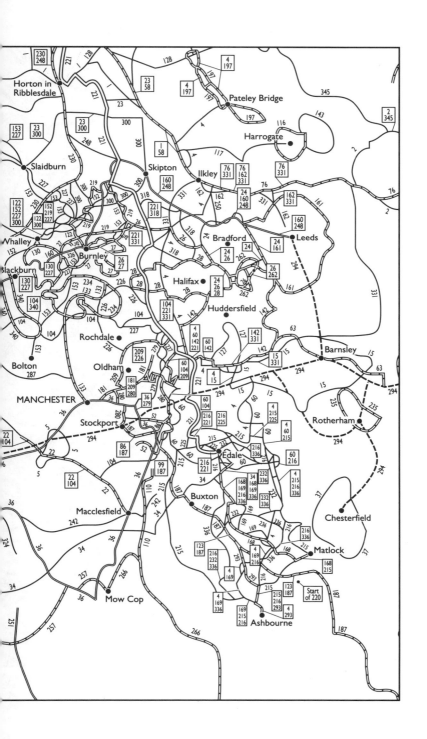

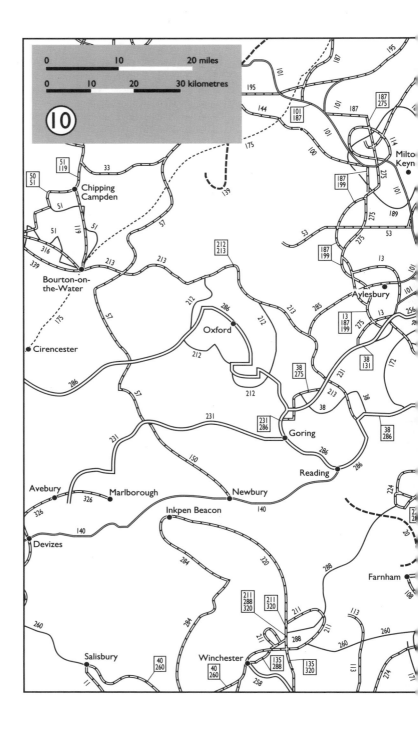

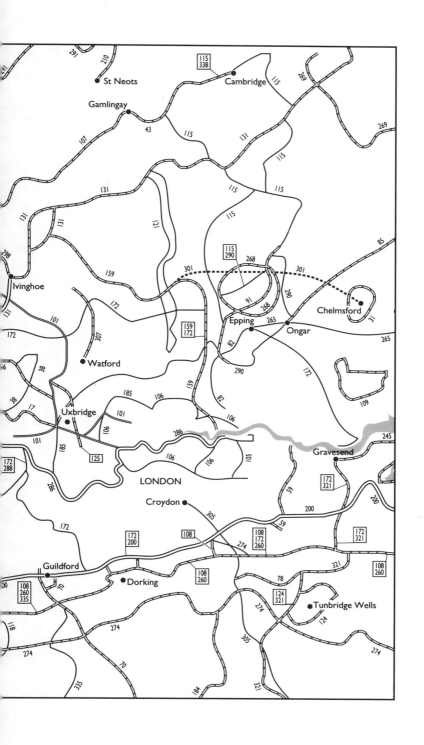

INDEX OF MAPS

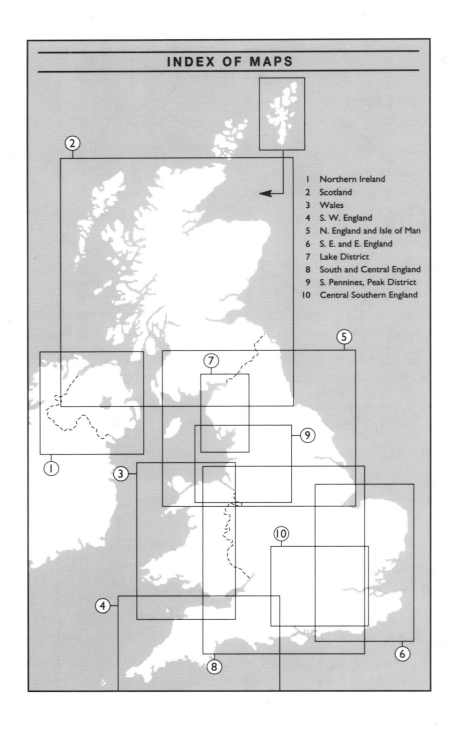

1   Northern Ireland
2   Scotland
3   Wales
4   S. W. England
5   N. England and Isle of Man
6   S. E. and E. England
7   Lake District
8   South and Central England
9   S. Pennines, Peak District
10 Central Southern England